Noise Control in Industry

NOISE CONTROL IN INDUSTRY

Third edition

Sound Research Laboratories Ltd

E. & F.N. Spon
An imprint of Chapman and Hall
London • New York • Tokyo • Melbourne • Madras

UK	Chapman and Hall, 2-6 Boundary Row, London SE1 8HN
USA	Van Nostrand Reinhold, 115 5th Avenue, New York NY10003
JAPAN	Chapman and Hall Japan, Thomson Publishing Japan, Hirakawacho Nemoto Building, 7F, 1-7-11 Hirakawa-cho, Chiyoda-ku, Tokyo 102
AUSTRALIA	Chapman and Hall Australia, Thomas Nelson Australia, 102 Dodds Street, South Melbourne, Victoria 3205
INDIA	Chapman and Hall India, R. Seshadri, 32 Second Main Road, CIT East, Madras 600 035

First edition 1976
Second edition 1978
Third edition 1991

© 1976, 1978, 1991 Sound Research Laboratories Ltd, Sudbury, Suffolk

Typeset by Image Print, Colchester, Essex.

Printed in Great Britain by Courier International Limited, Tiptree, Essex.

ISBN   0 419 17170 3   0 442 31341 1   (USA)

British Library Cataloguing in Publication Data
Noise Control in Industry – 3rd Ed.
1.   Industries. Noise. Control Measures
I.   Sound Research Laboratories
620.23
ISBN 0-419-17170-3

Contents

Introduction

This book is for all those in industry who find they have a noise problem or have been given the task of health and safety which includes an element of noise. Its aim is to provide a foundation of basic knowledge of acoustics tempered with examples of real life treatments in an attempt to dispel the "black art" image sometimes assigned to noise control.

With the ever increasing awareness of the quality of life and our environment, attention is paid to both the legal and health aspects of noise. More and more legislation is being developed within the UK, the EEC and worldwide to protect the individual and the environment from the dangerous pollutant –noise.

The first few chapters deal with the fundamental principles of acoustics and noise measurement, including legal aspects, the middle section covers basic noise control methods whilst the latter chapters show how these techniques are applied to particular problems. Inevitably there is some duplication between chapters, and with our other publication "Noise Control in Building Services." Nevertheless it is seen as a book of value to both the student and the practicing engineer in all industries, an essential reference for any bookcase.

SRL is a member of the Salex Group of Companies

Photographic Acknowledgements

The editor would like to thank the following companies for their help with photographs; and for permission to reproduce them in this book. They appear on the following pages:

Amplivox Limited 34
O.N. Beck & Co. Limited 170
British Steel 295
British Telecom 140
Bruel & Kjaer Laboratories Limited 115, 118, 124, 126
Burgess Industrial Silencing Limited 219, 347, 396
Comp Air Limited 270
Custom Coils Company 162
Dunlop Limited, Polymer Engineering Division 234
GEC Elliott Control Valves Limited 395
GEC Machines Limited 308
Massey Ferguson 388
Porvair Limited 167
Quietflo Engineering Limited 269
Sound Attenuators Limited 18, 80, 104, 156, 188, 189, 194, 196, 210, 211, 234, 235, 258, 284, 362, 388
Woods of Colchester Limited 332

1
Basic Physics of Sound

IF we burst a balloon, we cause a disturbance in the surrounding air which may be likened to the effect of throwing a stone in a pond. When the ripples caused by the explosion reach our ears we hear the sound of the balloon burst. It is these ripples travelling through the air that we generally regard as sound. Sound can also travel through solids and liquids, as anyone who has listened to a car engine with the aid of a screwdriver will know. In air, the sound is always transmitted as compression waves, but in solids other wave forms are possible.

If we imagine the piston in Fig 1 to be suddenly moved forward a short distance, the air immediately adjacent to its face will be compressed. This compressed region will in turn affect the region next to it and the disturbance will pass down the tube compressing subsequent sections of air in turn. The speed at which the disturbance will pass down the tube will depend upon the density of the air and its bulk modulus. For air at normal temperature the disturbance will travel at approximately 340m/sec (1120ft/sec).

Unless the action is very extreme, our single pulse of pressure will not produce an audible effect. However, if our piston is driven backwards and forwards by means of a crankshaft running at a suitable speed, it will produce a train of waves which will be audible.

The rotational speed of the crankshaft and the rate at which waves pass a fixed point will be the same, and is defined as the frequency. It is the frequency of a sound which determines its pitch; high frequency sounds are heard as high-pitched, and low frequency sounds as low-pitched. The unit of frequency is the Hertz (Hz). The frequency in

Hertz is equal to the repetition rate in cycles per second. The audible range of frequencies varies widely with circumstances, but for people of good hearing is normally considered to be between about 20Hz and 20 000Hz. In most practical noise control problems, however, it is possible to consider a rather narrower range of, say, 50Hz to 10 000Hz.

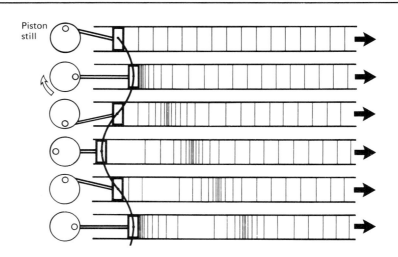

Figure 1. Mechanism of generating a sound wave

Wavelength   Taking again the example of a piston, the rate at which the piston is operated will not only determine the frequency of the sound waves but also their spacing. Since the waves travel at a fixed speed, the higher the frequency the closer the spacing. The spacing is related to:

$$\lambda = \frac{c}{f}$$

Where λ is the wavelength (i.e. the distance apart of successive waves).
and   c is the speed of sound in consistent units
       f is the frequency in Hz

For audible sounds, the wavelengths will vary from several metres to a few millimetres (Fig 2).

Sound Intensity   A sound wave transmits energy and so energy is required to produce a wave. The sound power of a source will govern the intensity of the waves produced. The greater the intensity of a given wave, the greater will be its loudness.

Sound Power and Sound Power Level   Under normal conditions, a given sound source will radiate energy more or less irrespective of its surroundings, in the same way that a 1kW electric fire will radiate 1kW

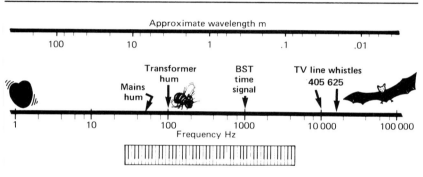

Figure 2.   Frequencies and wavelengths

of heat. The power in each case can be measured in watts. Real life sound sources can cover a range from about 10^{-12} watt up to many millions of watts.

The human ear does not tend to judge sound powers in absolute terms, but judges how many times greater one power is than another. This behaviour, combined with the very large range of powers involved, makes it convenient to use a logarithmic scale when dealing with sound power. This leads to the decibel (dB) scale of sound power level which is based on the logarithm to the base 10. This enables one source to be related in power to any other source.

In order to describe the power of a source in absolute terms, however, it is necessary to have a reference level. The normal one in use in this country is the picowatt (10^{-12} watt). (In America, a reference unit of 10^{-13} watt is sometimes still used but this is now obsolete.)

The Sound Power Level (SWL) is related to the sound power (W) of a source by:

$$SWL = 10 \log_{10} \frac{W}{W_0} \; dB$$

Where $W_0 = 10^{-12}$ watt

Acoustic Power watt	dB re 10^{-12}w	Typical Sources
100 000 000	200	Saturn Booster Rocket
10 000 000		
1 000 000	180	
100 000		
10 000	160	Boeing 707 - full power
1000		
100	140	75 Piece Orchestra
10		
1	120	Chain Saw
0.1		
0.01	100	
0.001		Average Motor Car
0.000 1	80	
0.000 01		Normal Voice
0.000 001	60	
0.000 000 1		
0.000 000 01	40	
0.000 000 001		Whisper
0.000 000 000 1	20	
0.000 000 000 01		
0.000 000 000 001	0	

Figure 3.   Acoustic power

The multiplier 10 is a scaling factor to produce a convenient size unit – the decibel, as opposed to the larger bel – in the same way that we can convert from cm to mm by relationship 10mm = 1cm.

For example, if the sound power level of a given source is 10^{-3}w, the sound power level is given by:

$$SWL = 10 \log_{10} \frac{10^{-3}}{10^{-12}}$$

$$= 10 \log_{10} 10^9 = 10 \times 9 = 90 \text{ dB re } 10^{-12} \text{ watt}$$

SWL(Sound Watt Level) and (PWL) Power Watt Level are both used to denote Sound Power Level. Throughout this book, SWL will be used. Examples of Sound Power Levels (SWL) are given in Fig 3.

Sound Pressure Level   The sound power from a source, as indicated previously, can be compared with the power from an electric fire. However, the temperature in the area in which the fire is located will depend upon the thermal properties of its surroundings. Similarly the sound pressure produced in given surroundings will depend on the acoustic properties of those surroundings (Fig 4). The sound produced in a confined space will be very different from that produced in the open air. Thus, the sound pressure does not depend entirely on the source but also on the surroundings. The range of sound pressures experienced in everyday life is very wide and is also conveniently expressed in a logarithmic form.

Sound power and sound pressure are related in a manner analogous to electrical power and voltage. The corresponding relationships are as follows:

Electrical Power   Sound Power

power $W = \dfrac{V^2}{R}$ power $W = \dfrac{p^2}{z}$

Where p is the sound pressure and z is the impedance of the transmitting medium.

Taking the acoustic case further:

$W = p^2 \times$ constant

Expressing this in logarithmic form relative to reference power and pressure, this becomes:

$$\text{Log } \frac{W}{W_0} = 2 \log_{10} \frac{p}{p_0} + \text{constant}$$

or, in decibel terms:

$$10 \log_{10} \frac{W}{W_0} = 20 \log \frac{p}{p_0} + \text{constant}$$

This is the equation relating the sound pressure level and sound power level in any given circumstances. The constant is defined by the circumstances. This leads to the definition of SPL.

$$\text{SPL} = 20 \log_{10} \frac{p}{p_0} \quad \text{where } p_0 = 2 \times 10^{-5} \text{N/m}^2$$

If a sound source with a sound power of W_1 in a given situation produces a sound pressure p, then 100 similar sources will increase the sound power 100 times, which is equivalent to 20dB. Thus $W_2 = 100W_1$ or $\text{SWL}_2 = \text{SWL}_1 + 20\text{dB}$. From the acoustic power equation above, it is seen that the sound pressure will only increase ten times. This ten times increase again corresponds to 20dB. $p_2 = 10_{p_1}$ or $\text{SPL}_2 = \text{SPL}_1 + 20\text{dB}$. The use of the multiplier 20 instead of 10 in the sound pressure scale makes the two units compatible.

Pure Tones So far, the sounds that we have discussed have been those corresponding to an idealised crank system which produces a pure sine wave consisting of one frequency only. Sounds of this type are relatively rare in nature but are important because, in theory, any sound can be regarded as consisting of a suitable mixture of these simple pure tone sounds.

Periodic Sounds Musical notes, the sound of a diesel engine, the hum of a transformer, or the screech of a circular saw consist of simple or complex mixtures of pure tones. The number of pure tones involved is finite and results in a sound whose wave form repeats itself regularly.

Such sounds are referred to as periodic. With the use of suitable analysis equipment it is possible to pick out the individual components.

Broad Band or Random Sounds   Many other sounds are composed of an infinite mixture of inseparable components which combine to produce a wave form which never repeats and is unpredictable in the

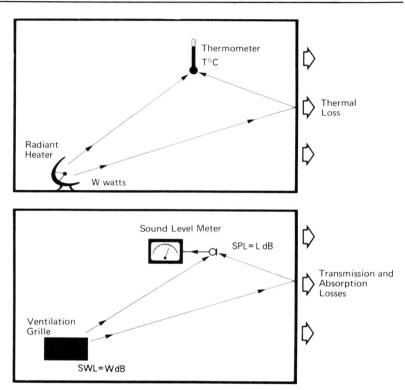

Figure 4.   Acoustic analogy

future. This applies to the noise of a fan, the roar of the wind, or the additive effects of a large number of unrelated sounds. With such sounds it is impossible to separate individual components. These sounds can only be divided up into bands of energy.

Because of the differing behaviour of long and short wavelength sounds, it is necessary to know whether high or low frequency sounds are present when dealing with a noise problem. It is therefore necessary to be able to divide sounds into suitable bands of frequency. For most purposes, division into octave bands is adequate. Octave bands are frequency bands which cover a two-to-one range of frequencies, e.g. the 1kHz covers the range from approximately 707 to 1414Hz. The nominal frequency of each band is equal to the geometric mean of the upper and lower frequencies. The standard octave bands are centred on 1kHz and have centre frequencies of 250Hz, 500Hz, 1kHz,

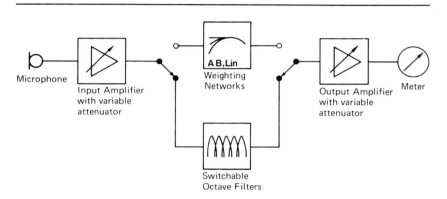

Figure 5. Simplified block diagram of a sound level meter

2kHz, etc. Where more detailed information is required, a finer subdivision may be used. Bands one-third octave wide are the most common of the finer subdivisions.

Basic Measurements   The basic instrument for measuring sound is the sound level meter, which consists of a microphone, input and output amplifiers and an indicating device. This arrangement is shown diagrammatically in Fig 5. The microphone transforms sound pressure waves into voltage fluctuations, which are again amplified sufficiently to activate the indicating device. It should be noted here that, just as a thermometer measures temperature and not the heat output of an electric fire, so the sound level meter registers sound pressure; it cannot read sound power directly. Range switching has to be incorporated to enable sound pressures covering a possible range of 10^{12} or more to be measured.

Since the ear is not equally sensitive to all frequencies, a meter which measured overall sound pressure level would not be a very good indication of the loudness of a sound (Fig 6). A reading of 70dB might represent either a nearly inaudible low frequency sound or a loud sound at middle frequencies. In order to make the sound level meter give readings which are representative of human response, a system of weighting networks is incorporated which biases the meter reading so

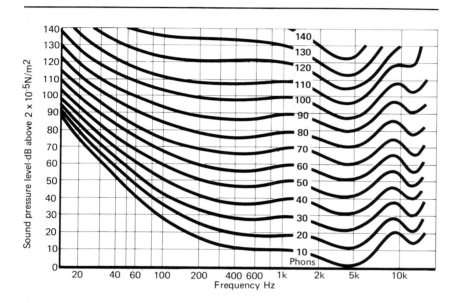

Figure 6.   Equal loudness contours after Robinson & Dadson

that the meter behaves in a manner comparable with the human ear. There are three principal weighting networks–'A', 'B' and 'C' (Fig 7). It was originally intended that the 'A' weighting which corresponds to the equal loudness contour passing through 1 kHz at 40dB should be used for sound pressure levels up to 55dB, the 'B' weighting for sound pressure levels between 55 and 85, and the 'C' weighting for higher sound pressure levels. However, nowadays, the 'A' weighting is used for all sounds regardless of level because it has been found that there is a good agreement between subjective reaction and the 'A' weighted sound level, regardless of level, for any generally similar noise sources.

Most industrial noise standards have been based upon the 'A' weighted decibel. As a method of measuring noise levels, it has the advantage that an assessment of the level can be made with a single reading of the meter. Unfortunately this simplicity is a disadvantage as far as detailed design and calculations are concerned. The information that a given noise source produces a level of XdBA gives no indication of whether the energy is concentrated at low frequencies or high frequencies. If

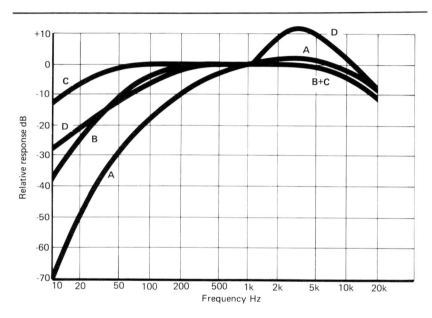

Figure 7. Standard weighting networks for the sound level meter

any curative measures or preventative design measures are required, it is necessary to know over what part of the frequency range the noise is concentrated, since the behaviour of high and low frequency sounds is very different.

By breaking the sounds down into octave bands, the relative importance of the different frequency bands can be determined. This can be done either by applying the weighting effect of the network to the individual octave bands, which enables the relative importance of the different bands to be assessed, or alternatively by comparing the octave bands with sets of standard rating curves. There are two sets of rating curves in common use; the noise criterion (NC) curves (Fig 8) which are widely used in America and in the heating and ventilating industry in the United Kingdom, and the noise rating (NR) curves (Fig 9) which are used on the continent of Europe and in the industrial field in the UK.

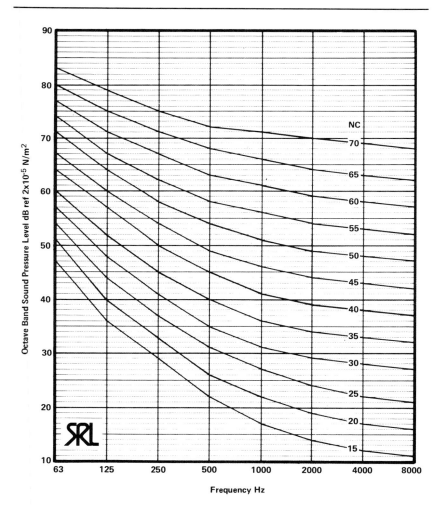

Figure 8. NC (Noise Criterion) curves

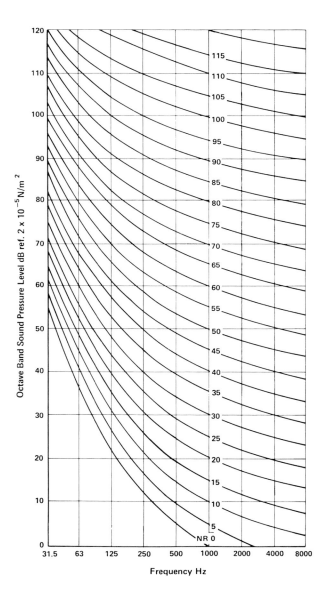

Figure 9. NR (Noise Rating) curves

In the United States, the American acoustics consultancy firm of Bolt, Beranek and Newman developed the noise criterion series of curves based on octave band measurements which were proposed as criteria for acceptability of noise. These curves were based on broad band noises and the procedure for rating any noise was to plot the individual octave band readings and the lowest of these contour curves which the measured spectrum did not cut was deemed the noise criterion or NC level for the noise. The splitting up of noise into octave bands makes the treatment very convenient for design purposes as it enables high and low frequency components of noises to be treated independently and appropriately. The measurement of NC levels is relatively simple, although the equipment is slightly more complicated than using straight sound level meter 'A', 'B' and 'C' weightings. It is this system of curves and noise ratings that is generally being used for selecting suitable background levels for air conditioning systems and other plant in buildings.

A similar system was developed in Europe by Kosten & Van Os in 1961. This system was based on a very large survey of external residential noise. The curves are generally similar to those of the NC system but differ slightly, particularly at the low frequency end. This system of curves has been partially adopted by the International Standards Organisation and is gaining favour in Europe as a rival to the American NC system.

One word of warning; the American NC system was originally based on the American Standard octave bands which were mentioned earlier. A modified version has since been published to correspond with the International Octave Bands and this is the form normally used in this country. Confusion does however sometimes arise when the values for the NC contours get mixed up. The NC and NR rating systems unfortunately appear to be slightly less reliable than the 'A' weighted sound level meter reading when compared with people's reactions for many applications.

A simple rule of thumb method for comparing measurements in dBA and NC/NR is that for most common broad band noises the dBA level is equal to NC/NR + 5 to 7. The exact relationship of course depends on the spectrum, but it is quite a useful conversion.

Although it is not possible to obtain frequency information directly from a single dBA reading, it is possible to calculate dBA values from octave or third octave bands. This is done by applying the appropriate weighting factors to each individual octave band and then combining the octave bands using the procedure given on Page 15.

Decibel Arithmetic – Addition and Subtraction   Since decibel scales are logarithmic, sound power levels and sound pressure levels cannot be added or subtracted in the way that normal numbers can. For example, if two sound sources of 100dB are to be added, the procedure is as follows:

Source A: 100dB re 10^{-12} watt = 0.01 watt
Source B: 100dB re 10^{-12} watt = 0.01 watt

$$\text{Total} \quad \overline{0.02 \text{ watt}}$$

$$
\begin{aligned}
0.02 \text{ watt} &= 2 \times 0.01 \text{ watt, or in decibel terms} \\
&= 10\,(\log 2 + \log 10^{10}) \\
&= 10\,(0.3 + 10) \\
&= 103 \text{dB}
\end{aligned}
$$

i.e. 100dB + 100dB = 103.

From this procedure, it can be seen that, when two identical levels are added, the result will be an increase in level of 3dB. When adding or subtracting decibels, therefore, the following table can be derived:

Addition – *If the levels differ by*	*The following should be added to the higher*
0 or 1dB	3dB
2 or 3dB	2dB
4 to 9dB	1dB
10dB or over	0dB

Subtraction – *If the levels differ by*	*The difference is the higher level minus*
More than 10dB	0dB
6 to 9dB	1dB
5 or 4dB	2dB
3dB	3dB
2dB	5dB (approx)
1dB	7dB (approx)

For example:

34dB + 37dB = 39dB
34dB + 39dB = 40dB

This rule can be used to combine individual octave band readings to obtain dBA. For example, if the following octave band readings were predicted in a design calculation, what would the dBA level be?

Frequency	31.5	63	125	250	500	1k	2k	4k	8k	Hz
Octave Band Readings	74	63	50	48	45	40	35	30	22	dB*
'A' Weighting (to nearest whole number)	−40	−26	−16	−9	−3	0	+1	+1	−1	

'A' Weighted Octave Band Levels

| 34 | 37 | 34 | 39 | 42 | 40 | 36 | 31 | 21 |

39   40   44   37

43   45

37

47dBA Total

*re 2×10^{-5}N/m²

Multiplication Where a large number of similar sources is to be combined, logarithmic multiplications can be used. For example, if one sound source has a sound power level of 90dB, what is the sound power level for five similar sources?

$$SWL_1 = 10\log_{10}W = 90dB$$
$$SWL_2 = 10\log_{10}(W \times 5)$$
$$= 10(\log_{10}W + \log_{10}5) \text{ (add logarithms to multiply)}$$
$$= 10(\log_{10}W + 0.7)$$
$$= 10\log_{10}W + 7$$
$$= 90 + 7 = 97dB$$

The Relationship between Sound Power Level and Sound Pressure Level If a source is radiating sound equally in all directions, the energy will be spread over an increasing area as the distance from the source increases, as indicated in Fig. 10.

The sound energy per unit area received at any point is inversely proportional to the square of the distance from the source. If the distance from the source is doubled the energy density is reduced to a quarter. This means, in terms of decibels, a decrease in level of 6dB for

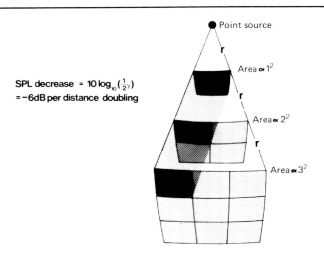

SPL decrease $= 10 \log_{10}(\frac{1}{2^2})$
$= -6dB$ per distance doubling

Point source

r

Area $\propto 1^2$

r

Area $\propto 2^2$

r

Area $\propto 3^2$

Figure 10.   Inverse square law

every doubling of distance. The sound pressure will fall linearly with distance from the source, so for each doubling of distance the pressure is halved, again leading to a 6dB drop for each doubling of distance (Fig 10). This law will only apply for external sound pressure levels (or free field conditions) since in an enclosed space the level will be affected by reflections from floors and walls, etc.

In Chapter 4 a chart is given to enable the sound pressure level to be calculated both for external and internal conditions.

For larger sources, the 'inverse square law', as it is known, does not apply close to the source. For a large source the sound pressure level remains constant until one is a distance (c/π) from the source. It then falls at 3dB until a distance (b/π) is reached, after which it falls at the normal 6dB per doubling of distance (Fig 11).

When one is beyond the distance (b/π) the sound pressure level is the same as would be produced by a compact source of the same power. Closer to the source the sound pressure level is less than would be

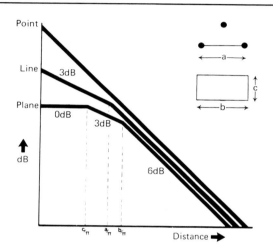

Figure 11. *Attenuation with distance from various sources*

expected for a small source of the same power, since the energy is spread over a greater area. This has the serious implication that the sound power level of large sources is often grossly underestimated by a casual observer who makes a subjective assessment based on the sound pressure level close to the source.

It must be realised that these rules are for ideal conditions and there-fore they are a guide only to average values, not specific ones.

Plate 1.   Ripples on a pond spread out in much the same way as sound radiates from a small source. Reflections and interference effects can also be simulated. Remember that sound in air is a longitudinal particle displacement wave whilst ripples in water are transverse displacement waves

2
Physiology and Psychology of Hearing

OF our five senses – hearing, sight, taste, smell and touch, we are most dependent on those of our eyes and ears. Sight allows us to move, to work, to live an active life. Hearing, together with sight, is of paramount importance at work and at play; it enables us, in combination with speech, to communicate with each other, to express opinions, to learn, to enjoy entertainment and life. It is also our most sensitive mechanism of warning and, in times past, when the environment was quieter, for locating prey. It is often said that the reason we have two ears is so that they can be used in a similar manner to our eyes in range finding, in that they can accurately locate sources of noise – a useful ability when hunting or being hunted!

The hearing mechanism is divided anatomically into three parts (Fig 1); the outer ear, middle ear and the inner ear. Functionally, the ear can be considered in two distinctly separate parts, the outer and middle ear joining together to collect the sound waves and transform the acoustic energy into mechanical energy. The inner ear transduces this mechanical energy into a series of nerve impulses which represent the acoustic events.

When a sound wave travelling through the air meets the open end of a small tube, the intensity of the sound wave which enters the tube will only be a fraction of the intensity of the wave outside. On its own, the auditory canal (meatus) has the same problem as a small tube. This problem is solved by the external flap of flesh generally called the ear, and known medically as the 'pinna'. By virtue of its shape, it reduces the abruptness of the change from free air as the sound wave meets the ear and helps to funnel more sound into the auditory canal. At the end of this canal, the sound wave meets the ear-drum (tympanic membrane), which it sets into vibration.

Connected to the ear-drum is a series of small bones in the air-filled cavity of the middle ear. These are known collectively as the 'ossicles' and consist of the hammer (malleus), the anvil (incus) and the stirrup (stapes). The hammer is connected to the ear-drum and, with the anvil,

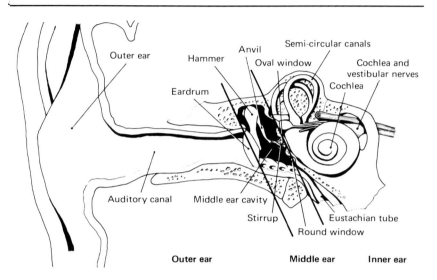

Figure 1. Anatomy of the ear after Bilsom International Ltd

forms a three-to-one mechanical advantage on the stirrup. The stirrup is attached to a section of the membrane separating the middle and inner ears, known as the 'oval window'. Also contained in the middle ear are two muscles which operate on the hammer and stirrup. These muscles contract in response to loud sounds. Their action reduces the amplitude of movement of the ossicles, thus limiting the sound intensity delivered to the inner ear. Connecting the middle ear to the back of the mouth and thus the outside atmosphere is a small channel known as the 'eustachian tube'. In order to function properly, the air pressure within the middle ear must be equal to the ambient atmospheric pressure. The tube, normally closed, opens on swallowing to allow the pressure on both sides of the ear-drum to be equalised. If for some reason the tube is blocked, the ear-drum is less able to vibrate freely, causing slight deafness. If the unbalanced pressure is great enough, the result is ear-ache. With a head cold, the eustachian tube and even the middle ear cavity will fill with mucus and pressure equalisation cannot take place. The middle ear often contains a little liquid which normally drains away via the eustachian tube on swallowing. However, if the tube is blocked, or if the middle ear cavity is filled with mucus, the

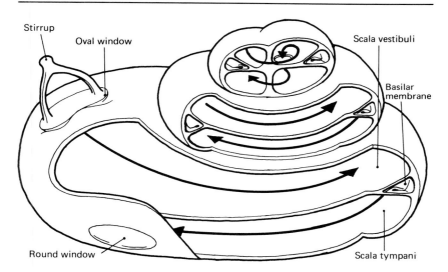

Figure 2. Bony cochlea section after Bilsom International Ltd

viscous drag exerted on the ossicles reduces hearing sensitivity, a common side effect of a head cold.

The final stage in the acoustic energy, to mechanical energy, to neural impulse link is the inner ear. The inner ear can be divided into two systems; the semicircular canals, which are the organs of balance, and the cochlea, the organ of hearing. The cochlea is a spiral organ which resembles a snail shell and which, when uncoiled, is about 35mm long and 3mm in diameter where the stirrup bone is attached at the oval window. Because of the relative size of the oval window to that of the ear-drum, the physical displacement of the ear-drum is amplified approximately 20 times at the oval window (Fig 2). The liquid-filled spiral cavity of the cochlea is divided into two by the basilar membrane which runs almost to the apex of the spiral and leaves a small gap at the end known as the 'helicotrema'. When a pressure is exerted by the stirrup on the oval window, fluid is displaced from the upper passage (scala vestibuli) through the helicotrema into the lower passage (scala tympani). The lower passage terminates in a membrane known as the 'round window' which deflects to relieve the pressure. This movement of the fluid causes a travelling wave up the cochlea duct, which deflects

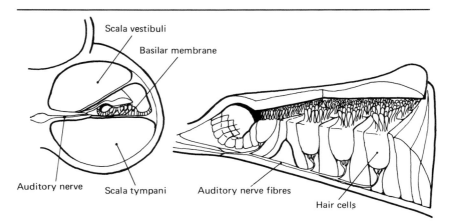

Figure 3. Section of cochlea (left) and basilar membrane with organ of corti after Bilsom International Ltd

and distorts the basilar membrane. On top of this membrane there are of the order of 30 000 highly sensitive hair cells which register the movement of the basilar membrane and translate this movement into neural impulses for transmission to the auditory centre of the brain by the auditory nerve. The response of the basilar membrane varies with frequency. Signals of different frequency produce maximum vibrations in different parts of the membrane. High frequency sounds cause a short response that does not extend far from the oval window, but as the frequency is lowered the area of maximum vibration moves progressively away from the oval window end of the membrane (Fig 3).

The human ear, because of its intricate construction of levers, diaphragms, canals, membranes and hair cells, can detect sounds over a vast range of intensities and frequencies. It can hear sounds the loudest of which can be ten billion times as intense as the softest. To use straightforward numerical values for measuring the intensity of sound heard by the ear would lead to the continual writing of zeros, hence the logarithmic systems of measurement introduced in Chapter 1. Similarly, the ear can analyse sounds over a range of frequencies with the highest almost a thousand times greater than the lowest.

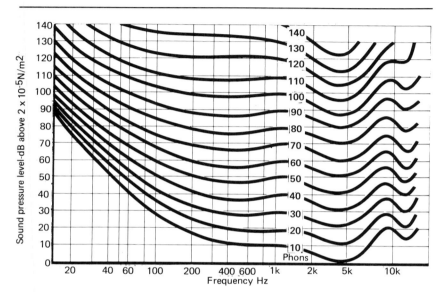

Figure 4.   Equal loudness contours after Robinson & Dadson

The threshold of hearing for a young person between 100Hz and 4000Hz is approximately 0dB, which corresponds to a sound pressure of 2×10^{-5}N/m². Above and below the frequency limits mentioned of 1000Hz and 4000Hz (the ear's most sensitive range) the sound intensity of the threshold of hearing changes. This can be seen in Fig 4 for example where the threshold at 100Hz is some 100 times greater, i.e. 20dB, than the threshold at 1000Hz. From these curves one can see that the ear is less sensitive to low frequency sound and is non-linear in its assessment of loudness. One would expect that upon doubling the sound pressure one would double the loudness. However, this is not the case. To obtain a subjective doubling of the loudness, the sound pressure level needs to be increased by about 10dB.

The threshold of feeling is generally taken to be around 120dB as indicated in Fig 7. The ear has two safety mechanisms which help to protect it against damage. The first is known as the aural reflex and is caused by the tightening of the tiny muscles attached to the ossicles and ear-drum. If the ear is subjected to a noise of more than approximately 90dB, a reflex action occurs which tightens these muscles and reduces the sensitivity of the ear to low and middle frequencies by stiffening up the mechanical action of the middle ear. This protection cannot, however, cope with sudden unexpected noises. The second protective device occurs when sounds above 140dB are sensed. In this instance the ossicles, instead of functioning in their normal to and fro manner, rock from side to side, thus reducing the pressure changes in the cochlea and the sensed level of sound.

Short periods of exposure to excessive noise levels produce varying degrees of inner ear damage which is initially reversible. This auditory fatigue is known as 'temporary threshold shift' (TTS). As its name implies, this type of exposure produces an elevation of the hearing threshold which progressively reduces with time after leaving the excessively noisy environment. The time taken to recover from the temporary threshold shift may be anything from a few minutes to days depending upon the degree of exposure. Permanent damage, known as 'noise induced hearing loss' (NIHL), occurs when exposure to excessive noise continues over a long period of time. The full relationship between temporary threshold shift and noise induced hearing loss is not fully understood. It is possible for a person with noise induced hearing loss to be affected by temporary threshold shift due to exposure to noise but the degree of temporary threshold shift is reduced by the extent of the noise induced hearing loss. Permanent noise induced hearing loss occurs because the nerve hairs in the cochlea become damaged and eventually die.

Both the temporary threshold shift and the permanent noise induced hearing loss are frequency dependent in so far that the greatest loss generally occurs at frequencies about one half to one octave higher than the frequency of the noise source. However, noise induced hearing loss generally occurs first in the 4000Hz octave band, mainly due to the fact that a lot of industrial noise occurs at frequencies between 1500Hz and 3500Hz. If exposure continues over a number of years, the hearing loss at 4000Hz increases along with losses in lower octave bands, as shown in Fig 5. Not everyone develops the same hearing loss when exposed to the same noise. Similarly, not everyone has the same level of threshold – anything up to ±20dB deviation from the accepted standard has been noted.

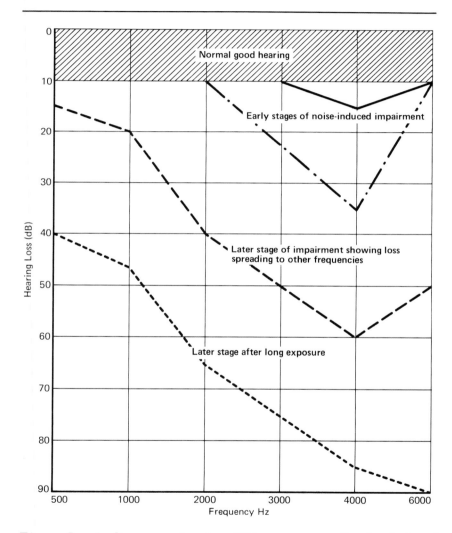

Figure 5. Audiograms showing different stages of noise induced hearing loss after Bell

Industrial noise in itself is not the only source of hearing loss (Fig 5). Blows on the head or explosive blasts near the ear may rupture the ear-drum, damage the hair cells or dislocate the ossicular chain. Disease can effect the middle ear or can even eat away at the nerve hair cells in the cochlea. Compacted wax or even foreign bodies can cause a conductive hearing loss by blocking the auditory canal or rupturing the drum. Certain drugs such as quinine or streptomycin can cause burns of the inner ear and deafness. Finally, like all organs of the body, there is an ageing process, in this case known as presbycousis. This again is frequency dependent and starts with the higher frequency octave bands and usually becomes noticeable at about the age of 30 years in men and 35 years in women. There is some discussion as to whether the difference between men and women is partially due to the higher exposure to noise of most men rather than a pure ageing effect. It is therefore generally taken for the whole population that the effect of presbycousis is nearer that shown in Fig 6.

Excessive noise is dangerous and a health hazard, but what is excessive? Exposure to noise in excess of 90dBA for eight hours in any 24 hours for five days a week can lead to permanent hearing damage if exposure continues over a period of say 30 to 40 years. Because of the variation in the susceptibility of individual ears, this norm will only protect up to 80% of the population. The remaining 20% may have their hearing affected by exposure to noise levels between 80dBA and 90dBA but obviously to a lesser extent than exposure to levels above 90dBA. Exposure to noise levels below 80dBA over any period of time is not thought to cause hearing damage. It is generally recommended that no person at any time should be exposed to noise levels in excess of 120dB without proper hearing protection and should not be exposed under any conditions to levels in excess of 140dB. These levels assume that the noise is steady and broad band. Exposure to impulsive noise of 150dB or above can cause rupture of the ear-drum beyong repair – the ossicles can be broken or displaced or even penetrate the oval window.

The term dBA is used to describe in one value the level at which noise must be considered a hazard. It is described in more detail in an earlier chapter. It is sufficient to say here that the weighting of each separate octave band from 63Hz to 8000Hz to produce the 'A' weighting curve is similar to the sensitivity of the ear at these frequencies. This value therefore gives a very good approximation to the physical effect a noise

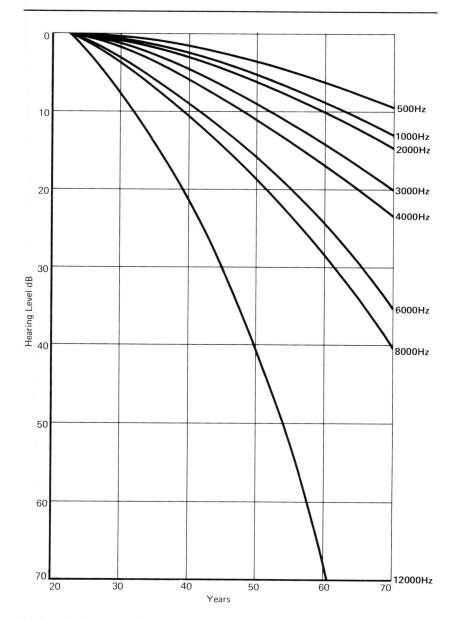

Figure 6. Hearing loss with age after Hinchcliffe 1958

has on the delicate hair cells of the cochlea. The values of sound pressure levels in specified octave bands which indicate a hazard to hearing for a duration of approximately eight hours a day are shown in Table 1.

These levels are not to be regarded as acceptable maximum noise levels but as defining an arbitrary level of hazard to hearing. The damage risk criterion of 90dBA has been expressed in terms of a steady and broad band noise. However noise, particularly industrial

Table 1 Maximum Recommended Octave Band Sound Pressure Levels

Octave Band Centre Frequency (Hz)	Sound Pressure Level (dB)
63	97
125	91
250	87
500	84
1000	82
2000	80
4000	79
8000	78

noise, fluctuates in strength and frequency with the number and types of machines in operation. A person's exposure during an eight hour day may vary from a noisy process to a relatively quiet one. It was with this situation in mind that the Equivalent Continuous Noise Level (L_{eq}) was introduced to enable assessment of hearing risk to persons employed in a situation of varying noise levels. It is, as its name implies, a mathematical method of obtaining a measurement of a person's noise exposure to varying noise which is equivalent to a continuous level of noise. This is based on the hypothesis that the damage caused by a varying noise level is equal to the damage caused by a steady noise of equivalent energy. Thus, if the time of exposure to the noise is halved, the maximum permitted energy level may be doubled, but since it is measured on a logarithmic basis this only represents an increase in the maximum level from 90dBA to 93dBA. This can be continued in both directions, as shown in Table 2.

Tables 1 and 2 form the basis of the recommended maximum limits of the Health and Safety Executive.

Noise is a very subjective thing – that which appears loud and objectionable to one person will be quite acceptable to another. The spread of hearing theshold shows just one factor in the individuality of human

Table 2 Maximum Exposure Times for Varying Sound Pressure Levels based on Second Action Level of 90dBA

Sound Pressure Level (dBA)	Maximum Exposure in any 24 hours
85	24 hours
87	16 hours
90	8 hours
93	4 hours
96	2 hours
99	1 hour
102	30 mins
105	15 mins
108	7½ mins
111	3¾ mins

response to noise. The degree of annoyance is not necessarily related to the intensity of sound, although quite often it is. It may be influenced by subjective factors and noise patterns containing distinct pure tones or particular characteristics. Annoyance is largely an individual response and varies with each person. Their situation, health, attitude of mind and environment are all important. Sounds outside the normal hearing range of the human ear can also cause physical discomfort and annoyance. It has been suggested that ultrasonic frequencies (above 20 000Hz), increasingly used in industry, can seriously damage the human ear even though the ear does not register their presence. Exposure to powerful ultrasonics can effect the nerve cells in the brain and spinal chords and can cause a feeling of nausea or a burning sensation of the auditory canals. Similarly, infrasound frequencies, i.e. below 20Hz, if sufficiently intense, can effect the sense of balance, cause fatigue, irritation and nausea. The brain is particularly sensitive to infrasound of 7Hz which coincides with the brain alpha waves. Exposure to this type of sound can prevent clear thought or concentration. Intense infrasound can cause internal bleeding if exposure continues over a length of time.

The main physiological effect of noise is that the inner ear becomes damaged, either acutely, due to sounds of very high intensity such as explosions, or gradually as a result of long exposure to high industrial noise levels. Other effects observed in humans are changes in the electrical conductivity of the skin, in the electrical activity of the brain (EEG), in heart and respiration rate, and in gross motor activity. Other effects have been noted during tests on animals and there is no reason why these same effects could not be present in man, but they have not as yet been documented. These have included changes in the size of several of the glands of the endocrine system, blood pressure changes, constriction of the blood vessels, dilation of the pupil of the eye. Observations of irritability, nausea, fatigue, anxiety, insomnia, also reduction of sexual urge and reduction of appetite have been noted in animals.

Apart from these physical changes, noise can cause psychological disturbances. Interruption of sleep by noise can cause people to become irritable and resentful against the cause of the noise. Speech communication can be impaired by noise masking resulting in inefficiency, a feeling of isolation, and more seriously can result in accidents. Warning bells on machinery, hooters on factory trucks or even motor cars, shouted warnings, can be missed because of their submergence in the overall noise. In several tests it has been established that productivity and efficiency can be seriously affected by high noise levels and that fewer mistakes are made when noise levels are reduced, although this is by no means always the case. When this occurs it is a direct result of the mental fatigue caused by noise which makes people disagreeable and has been shown to be a direct cause of absenteeism. There has also been a number of cases where the poor state of mental health of an individual has been directly attributed to high and subjectively annoying noise levels.

Noise can therefore be the cause of hearing loss, mental illness, reduction in productivity, or even loss of life. To protect the individual there are various devices which can be worn over or in the ears to reduce the level of noise received by the sensory system. These can be divided into two groups – those worn in the ear (auditory canal) and those covering the ear (pinna). The first type provides a very convenient form of hearing protection but not to the same degree as ear muffs. Dry cotton wool has little or no useful noise reduction effect when inserted into the ear, as is shown on Fig 8. Glass down, which can be supplied in easily dispensable packs, provides good protection but must be disposed of after each use. Rubber ear plugs can be re-used but attention

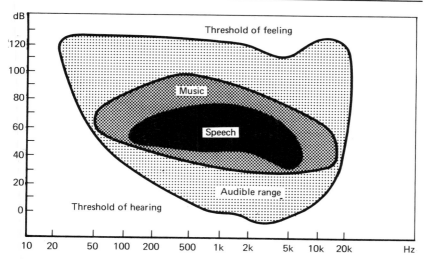

Figure 7. The important areas of hearing after Bilsom International Ltd

must be paid to hygiene. With all ear plugs there is a question of discomfort to the wearer. There is a saying which goes 'if it hurts, it works'. However, there is a relatively new development in ear plugs which expands into the auditory canal, after compression by the fingers, to provide a firm but not uncomfortable seal and thus good attenuation performance. Ear muffs come in a variety of types, each with its own level of performance. The seal around the edge of the cup is a very important factor in the muff's performance, foam filled seals being generally less effective than fluid seals. However, the latter can get punctured, causing a rather messy situation. The second factor is the weight of the cup itself; the heavier it is, generally the better the

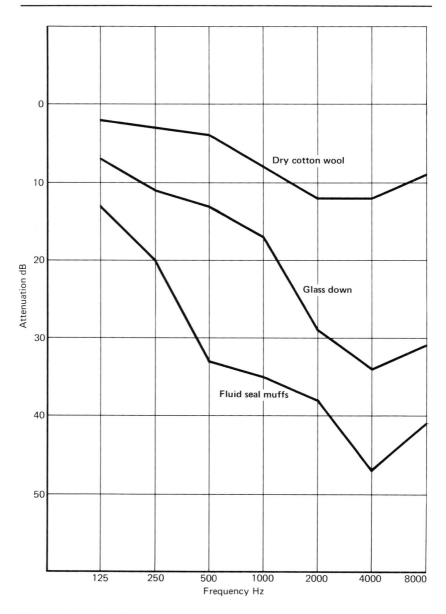

Figure 8.   The effects of ear muffs, glass down and cotton wool

attenuation performance. Although the ear muff does provide for better protection of the ear, it does have the disadvantage of weight and the problems associated with the seal around the ear. This seal can be disturbed, resulting in loss of performance, by the wearing of glasses or even long hair (Fig 8).

Whatever the hearing protection worn, if any, it is useful and possibly essential for people exposed to high noise levels to have their hearing checked at regular intervals (twelve months maximum). Remembering that loss of hearing can result from blows on the head, from other medical reasons and from factors outside the working environment such as sports, it is useful for the employee and his employer to know the level of his hearing threshold before exposure to high noise levels. It can be used as an indicator of the level of risk to which employees are being exposed and can prevent small levels of noise induced hearing loss becoming significant by drawing attention to particular processes and the need for the wearing of ear defenders, or even a change in job location for the person affected. Audiometry can also protect the employer from false claims for compensation due to noise induced hearing loss by unscrupulous employees or from employees not realising that they had a hearing impediment before joining the company. Audiometry can work for both the employee and the employer. The main problems are the practical ones of fitting the measuring sessions into a normal working week without undue disruption of work patterns. Because measurements can only be made after the person has been away from a noisy environment at least overnight, they can only be made first thing in the morning before the employee enters his normal work area. This restricts the number of people that can be checked each day.

Plate 1. Muff type ear defenders. The version shown is fitted directly to the normal industrial safety helmet. Ear defenders should be used where noise levels exceed NR 85 or 90dBA

3
Noise and the Law

NOISE produced by Industry affects people in two main ways. It causes annoyance to neighbours, particularly in mixed residential/industrial areas, and it causes actual damage to hearing of workers due to over-exposure at the workplace. There is a growing structure of legislation aimed at setting acceptable standards in both areas.

This chapter serves as an introductory guide to engineers; it does not attempt to offer definitive legal advice. Professional advice must be sought where legal action might be involved.

Several topics are discussed, directly concerned or associated with the following aspect of industrial noise:-

> Environmental noise and planning
> Noise on construction sites
> Workplace noise
> Occupational deafness
> Audiometry

Environmental Noise When environmental noise from a factory, say, can be heard in neighbouring houses it may constitute a legal nuisance. Legal nuisance is described as "an unlawful interference with a person's use or enjoyment of land". Along with smells, smoke fumes, dust, liquid effluent, etc, both noise and vibration emitted by Industry can be a nuisance to the neighbourhood.

There are basically three types of legal nuisance:-
1. Public Nuisance, in which inconvenience or damage is caused to a number of people. Action in this case may only be taken by the Attorney General and is relatively rare.
2. Private Nuisance, in which inconvenience or damage is caused to a single person's use or enjoyment of land. Action may be taken by this person (the plaintiff) but this is usually only done if the plaintiff is able to afford the high cost of the legal action. Both of the above nuisances – public or private – can overlap considerably and together they constitute a Nuisance at Common Law (see also later).
3. Statutory Nuisance – the most common form of nuisance – is defined as nuisance which has been designated by statute, such as the Control of Pollution Act 1974. This act incorporates a wide range of provisions including noise.

Action with regard to Statutory Nuisance generally follows complaints from householders being received by the Local Authority's Health Department. The latter is obliged under statutory duty to investigate all such complaints and to take whatever action is deemed necessary.

In cases where the Local Authority is agreed that a noise nuisance exists or is likely to re-occur, then they are able to issue a "Section 58 Notice" against the offender requiring the nuisance to be stopped. British Standard BS 4142, "Method of Rating Industrial Noise Affecting Mixed Residential and Industrial Areas", may be used for guidance. Corresponding noise nuisance from construction sites is controlled via a "Section 60 Notice".

In issuing an Abatement Notice under Section 58 of the Control of Pollution Act, the local authority may well specify the reduction in noise level required, an acceptable time limit, and even the actual steps to be taken. However, increasingly the offender is advised to seek specialist help from outside. In the event that the target noise level cannot be reached, it is an acceptable defence to demonstrate that the best practicable means has been applied to prevent or minimise the noise nuisance.

Appeal may be made within 21 days against an Abatement Notice on various grounds. Failure to comply with the Abatement Notice renders the person/firm causing the nuisance guilty of an offence under Part III of the Act and fines can be levied. Further, if the works specified in the Abatement Notice are not carried out correctly, the local authority can take steps to execute the works and recover the costs from the defaulter.

Planning and Development The Town and Country Planning (Assessment of Environmental Effects) Regulations came into force in the United Kingdom in July 1988. These regulations conform to Directive No 85/337/EEC and are described within Department of Environment Circular 15/88.

The Regulations require that projects which are likely to have significant effects on the environment by virtue of their nature, size or location, shall be subject to an assessment of those effects, in many case before planning permission is granted. Noise is one of the many factors to be considered, together with effects on flora, fauna, soil, water, air, etc.

Assessment of noise impact is carried out in line with Department of Environment Circular 10/73, "Planning and Noise". Paragraphs 24 to 36 of the Circular address the subject of noise from industrial premises and other fixed installations. Use is also made of British Standard BS 4142 as discussed earlier, in order to quantify noise "nuisance", the standard specifying measuring technique, correction and rating of individual noise.

The guidance given in Circular 10/73 and BS 4142 primarily relates to noise from industry as it affects residential development. In the event that there are schools, hospitals, offices etc nearby, guidance can be found in British Standard BS 8233. "Sound insulation and noise reduction in buildings".

Noise from Construction Sites Construction (and demolition) sites are subject to the Control of Pollution act 1974, usually as a condition imposed by the the Planning Consent. Such a condition typically specifies acceptable noise levels, the hours of working, any restriction of methods of working, types of machinery which may be used, and any other detailed constraints.

Guidelines on noise emission and control may be found in British standard BS 5228, "Noise Control on Construction and Open Sites".

An ever-increasing range of machine types used in building construction work, such as compressors, road drills, bull-dozers, excavators, and many others require type approval of their noise emission in order that they may be used within the European Community. Maximum acceptable sound power limits are specified dependent upon machine type and size, and testing takes place under strict measurement and load conditions. Machines which comply with the requirements are entitled to wear a plate as evidence of the fact.

Practical Aspects of the Law on Environmental Noise   Two case histories showing how local authorities operate in practice follow. The first describes noise control requirements as a remedy after construction and commissioning. The second show how level requirements were made at the planning level of a plant.

a) A large animal feed mill had been built on a small new industrial estate at the edge of a country town. No conditions on noise levels had been applied in the planning permission, although there were houses on a new estate only 150 metres from the finalised position of the mill building. The original preferred position of the mill was further away from these houses and the planning authorities apparently moved it to its present site for visual or other reasons.

When the mill began to operate, immediate complaints were received from the occupants of the nearby houses. Measurements were made near the houses and it was discovered that the normal operative noise level at night was 57dBA with a strong and objectionable pure tone component. The normal pre-existing background noise level was in the region of 30 to 35dBA.

Some noise control work was carried out initially to reduce the noise level down to 53dBA.

At this stage the Environmental Health Department of the Local Authority issued a notice under the Control of Pollution Act 1974, requiring works to be carried out to reduce the noise level at the houses to a maximum of 10dBA greater than the previous background noise (which was agreed to be 35dBA).

A great deal of noise control work was carried out on individual noise sources and on the building cladding, which resulted in a final night time operating noise of 41dBA. This level was accepted by the local authority and complaints about noise ceased.

b)A small capacity asphalt plant was being replaced by a larger new plant on a site by a railway and main road, with a few houses at the edge of the site near the road.

Planning permission had been given with a condition on noise attached: "The corrected noise level (in accordance with British Standard 4142: 1967) from operations conducted on the premises shall not exceed 48dBA as measured at the southern boundary of the application site between the hours of 0800 and 1800 Mondays to Saturdays, and 40dBA at any other time."

The reasons for the conditions were to ensure that the noise levels would not cause nuisance to nearby residents.

There were two important points inherent in this condition. Firstly, the normal start-up time for the asphalt plant was early in the morning at 0600 to 0700 hours.
Secondly, the existing old and rather noisy plant had been operating without complaints for at least six years. The noise in the early morning from heavy traffic on the main road was 50dBA, with peaks up to 70dBA.

Representation was made to the local Authority, resulting in a meeting with the Environmental Health Department at which a compromise was reached. A revised planning permission was granted in which the noise levels remained the same but the time limits were changed to 0600-1600 hours.

A basic asphalt plant without environmental emission controls is relatively noisy and produces atmospheric pollution in the form of dust, smoke and fumes, etc. To counteract this, a special scrubber is usually added to the exhaust and this normally has a noisy fan requiring careful attenuation.

For reasons of noise and pollution control, a special new type of plant was chosen for the project which was inherently quieter and could meet the planning authority's requirements without major modification. The plant was installed and proved acceptable in that no complants were received from the local residents, thus satisfying the Local Authority.

Workplace Noise and Damage to Hearing While it has been recognised for very many years that the exposure of work-people to noise is hazardous and that noise-induced hearing loss cannot be corrected to any significant degree by means of medical treatment. Only in the last few years has research been conducted to quantify the relationship between noise exposure and deafness. The introduction of Statute Law to impose controls on noise exposure is even more recent. For example, between 1974 and 1989 the only areas of industry which were subjected to noise control by law were the Woodworking Industry, Agricultural Tractor Cabs, and the Offshore oil and gas industry. There was an absence of legal control of exposure to noise at the workplace until 1 January 1990 when all Member States of the European Community were required to implement national legislation. The objective is to safeguard the hearing of people at work by imposing a wide range of specific duties upon employers, employees, and manufacturers of new machinery.

The UK's Noise at Work Regulations 1989 specify a series of requirements which are to be applied where noise exposure of a worker is likely to be at or above any of three "Action Levels". These requirements and their corresponding Action Levels are summarised in Appendix 3.

The term $L_{EP,d}$ is the "daily personal noise exposure level" and is derived from both noise levels and durations of exposure to which the person is exposed in the course of his work-day. The First and Second Action Levels are normalised to an 8 hour working day. Daily personal noise exposure is ascertained using the formula:

$$L_{EP,d} = 10 \log_{10} \frac{1}{To} \int_{o}^{Te} \left[\frac{pA(t)}{po}\right]^{2} dt$$

where Te = duration of the persons personal exposure to noise
       To = 8 Hours
       pA(t) = the time-varying value of A-weighted instantaneous
              sound pressure, Pa
       po = 20×10^{-6} Pa

It will be seen that this formula takes into account both shorter and longer exposure periods, such as for example, a twelve hour shift. In simple terms, exposure to a steady level of 85dBA for a period of eight hours has the same effect as 88dBA for four hours or 82dBA for sixteen hours. On this basis – permitting an additional 3dBA for each halving of the duration of exposure – a person working in a steady environment of 102 dBA will reach the First Action Level in less than 10 minutes and the Second Action Level in 30 minutes. While it is clear that personal ear protection must be provided in such circumstances, no account must be taken of the protective benefit in assessing a daily personal noise exposure.

Table 2 illustrates how a worker's daily personal noise exposure is assessed from his work pattern including both total duration and noise level of each task. The nomogram presented in Appendix 4 can be used in place of the $L_{EP,d}$ formula if required. The procedure is to take a straight line between the exposure time and the equivalent continuous sound level (L_{eq}) of each task or element of the work pattern. This straight line intersects the centre scale on which the appropriate fractional exposure can be read. For example, 2 hours exposure at a level of 102dBA gives a fractional exposure of 4.0.

Table 2
Work pattern of Steel Fabricator

NAME:	CLOCK NUMBER:	DEPARTMENT	
Description of Task	Time	Noise Exposure Level, dBA	Fractional Exposure
Work Preparation	1 hr 30 min	87	0.10
Welding	3 hr 45 min	94	1.20
Shot Blasting	1 hr 25 min	102	2.75
Record-keeping	45 min	85	0.03
Breaks, etc	35 min	<65	0.00

TOTAL FRACTIONAL EXPOSURE = 4.08

from nomogram, 8 hour $L_{EP,d}$ = 96dBA

In order to reduce this worker's daily noise exposure level to below 90dBA, the Second Action Level, his fractional exposure would need to be less than 1.0. The same nomogram can be used in making assessments in relation to the 85dBA First Action Level but in this case the fractional exposure limit would be 0.31.

The Noise at Work Regulations 1989 are supported by a series of noise Guides issued by the Health and Safety Executive. These serve to provide interpretation of the legal duties as laid down in the Regulations, and general guidance on noise surveying, noise control by engineering means, personal ear protectors, training of competent persons to undertake noise assessment and control programmes, noise testing of machinery, exemption procedures and so on.

Occupational Deafness Prior to The Noise at Work Regulations 1989, most claims for industrial deafness would appear to have been settled out of court and there is little case law available on which to base definite guidance regarding the likelihood of any particular claim being successful.

While it has been known for well over 100 years that the exposure to excessive noise is responsible for hearing loss, only since the publication of "Noise and the Worker", Safety, Health and Welfare new series No 25, in 1963, has there been a definitive point in time after which employees are expected to be adequately aware of the risks and the remedial measures necessary to minimise them. This "State of Knowledge" has been tested in the courts but with varying degrees of success.

There are several references available to the claim of industrial deafness. These include **causation** where the plaintiff must show that on the balance of probabilities his loss of hearing is due to exposure to noise at his place of work. **No breach of duty** may be a defence where the plaintiff was adequately protected, where levels of noise and durations were not excessive, and where the plaintiff's exposure to noise occurred before the defendant could reasonably be expected to be aware of the risks. **Contributory negligence** perhaps occurring when the plaintiff has not worn the personal ear protection provided, may well be an appropriate defence.

In view of the slow and progressive way in which hearing loss can arise, a defence may be presented under the **Limitation Act 1980,** which states that a claim has to be brought within three years from the injury occurring or the plaintiff first learning that his hearing loss was significant.

It remains to be seen how the Legal Profession will be required to act in response to future claims for compensation by sufferers of noise induced hearing loss; it is likely that as awareness of the law and the duties placed on employers grows, so there will be more claims and cases. The need for irrefutable evidence, will, in turn become more significant and the keeping of accurate records will be just as important as the actual implementation of hearing conservation and noise reduction programmes.

Audiometry Audiometry is the science of the measurement of hearing. In the United Kingdom it is not a requirement of The Noise at Work Regulations 1989 to conduct testing of employee's hearing. The European Community Directive 86/88/EEC, however, requires facilities to be made available for audiometric testing. The explanation of this apparent anomaly is that British Law avoids duplication. All citizens are already able to request a hearing test from their General Practitioner under The National Health Service. In practice, such is the heavy load on the NHS that the waiting list for hearing testing can be between five months and over two years.

For information, the standard method used for testing a person's hearing is 'Pure Tone Audiometry' and is a means whereby the patient's threshold of hearing is established at discrete tonal frequencies. The test takes place in a sound-proof booth with the patient wearing headphones. He has a button to press whenever he hears a tone played into one ear at a time. The frequencies normally used are in octave steps from 125Hz to 8kHz, often with an additional tone at 3kHz, this being important in the intelligibility of speech. Sound level steps are generally in 5 decibel increments.

Examples of hearing loss as measured by audiometric testing are presented in Chapter 2, Figures 5 and, in idealised form, Figure 6.

Plate 1. A fragmentation plant for efficient breaking down of scrap cars into their constituent materials – ferrous and non-ferrous metals, plastic, etc. Such a plant can be a serious noise problem to nearby residents

4
Sound in Rooms

IN Chapter 1, the concept of the Inverse Square Law was introduced. The principle of this is that for a free progressive wave, as the distance from the source increases, the available area of the wave front over which the energy is spread also increases and, consequently, the resulting sound intensity (sound energy per unit area) is reduced.

When the sound field is spherical (i.e. sound spreading out in all directions), we may write:

$$I = \frac{W}{4\pi r^2} \qquad\qquad (4.1)$$

where I = sound intensity
$\quad\quad W$ = sound power

As sound intensity is related to sound pressure and taking logarithms to the base 10, we can determine that:

$$\begin{aligned} SPL &= SWL - 20 \log r - 10 \log 4\pi \\ &= SWL - 20 \log r - 11dB \end{aligned} \qquad (4.2)$$

where $\quad$ SPL $\;=$ sound pressure level re $2 \times 10^{-5} N/m^2$
$\qquad$ SWL $=$ sound power level re 10^{-12} watt
$\qquad\;\; r \quad\;\;=$ distance from source (metres)
or in Imperial units
$SPL = SWL - 20 \log r$
where $r =$ distance from source (ft)

It can therefore be seen that for spherical radiation, the sound pressure level is reduced by 6dB for every doubling of the distance from the source. In a room, however, sound is not free to travel unconstrained (at least not for long) because in a very short time after the source begins to emit sound the wave front will encounter the boundaries of the room.

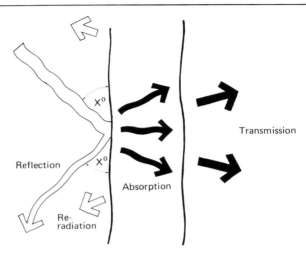

Figure 1. Reflection, absorption and transmission at a barrier

Three important things take place when this occurs and these are depicted in Fig 1. Some of the energy is transmitted through the structure, some of it is absorbed within the material, and the remaining part is reflected back into the room. From the law of energy conservation, we may therefore write:

$$E_i = E_t + E_a + E_r \qquad\qquad (4.3)$$

(energy incident) = (energy transmitted, absorbed and reflected)

Sound Transmission   The energy which is transmitted will give rise to a new sound field on the other side of the boundary. The degree and methods by which this transmitted sound can be controlled will be dealt with fully in Chapter 5.

Sound Absorption   The energy which is absorbed is usually the result of being converted into another form of mechanical energy which is generally heat and this may be achieved in several different ways. The amount of sound energy which is absorbed is described as the ratio of sound energy absorbed to the sound energy incident, and is termed the 'sound absorption coefficient'. Using the same notation as for (4.3), we may write:

$$\alpha = \frac{E_i - E_r}{E_i} \qquad\qquad (4.4)$$

where α = sound absorption coefficient

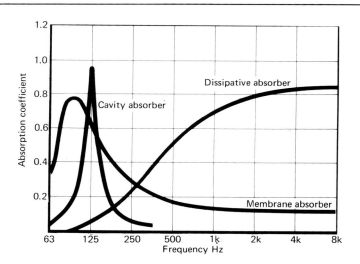

Figure 2. Absorber response curves

Fig 2 shows the typical absorption coefficients for three common types of sound absorbers. Dissipative or porous absorbers, such as glass fibre or mineral wool blankets, open cell foams and acoustic tile type materials, are so called because the sound energy is dissipated in the interstices of the fibres. It can be seen that their maximum efficiency occurs at the higher frequencies where the wavelengths of sound are comparable with the typical thicknesses of these materials that are used in practice. Absorption coefficients for common materials are given in Appendix 1.

Membrane or panel absorbers convert sound energy into heat as a result of bending deformations associated with the vibrations of the panel which are excited by the incident sound. As can be seen, the sound absorption of membrane absorbers is predominant at the lower frequencies. The frequency of maximum absorption (known as the resonant frequency) is determined by the mass of the panel and the stiffness and depth of airspace behind it from the following expression:

$$f_{res} = \frac{60}{\sqrt{md}} \qquad\qquad (4.5)$$

f_{res} = frequency of maximum absorption
where m = mass of the panel kg/m^2
        d = depth of the airspace in metres
or

$$f_{res} = \frac{49}{\sqrt{md}}$$

where m is in lb/ft^2 and d is in ft.

The value of the peak absorption coefficient is dependent upon the degree of damping in the system. Increasing the damping can actually reduce the absorption coefficient, although the band of frequencies covered is widened (Fig 3) and it is not therefore correct to assume that placing mineral wool or glass fibre behind a panel will necessarily result in increasing the absorption coefficient.

Care must be taken when the wavelength of the resonant frequency is greater than the lateral dimensions of the panel to ensure that the airspace is well sealed. Failure to observe this will result in a lowering of the stiffness of the air and a consequent reduction of the resonant frequency.

It is not a simple process to determine the maximum absorption coefficient at the resonant frequency because there are many not readily quantifiable factors involved. However, it would be safe to assume not more than about 0.4 as representative for the type of panels which may be used in industry. Sound absorbers which exhibit the combined characteristics of both the panel and dissipative types can be constructed. Such an absorber, which could have a good absorption coefficient over a wide range of frequencies, would be formed by having a perforated panel of, for example, 20% open area 3mm (⅛in) hardboard over a porous material of 25-50mm (1-2in) thickness.

Cavity or Helmholtz resonator absorbers provide a very high absorption coefficient but over a very narrow band of frequencies. Because of this, they are not so commonly used but could well have more use for industrial applications where it is necessary to reduce the effect of pure tones. The absorption is obtained as a result of the tiny slug of air in the neck of the opening being forced to oscillate at a frequency determined by the size of the opening and the volume of the enclosed cavity. The

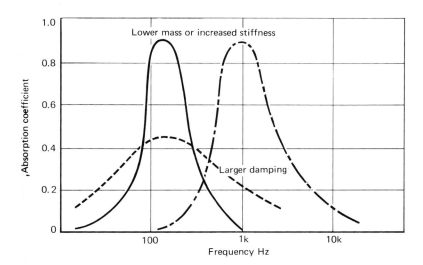

Figure 3. Changes affecting the performance of membrane absorbers after Day, Ford & Lord

resonant frequency can be calculated from the approximate expression:

$$f_{res} = \frac{c}{2\pi} \sqrt{\frac{s}{lv}} \qquad (4.6)$$

where c = speed of sound (approx. 344m/sec (1130ft/sec)
        at 20°C)
    s = cross-sectional area of neck opening
    l = length of neck
    v = volume of cavity
all in consistent units

Sound Reflection The sound energy which is reflected off a boundary does so in a manner which is determined by the angle of incidence of the sound wave and the shape of the surface. In this context, an analogy can be drawn with optics and Fig 4 shows the reflection sequences that can be expected. The first example shows that, for a plane reflecting surface, the angle of reflection of the sound wave is equal to the angle of incidence and, depending upon the proximity of the source to the surface, divergence takes place. The second example shows a convex surface where dispersion occurs, and finally the third example is a concave surface where the sound is concentrated and focusing results.

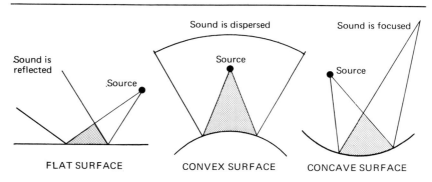

Figure 4. Reflection from different surface shapes

However, these generalised reflection patterns are subject to certain limits:

a) The wavelengths of the incident sound must be small compared with the size of the reflecting surfaces, otherwise diffraction may occur. Therefore it is found that for very low frequencies sound is only reflected well in large spaces off large surfaces.

b) The reflective surface is smooth, i.e. any surface modelling must be large or very small in relation to the wavelength. Any surface irregularities with dimensions similar to the wavelengths of incident will cause scattering, resulting in complicated reflections in all directions.

Reverberant Sound When a source of sound starts up in a room, the first sound a listener hears is that which arrives directly from the source. This is not affected by the boundaries of the room and is attenuated only in accordance with the inverse square law. The next sound which is heard is that which is reflected once and, in addition to distance attenuation, it is also affected by the sound absorptive quality of the surface. Then there is the sound which arrives after two, three or more reflections, each one arriving successively later and in a characteristic manner determined by the absorption of the surfaces from which they have been reflected and the size of the space (Fig 5).

These multiple reflected or reverberant sounds combine together, and with the direct sound, to form the resulting sound pressure level. Close

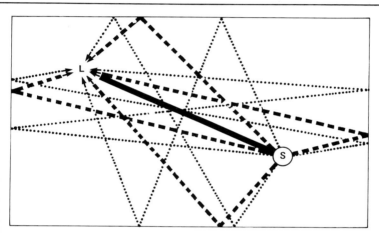

Figure 5. Development of sound field

to the source, the direct sound will predominate and will reduce with increasing distance from the source until the reverberant sound becomes dominant, when the sound pressure level will remain reasonably constant, irrespective of increasing distance. It is to be expected that, if sound energy is continuously introduced into a room, the resulting sound pressure level will rise until an equilibrium state is achieved. At this point the rate of energy input from the source will be the same as that absorbed either through or in the boundary materials. Consequently, a room with hard reflective walls and little sound absorption in it is termed 'live' and will have a higher reverberant sound pressure level than a room of the same size with a lot of sound absorption which is called 'dead' (Fig 6).

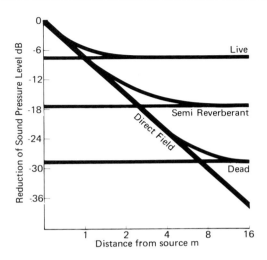

Figure 6. Components of sound fields

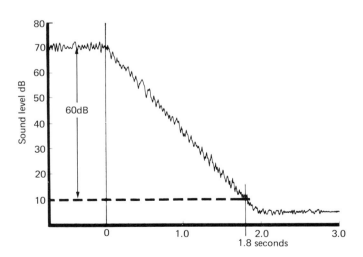

Figure 7. Reverberation time

Reverberation Time It has been indicated that the sound absorptive qualities of a room influence the way in which the sound field in a room is built up when a source is switched on. Likewise, when a source is stopped, the sound heard does not cease immediately but there is a finite time for it to be reflected off each surface where part of it is gradually absorbed. The time taken for this decay, which can be measured, calculated or estimated, is also dependent upon the sound absorption within a room. It is therefore a useful means for determining these qualities and for making comparisons of the acoustical conditions of different spaces. Specifically, this sound decay or reverberation time, as it is called, is the time taken for the sound energy to decay by 60dB or to 10^{-6} of its original intensity (Fig 7).

The reverberation time may be measured directly by charting the decay of sound following a gun shot or balloon burst, or it may be estimated from:

$$R = \frac{0.16V}{S\bar{\alpha}} \qquad\qquad (4.7)$$

where R = the reverberation time (sec)
        V = room volume (m³)
        S = surface area of the room (m²)
        $\bar{\alpha}$ = average room absorption coefficient

or

$$R = \frac{0.049}{S\bar{\alpha}}$$

where V is in ft³ and S in ft²

Room Sound Pressure Level Calculations It was shown in expression (4.1) that:

$$I = \frac{W}{4\pi r^2}$$

where I = sound intensity in the direct field
Likewise, the sound intensity in the reverberant field may be expressed as:

$$I = \frac{4W}{R} \qquad\qquad (4.8)$$

where R, room constant = $S\bar{\alpha}/(1 - \bar{\alpha})$ where S = total room surface (m²) and $\bar{\alpha}$ = average room absorption coefficient

These two expressions may be combined as:

$$I = \frac{WQ}{4\pi r^2} + \frac{4W}{R}$$

$$= W \left(\frac{Q}{4\pi r^2} + \frac{4}{R} \right) \tag{4.9}$$

where Q = directivity factor (see Table 1 and Fig 8)

Where as previously it was assumed that the source was in free space and radiated spherically in all directions, in practice this situation is rarely found. More often the source of sound is situated on the ground and consequently twice as much sound power is radiated in a given direction (i.e. that reflected off the ground is added to that already radiating outwards). Likewise, if a source is located at the junction of a floor and wall, four times as much power is radiated. This phenomenon is taken into account in the expression by means of the directivity factors as follows:

Table 1

Source Location	Directivity Factor Q
In free space (i.e. suspended well below ceiling)	1
On a flat plane (i.e. on the floor)	2
Junction of two planes (i.e. floor and wall)	4
Junction of three planes (i.e. floor and two walls) (Fig 8)	8

Taking logarithms$_{10}$ of (4.9) and expressing in terms of sound pressure gives:

$$SPL = SWL + 10 \log \left(\frac{Q}{4\pi r^2} + \frac{4}{R} \right) dB \tag{4.10}$$

using metric units

$$SPL = SWL + 10 \log \left(\frac{Q}{4\pi r^2} + \frac{4}{R} \right) + 10dB$$

using imperial units

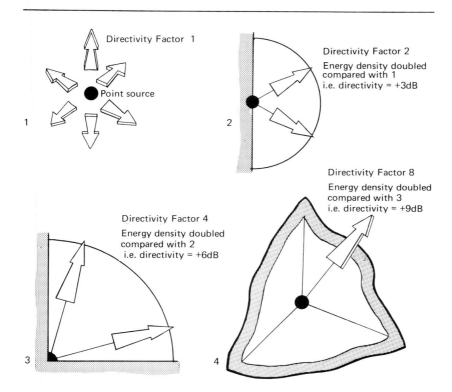

Figure 8. Directivity patterns of noise sources

It will be obvious that, for any position in a room, the closer to the source the greater will be the effect of the direct sound, but at some point both the direct and reverberant components will be equal. At this point, which is called the 'room radius':

$$\frac{Q}{4\pi r^2} = \frac{4}{R}$$

and therefore it can be deduced that the room radius is equal to

$$\sqrt{\frac{RQ}{16\pi}} \tag{4.11}$$

Sound Pressure Level Calculations To avoid the necessity for calculation on each occasion, both expressions (4.10) and (4.11) have been combined into a chart (Fig 9) whereby the relative sound pressure level can be determined from a knowledge of the room volume, its reverberation time or room constant, the distance from and directivity of the source.

Example Consider a machine of sound power 90dB situated on the floor and against the wall of a small factory space of 3000m³ with a reverberation time of 2sec. What will be the sound pressure level 5m from the source?

Enter the graph on the distance axis at 5m and rise obliquely until the intersection of the directivity ordinate 4 (Table 1). The vertical line from this point rises until it intersects the horizontal line from the right, which itself has originated from the intersection of the vertical ordinate from 3000m³ and the oblique ordinate for 2sec. At the point which the vertical (from distance and directivity) and horizontal (from room characteristics) lines converge, read −15dB on the relative sound pressure level scale. The resulting sound pressure level at 5m is therefore 90dB−15dB = 75dB. For external noise sources the same procedure is followed except that the room characteristic is given by the R = ∞ line

For room volumes or reverberation times not given in Fig 9, the reverberant sound pressure level below the sound power level may be calculated from:

$$SPL = SWL - 10 \log_{10}V + 10 \log_{10}R_t + 14dB \qquad (4.12)$$
(dimensions in metres)
$$SPL = SWL - 10 \log_{10}V + 10 \log_{10}R_t + 29dB$$
(dimensions in ft)

The achievement of the reverberant component of the sound pressure level in a room is only possible when the multiple reflection process of sound between the boundaries of space is not inhibited. In the case of a very large enclosure, particularly if it has a low ceiling, when the ratio of the smallest lateral dimension to the height is 10:1 or more, the previous assumptions do not hold. Such rooms are often described as two-dimensional. Under these conditions, the sound from the source

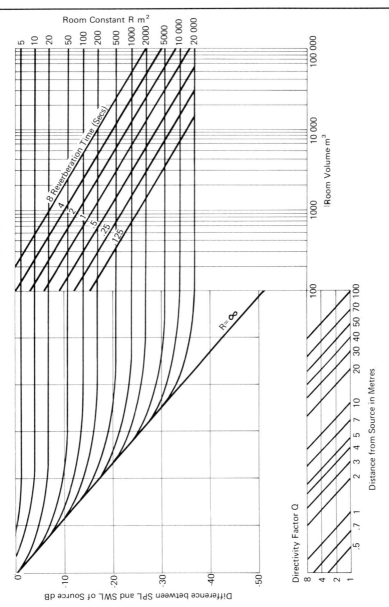

Figure 9. Calculation chart for estimating overall SPL in enclosed spaces

has to travel so far before it is reflected from one of the walls that it is effectively attenuated and does not contribute to the reverberant field. The sound pressure level at any point is therefore dominated by the direct sound field, although this may be modified by reflections from the ceiling or intermediate obstacles. The sound decay does not normally achieve the 6dB for doubling of distance as would the direct

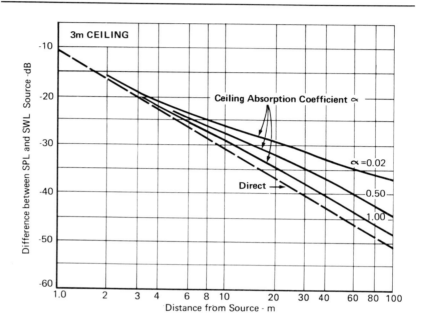

Figure 10. Approximate SPL between floor and ceiling in a 'two dimensional' room 3m high

field, but is generally between 4dB or 5dB depending upon the sound absorption of the ceiling. Fig 10 indicates typical attenuations for distance with different ceiling absorption coefficients for a height of 3m.

If there are a number of sources of sound in one space and they are all operating, it is comparatively easy to work out the resulting reverberant sound pressure level by combining logarithmically the various sound power levels and then making the room corrections as already

indicated. However, in two-dimensional rooms it is not so straightforward to combine the effects of a number of different sources and Fig 11
gives a graphic method for finding the approximate sound pressure
level under such circumstances with two different ceiling heights.
Ceiling absorptions different from those shown may be interpolated.

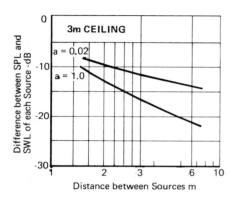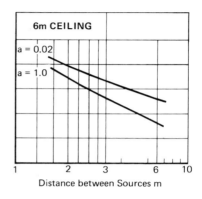

*Figure 11. Approximate SPL at centre of a uniform square array of
equal sources in a 'two dimensional' space in terms of the centre
spacing of the sources*

Acoustical Faults Although acoustical faults are not really problemat-
ical in industrial situations, apart from excessive noise of course, a brief
review of these will be given to enable an industrial engineer to fully
understand his acoustic environment.

Echoes are probably the most well known and occur when a listener
hears a reflected sound so long after the direct sound and so loudly as
to sound separate. Many factors determine whether or not an echo will
be audible but in general, if they are to be avoided, a path difference
(reflected–direct path) of about 15m should not be exceeded. (Fig.
12)

Flutter echoes can be heard when an impulsive sound occurs between
surfaces such that the sound is reflected backwards and forwards many
times along the same path. This is normally between two parallel

surfaces which are 'hard' acoustically, although other boundary configurations can lead to the same effect. The effect is generally heard as
a 'buzzing'. (Fig. 13)

Focusing, as was described in the section on sound reflection, occurs
when sound is reflected from a concave surface. The effect is that, at
the point of focus, the sound pressure is increased and 'hot spots'
result.

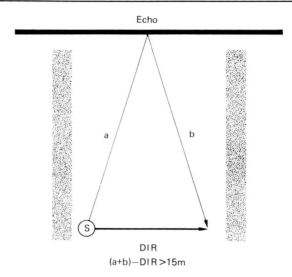

Figure 12. Echoes

All three of the foregoing faults can be overcome by ensuring that the
sound is not so readily reflected off the particular surfaces. This can be
done by increasing the sound absorption on the surface at the disturbing frequencies, or by making the surfaces diffuse so that the sound is
reflected at random.

Shadowing occurs when screens or overhangs result in areas where
sound reflections are prevented from reaching and the sound pressure
level is actually reduced or changed in character. Although this causes
a disturbance to the normal sound field and may therefore be considered a fault, this can actually be used to advantage. In Chapter 12 it

will be shown how screening can be used to reduce the output from machinery to the benefit of personnel who might otherwise be disturbed or even subjected to a health hazard.

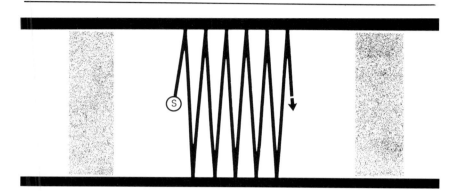

Figure 13. Flutter echoes

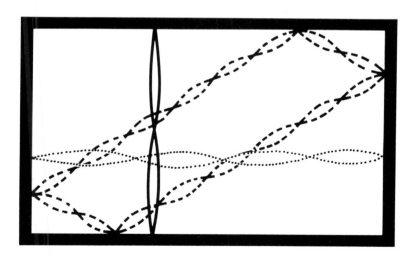

Figure 14. Standing waves

Standing Waves It has been shown in Chapter 1 that every frequency of sound has a corresponding wavelength and that the lower the frequency the longer the wavelength. At some frequencies, and especially in smaller rooms, multiples of the half wavelength of a particular frequency will match the dimension between two opposite reflecting walls. When this occurs, a standing wave or room mode is set up whereby the sound pressure is reinforced and also decays more slowly if the sound is switched off. Other axial standing waves can also occur between the other opposite pairs of boundaries while tangential and oblique modes can occur between even more of the boundaries. At low frequencies, the room modes are widely spaced and, if excited by a sound source, can easily be distinguished by the presence of regions of high and low noise level corresponding to the position of the wave in the room. At higher frequencies or in larger rooms, multiples of the wavelengths fit the room's dimensions with the result that very many standing waves occur close together and so they are not so noticeable. (Fig. 14)

Plate 1. A typical modern factory building showing the hard reflective surfaces which promote highly reverberant conditions – concrete floor, brick walls and plastic faced plaster board roof linings

5
Sound Insulation

IT was indicated in Chapter 4 that of the sound energy incident on a room boundary some is transmitted through the partition to adjacent areas. The transmitted sound will give rise to a new sound field which, if it is of a particular amplitude and frequency, may cause noise problems.

The ability of a partition to resist the flow of sound energy through it is termed its sound insulation and this is largely determined by its mass.

Mass Law Most of the principles involved in direct sound transmission are revealed by considering a single leaf wall. Chapter 1 on the fundamentals of acoustics showed that acoustic wave motion is transmitted through air in the form of successive compressions and rarefactions travelling at a speed of approximately 340m/sec (1120ft/sec) in the direction of propagation of the sound waves. In other words, air is able to transmit longitudinal wave motion by virtue of its compressibility. A wall, however, is constructed from an incompressible material and, as such, clearly cannot transmit acoustic wave motions in the manner of the surrounding air. Fig 1 illustrates how the incident sound wave acts on the partition – through its pressure fluctuations – and sets it into flexible or bending movements. These movements are usually extremely small but they radiate sound from the opposite side of the partition and also set supporting structural members into vibration. The flexible motions can be likened to ripples travelling across the surface of the partition with velocities very much higher than the speed of sound in air.

The amplitude of the sound waves radiated into the receiving room depends only upon the amplitude of vibrations in the wall and not on any other properties of the wall. In turn, the amplitude of the wall vibrations will depend on the amplitude of the pressure oscillations in the source room which acts on the wall. According to Newton's Law of Motion:

Force = Mass×Acceleration

and in an oscillatory system, amplitude and acceleration are proportional to one another. Thus the amplitude of wall vibrations is inversely proportional to the mass of the wall and it follows that the amplitude of

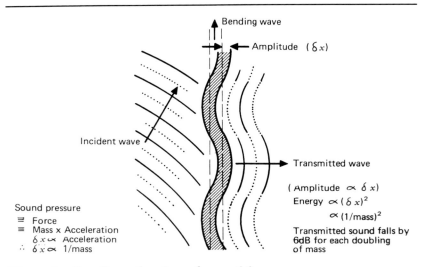

Figure 1. Bending vibration of a partition

sound waves radiated into the receiving room is similarly inversely proportional to the mass of the wall. Sound transmission is measured in terms of the energy reaching the receiving room. Since energy is proportional to the square of the velocity, and thus to the square of the amplitude, the transmitted sound is inversely proportional to the square of the mass of the wall. This means that, by doubling the mass of the wall, sound transmission is reduced by one quarter. In decibel measure, the insulation is increased by:

$$10 \log_{10}4 = 6dB$$

and by extending this argument it can be shown that a doubling in frequency will also produce a 6dB increase in insulation. Broadly,

these two statements about the effects of changes in mass and frequency constitute the Acoustic Mass Law. Later sections of this chapter will show other physical phenomena have an effect on the insulating performance of any structure and a more realistic statement of the
Mass Law would be to claim a 5dB improvement in insulation for each
doubling of weight or doubling of frequency.

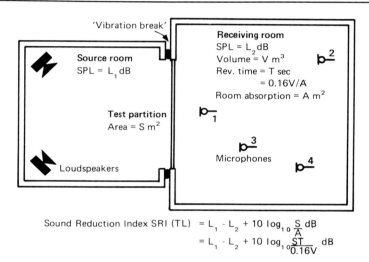

Sound Reduction Index SRI (TL) $= L_1 - L_2 + 10 \log_{10} \frac{S}{A}$ dB

$\qquad\qquad\qquad\qquad\qquad = L_1 - L_2 + 10 \log_{10} \frac{ST}{0.16V}$ dB

Figure 2. Measurement of SRI in laboratory

Sound Reduction Index Measurements of sound reduction index
require to be undertaken in special laboratories where the test procedure ensures that the sound transmission only takes place through a
partition under test and not via a flanking path. This can involve the
construction of complex laboratory installations which must conform
to the recommendations of BS2750 or ISO140. A diagrammatic
layout of a partition test is shown in Fig 2. The sound insulation
will be simply represented by the difference in the average sound
pressure levels in the two rooms at any given frequency:

Sound Insulation $= (L_1 - L_2)$ dB

The sound reduction index of the partition will be represented by the
measured sound insulation, adjusted to make the test result independent of the two variables that can affect the measured sound pressure

levels in the receiving room – the area of the test partition and the amount of absorption in the room. It will be evident that the transmitted sound pressure level L_2 will be directly proportional to the area of the partition under test. If the area of the partition were increased, more acoustic energy would be communicated to the receiving room and the measured sound pressure level L_2 would increase. Similarly, if the residual absorption A_2 of the room were increased, the net outflow of energy from the receiving room would increase and the measured sound pressure level would drop. Therefore the final expression of sound reduction index is:

$$SRI = L_1 - L_2 + 10 \log_{10}(S/A_2) \text{ dB}$$

Measurements are usually made at intervals of one third octave throughout the entire audio frequency band width. When discussing the performance of partitions in a general sense, it is normal to speak of the average sound reduction index as represented by the aggregate of the 16 measured values at one third octave intervals between 100Hz and 3150Hz. This will invariably be found to be similar to the single value measured at 500Hz. It is often convenient to use such average values for initial design calculations.

Absorption and Insulation By now it should be clear that there is a distinct difference between sound absorption and sound insulation. The best available sound absorber treatments for rooms provide approximately 70% absorption of low frequency sound and up to 95% absorption at high frequencies. However, sound absorption is rated on a linear scale and sound insulation on a logarithmic scale. Fig 3 and the

Table 1

Absorption or Loss Efficiency %	Insulation dB	Incident Energy Transmitted %
10	0.5	90
70	5	30
90	10	10
99	20	1
99.9	30	0.1
99.99	40	0.01

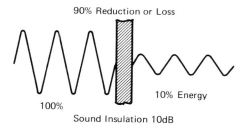

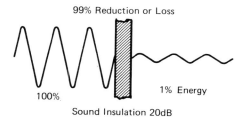

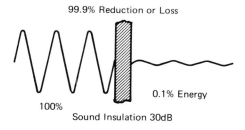

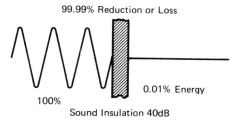

Figure 3.   Absorption versus insulation

following table show how the average sound absorbent treatment provides virtually no transmission loss and how exceedingly high absorption efficiencies would be required to give useful sound reductions.

Factors Affecting Sound Insulation The effectiveness of any structure as an insulator is determined by the following four parameters:
1. Weight
2. Homogeneity and uniformity
3. Stiffness
4. Discontinuity or isolation
Let us consider each of these features in turn.

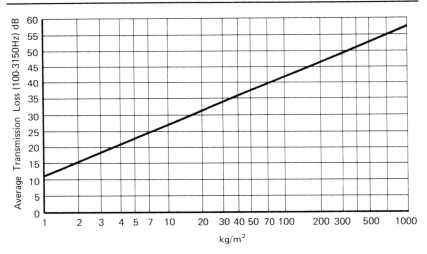

Figure 4. Mass Law Curve

Weight As noted in the introduction, the Acoustic Mass Law relates the superficial weight of a partition to its sound reduction index. This is quantified in Fig 4 where the average sound reduction indices of solid partitions are plotted against their weight per unit area. It will be seen that in general there is an increase in insulation of about 5dB for each doubling of weight.

In terms of imperial units only, a convenient way of remembering the Mass Law performance of medium and heavy weight partitions is to consider the performance of a single brick wall. A partition constructed of a single thickness of building brick will have a thickness of 4.5in, a superficial weight of 45lb/ft² and an average sound reduction index of 45dB. Consequently, the performance of a 9in brick wall will be represented by a doubling in the weight and an increase of 5dB, i.e. a 9in brick wall will give an average sound reduction index of 50dB. Similar extrapolations can be made by further redoubling or halving the performance noted here.

Since the average sound reduction index of a partition is very nearly equal to the performance at 500Hz, the performance at other frequencies can be determined knowing that the transmission loss increases by about 5dB for each doubling of frequency. For our single thickness brick wall, the sound reduction index at 1000Hz will be equal to 45+5dB = 50dB and at 250Hz will be equal to 45−5dB = 40dB. Further extrapolations up and down the audio frequency range are possible with a fair degree of accuracy.

It will be shown later that improvements in insulation can be obtained by complex discontinuous wall structures, but it should be noted that there is no such thing as an ultra-lightweight high efficiency acoustic partition. The weight of a wall is the primary consideration in all designs for sound insulation. Whenever it is likely that acoustically insulating partitions are required in a building structure, their weight should never be underestimated and provisions for supporting the mass of heavy partitions should be made in the preliminary planning stage.

Homogeneity The efficiency of sound insulation depends not only on the weight but on the completeness and uniformity of the structure. If there is a hole in the barrier, the sound energy or pressure is released and 'flanking' transmissions will pass through the hole, seriously degrading the total performance of the partition. As an example, a 40dB partition transmits only 0.01% of the sound energy incident on it. An air gap of only 0.01 of the area of such a partition (e.g. a gap of 1mm along the edge of a panel 10m×10m) will transmit as much energy as the partition, resulting in a 3dB loss in overall insulation. Where higher insulations are required. the potential reduction of performance due to air leaks becomes even more significant.

Stiffness Fig 5 represents, in idealised form, the frequency response of a typical partition. The performance is divided into three regions which are respectively:

Region 1   Stiffness controlled and resonances
Region 2   Mass controlled
Region 3   Wave-coincidence controlled

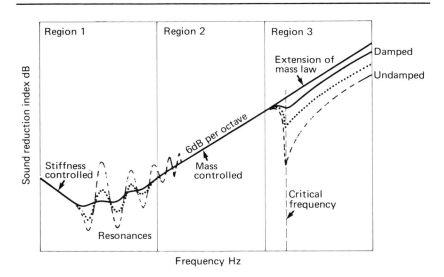

Figure 5.   *Mass Law + Stiffness + Coincidence*

The stiffness of the partition will have a bearing on the performance in both Regions 1 and 3. In Region 1 at low frequencies, partitions tend to exhibit bending motions whereby they tend to move as a membrane. Obviously the more resistance there is to the amplitude of this membrane vibration, the greater will be the low frequency insulation. Complex lightweight partitions having rigid foam plastic or honeycomb cores will often be found to exhibit very good low frequency insulation due to their inherent stiffness. However, such materials also exhibit a complex series of natural resonances which tends to reduce their performance at middle frequencies.

A further reduction in partition performance in Region 3 is known as the 'coincidence loss'. The loss arises when a plane wave approaching at an oblique angle produces a forced motion in the wall (Fig 6) which has a greater wavelength (the trace wavelength) than that of the incident waves in air. Normally the sound field incident upon a wall is regarded as 'diffuse' and may be visualised as being composed of multiple plane waves approaching the wall from all possible directions. Certain components of this sound field will impinge at oblique angles of incidence and, if of a given frequency range, will give rise to the 'coincidence loss'. It was noted earlier that it is possible for free bending waves to propagate in a wall because of its inherent stiffness.

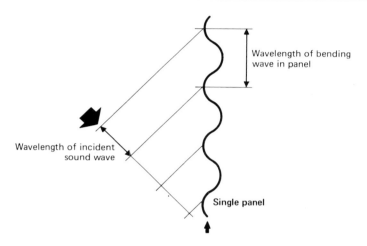

Figure 6. Coincidence effect

The amplitude of wall vibrations is greatly magnified when the wavelength of the free bending waves is near to that of the wave impressed on the wall by the incident sound wave. This, in its turn, results in greater energy transmission to the receiving room and hence an effective reduction in sound insulation. Wave coincidence can only occur when the wavelength of the free bending waves in the partition is greater than the wavelength of the airborne excitation. The frequency where these two wavelengths are equal is known as the 'critical frequency'. Above this frequency, sound transmission is dominated by coincidence. Near the critical frequency, coincidence occurs for glancing waves (see Fig 6). Thus in Region 3 of Fig 5 two effects which lead to high transmission act together and there is a large decrease in insulation.

The undesirable effects of both stiffness and coincidence can be reduced by increasing the damping of a partition and Fig 5 shows the improvements that are possible. Where high insulation performance is required, partitions which have mass, low stiffness and high damping are usually preferred. Sheet lead is a very good example of a material possessing these properties.

Flanking Transmission The sound reduction index expression given earlier considers only the transmission of sound energy directly from one space to another via the intervening partition. Sound which reaches the receiving room via more devious paths is termed 'flanking' or 'indirect' sound transmission. The example in the previous section demonstrated the significance of even small air paths in an insulating partition, and in practice many paths of airborne flanking may exist, such as gaps around demountable partitions, doors and windows, poor joints in builders' work, common ceiling voids and ventilation duct-work with openings into both spaces, etc.

A more basic limitation on the achievable insulation between spaces in the same building is the presence of structural flanking paths. Fig 7 shows diagrammatically four rooms (in plan or section) in a building of conventional continuous construction.

So far we have only considered the sound transmitted directly via the partition. However, the sound field in the source room A will cause vibration of all the internal surfaces of the room, which will be transmitted via the structure not only to room B, bypassing the partition, but also to rooms such as C and D with no common wall area with A. In practice, energy transmitted by structural flanking will limit the insulation between rooms such as A and B to about 50 to 55dB, although the partition separating the rooms may have a higher sound reduction index than this value. Between rooms such as A and C or A and D, with conventional construction, the insulation may be no more than 60dB. Improvements of 10 to 15dB may be achieved by structural discontinuities at wall-floor-ceiling joints. In extreme cases where insulation in excess of 60dB is required (e.g. studios, acoustic test laboratories) it may be necessary to construct a room completely isolated from the structure by resilient mountings.

Cavity Construction The sound reduction index of most partitions can be increased for the mass per unit area by the use of cavity construction. The principle is shown in Fig 8. If we consider the transmission of sound through two successive 115mm brick walls placed at a large distance apart, the overall average sound reduction index would be expected to be the sum of the SRI of the two components, i.e. 45+45 = 90dB (the two walls built together as a single 230mm wall would only provide an SRI of 50dB). Unfortunately, this great

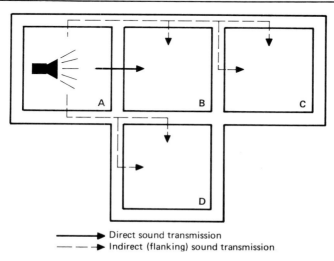

Direct sound transmission
Indirect (flanking) sound transmission

Figure 7. Flanking between rooms

improvement in insulation is not achieved in practice. The presence of structural flanking paths via edge supports, flanking walls and other mechanical connections between the leaves, limits the overall insulation. Also, it is not generally feasible to provide cavities of more than a few centimetres in width; the air contained within a narrow cavity is quite 'stiff' and transmits vibration from one leaf to the other, particularly at frequencies whose acoustic wavelengths are much longer than the cavity widths (i.e. at low frequencies). Also the insulating performance is further degraded by resonances of the mass-spring-mass system represented by the walls separated by an enclosed air filled cavity. In some cases the effect of such resonances can be reduced by the inclusion of absorbent material in the cavity. The net result of these

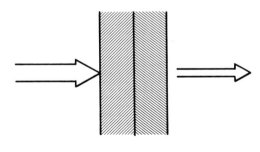

Single Wall   SRI = 50dB

Theoretical Cavity Wall   SRI = 90dB

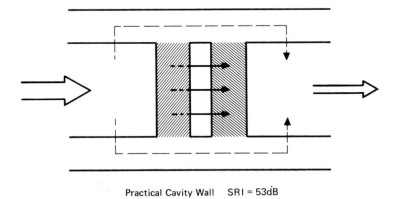

Practical Cavity Wall   SRI = 53dB

Figure 8.   Cavity versus single wall

factors on the insulating performance of a conventional 280mm cavity brick wall using 'butterfly' wire ties is to increase the average SRI to only 52 to 53dB compared with the 50dB provided by a 230mm solid brick wall.

The use of cavity construction is more effective when applied to materials of lower density, since the energy transmitted via flanking paths is less significant at the lower values of insulation achieved by such materials. A good example is a double glazed window. For a significant improvement in insulation over the same weight of glass in a single pane, cavity widths of at least 100mm and up to 300mm or more are necessary. Cavity absorption should be provided by the use of absorbent linings at the reveals and each pane should be airtight. For high performance windows, the use of resilient mountings for one or both panes may provide a small improvement. As explained earlier, the insulation performance of materials such as glass is degraded at mid to high frequencies by coincidence loss. To minimise the effect of this loss on the overall performance of double glazing, it is useful to specify panes of different thickness to ensure different critical frequencies.

Acoustic Performance of Typical Structures Fig 9 displays the average sound reduction indices of various building structures in relation to the mass law curve. It will be noted that certain compound discontinuous structures exceed the performance indicated by the mass law for single homogeneous slabs by up to 12dB. However, other partitions fail to meet the mass law performance either by virtue of panel resonances or coincidence losses or by leakage through the material or around its edges, as in the case of doors and windows. In addition, Appendix 2 gives in tabular form the SRIs of common building materials.

Calculations Involving Sound Insulation The value to the industrialist of knowing about the principles of sound insulation is so that he can assess whether a noisy machine or process is likely to cause problems to other people in the factory or adjacent neighbourhood. Chapter 4 discussed how to calculate the sound pressure level in a space knowing details of the sound power (SWL) of a machine or machines and of the room characteristics. This section of this chapter will show how to calculate how much noise from one area reaches another area in order that an assessment of its tolerability can be made.

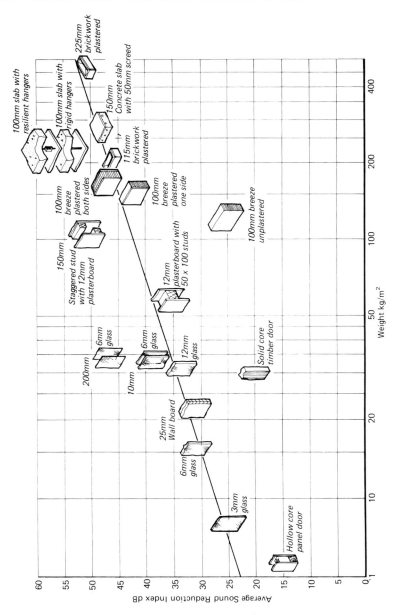

Figure 9. *Mass Law for common materials*

Case 1 – Room to Room Consider the case of a noisy workshop with a foreman's office to one side of it, separated by a partition. How much noise from the workshop will get into the foreman's office? The expression used to determine this is:

$$SPL_2 = SPL_1 - SRI + 10 \log_{10}S + 10 \log_{10}A \qquad (5.1)$$

where SPL_2 = resulting sound pressure level in the receiving room
$\quad\quad SPL_1$ = reverberant sound pressure level in the source room
$\quad\quad SRI$ = sound reduction index of the common partition
$\quad\quad S$ = area of the partition (m²)
$\quad\quad A$ = total absorption in the office $\dfrac{0.16V}{T}$

where V = office volume (m³)
$\quad\quad T$ = office reverberation time (s)

Example 1
Assume the workshop as in Chapter 4 of 3000m³ with a reverberation time of 2sec. The reverberant sound pressure level (SPL) in this case is 18dB below the sound power level of 90dB, i.e. 72dB. The SRI of the partition, which is of a typical demountable metal construction, is 35dB and its area is 10m². The office has a volume of 30m³ and a reverberation time of 1sec, but in this instance we do not need to know the SPL at any particular distance but rather the reverberant sound pressure level.

Starting with workshop reverberant SPL	72 dB
Partition average SRI	−35 dB
Partition area ($10 \log_{10} 10$ m²)	+10 dB
Room absorption correction	−7 dB
Office reverberant SPL	40 dB

Although this example has been shown in terms of average figures, it is in fact necessary to perform the calculation for each octave band in order to determine what is happening over the frequency range.

The final octave band levels may then be compared with the selected NC or NR criterion to determine their acceptability.

It was assumed in this example that the whole of the partition was of the same construction. It is likely that such a partition would have at least a door and possibly a window, each element of which would have a different SRI. In such a case, it is necessary to take the performance of each element into account in arriving at the overall performance of the partition. Fig 10 is a chart which can be used to find the combined performance of different elements.

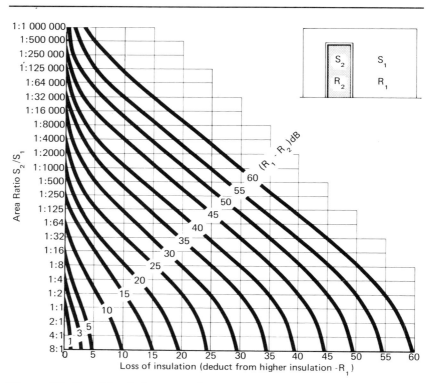

Figure 10. Combined elements chart

Example 2

The foreman's office partition is 10m² in total. Of this, the door of average 20dB SRI is 2m² and glazing of average 27dB SRI is 4m². The metal partition of average 35dB SRI is also 4m². Starting with the two larger areas, i.e. ratio 1:1 and difference of 8dB, determine from Fig 10 that the combined value is 6dB below the higher value, i.e. 35−6 = 29dB. The ratio of the door to the rest of the partition is 1:4 and the difference in average SRI is 9dB, i.e. 29dB−20dB. This gives from the chart a value of 4dB below the higher value, i.e. 29=4 = 25dB. Therefore the combined insulation of the three element partition is only 25dB compared with the 35dB of the metal partition alone. This shows what a dramatic effect lower SRI value elements can have when combined with otherwise high value constructions.

If in this case it was essential that the overall performance of the partition was not less than 35dB, it would be necessary to improve the performance of the door and glazing elements to 35dB also. Failing this, the performance of the partition would have to be improved such that the combined performance of three elements was acceptable.

Case 2 – Room to Outside Assume that the factory workshop has an external wall 3m high and 10m long, 30m from which is the rear wall of a dwelling. The wall is constructed of corrugated aluminium with an average SRI of 20dB. The industrialist needs to know how much noise from his factory will be incident on the rear wall of the dwelling and whether this is likely to provoke complaints. The expression is:

$$SPL_2 = SPL_1 - SRI + 10 \log_{10}S + 10 \log \left(\frac{Q}{4\pi r^2} \right) - 6dB$$

with S and r in consistent units

where SPL_2 = the sound pressure level at the dwelling facade
SPL_1 = the reverberant sound pressure level in the workshop
S = the area of the wall
$\frac{Q}{4\pi r^2}$ = directivity and distance corrections

The 6dB term occurs because there is no reverberant sound field in the open.

Assuming the same SPL in the workshop of	72dB
Wall average SRI	−20dB
Area of wall ($10\log_{10}30$).	+15dB
Directivity and distance Q = 2, r = 30m	−37dB
Non reverberant correction	−6dB
Facade SPL	24dB

Again, this procedure has to be carried out at each octave band so that a comparison with a criterion may be made.

Plate 1.   Close-up of the threshold of a sound resistant door used to maintain the sound insulation properties of enclosures and plant-rooms which contain noisy equipment near to critical areas. The perforated absorbent section shown obviates the necessity for a dirt collecting threshold board and gasket seal along the bottom

6
Vibration Theory

JUST as we are surrounded by noise, we are also surrounded by vibration. Vibration here is meant to describe the movement of solid materials such as the ground, walls of a building, or other items, in contrast to airborne audible noise. These structure-borne vibrations may be low frequency movements that we can sense with our finger-tips, or even see. On the other hand, they may extend in frequency up to the audible region, in which case we will detect them from the sound emitted. The basic principles are the same for both high and low frequencies and are outlined in chapter one – the Physics of Sound. The structural vibrations usually come from mechanical sources, possibly for reasons inherent in the design of the unit, or accidentally due to manufacturing modifications.

In general we have two situations (Fig 1); the first (Case A) in which we have a machine producing the vibration which we want to separate from the surrounding structure to protect the structure, and the second (Case B) in which we have a piece of equipment, such as a precision grinder, which we want to protect from vibrations in the structure caused by other operations. To overcome both of these problems, we will place a resilient member between the machine and the supporting structure shown in Case B. The selection and installation of such resilient members will form the basis of this chapter.

One of the consequences of separating the equipment from the structure in this way is that it is no longer rigidly tied to the structure and is therefore free to vibrate separately. It is therefore necessary in the first case that, not only should we minimise the force transfer between the equipment and the structure, but we must also minimise the vibration of the equipment (Fig 2). As a starting point, we will consider only the simple case of motion in one direction and we will consider the supporting structure to be exceedingly rigid. Later we will see that these two assumptions are not normally valid and it is necessary to modify the selection techniques to take these effects into account.

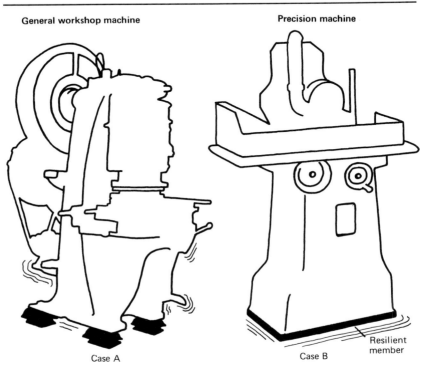

General workshop machine   **Precision machine**

Case A   Case B   Resilient member

Figure 1. The two basic vibration situations

Transmissibility In both cases considered earlier, the aim of vibration isolation is to reduce the force transmitted from the disturbing item. The transmissibility which, for the first case, is defined as:

$$T = \frac{\text{Transmitted force}}{\text{Disturbing force}} = \frac{F_t}{F_0}$$

is a criterion of the success of the operation. For the operation to be successful, T must be less than 1.

When we are protecting equipment from structureborne vibration, we have a similar definition based on the relative movements of the structure and the isolated equipment:

$$T = \frac{\text{Dynamic movement of isolated equipment}}{\text{Dynamic movement of supporting structure}} = \frac{X}{X_0}$$

The mathematics of these two situations is essentially identical. The transmissibility can be expressed either in fractional, decimal or percentage terms, e.g. $\frac{1}{10}$, 0.1 or 10%.

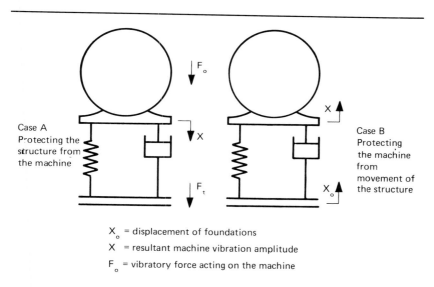

Case A
Protecting the structure from the machine

Case B
Protecting the machine from movement of the structure

X_0 = displacement of foundations
X = resultant machine vibration amplitude
F_0 = vibratory force acting on the machine

Figure 2. The two basic vibration situations

Efficiency Sometimes the complimentary term 'isolation efficiency' is used instead of 'transmissibility':

$$\eta = 1 - T$$

Whilst the term 'efficiency' gives an idea of the effectiveness of a system, it can be misleading. For instance, an increase in isolation efficiency from 98% to 99% might at first seem insignificant, even though this represents an improvement in transmissibility from 2% to 1%, which is a very significant improvement.

Reducing Vibration Transfer Ideally, one would know the vibrating forces produced by the source machine and also how much force can be tolerated by the supporting structure. From this information, the permissible transmissibility could be calculated and a system designed to achieve this. In practice, however, this is not generally feasible, since although the out-of-balance forces are calculable for internal combustion engines and similar equipment, they are not known for the majority of plant items. Similarly, the structural engineer rarely knows the forces that he can tolerate at any particular point in his structure.

However, experience with certain machines and structures has made it possible to produce guide tables such as Tables 1 and 2 which indicate appropriate transmissibilities for particular situations.

Achieving the Required Transmissibility In order to approach the subject, we must start with three simplifications:
1. The vibrating motion is in one direction only – conventionally vertical
2. The supporting structure is rigid
3. Linear springs, i.e. the deflection is proportional to the applied force.

These simplifications are not generally all true in practice and a blind assumption of them can lead to disasters. However, the assumptions simplify the understanding of the basic problem.

Natural Frequency f_0 The movement of a piece of equipment mounted on springs is governed by the out-of-balance forces which tend to produce motion, opposed by the stiffness of the springs, the mass of the equipment and any frictional effects which will tend to resist the motion. At low frequencies, the motion will be resisted primarily by the stiffness of the supporting springs. As the disturbing frequency tends towards zero, the movement of the equipment will be equal to the disturbing force divided by the spring stiffness. However, if the disturbing frequency is very high, the movement will be resisted by the mass effect of the mounted equipment. The motion will be reversing so rapidly that the whole disturbing force will be necessary to overcome the inertia of the mass and to provide the rapid changes in direction. Under these conditions, the effects of the spring stiffness will be negligible. From this it is seen that we have two totally different regions of behaviour. In the first, the system is said to be stiffness

Table 1
Recommended Isolation Efficiencies 150mm (6inch) Concrete Floor Slab

Critical Areas		Transmissibility %	Isolation Efficiency %
Centrifugal compressors		0.5	99.5
Centrifugal fans	greater than 25HP	2	98
Reciprocating compressors	greater than 50HP		
Pumps	greater than 5HP		
Axial flow fans	greater than 50HP	4	96
Centrifugal fans	5 to 25HP		
Reciprocating compressors	10 to 50HP		
Pumps	3 to 5HP		
Unit air conditioners	supported		
Fan coil units	supported		
Axial flow fans	10 to 50HP	6	94
Centrifugal fans	up to 5HP		
Reciprocating compressors	up to 10HP		
Pumps	up to 3HP		
Air handling units			
Axial flow fans	up to 10HP	10	90
Unit air conditioners	hung		
Fan coil units	hung		
Pipes	hung		
Gas fired boilers (more than 100 000BThU, 25kW)		7 to 12Hz	
Oil fired boilers (more than 60 000BThU, 15kW)		4 to 7Hz	

Table 2
Recommended Isolation Efficiencies (150mm (6inch) Concrete Floor Slab)

Less Critical Areas		Transmissibility %	Isolation Efficiency %
Centrifugal compressors		6	94
Centrifugal fans	greater than 25HP	10	90
Reciprocating compressors	greater than 50HP		
Pumps	greater than 5HP		
Unit air conditioners	supported		
Fan coil units	supported		
Axial flow fans	greater than 50HP	20	80
Centrifugal fans	5 to 25HP		
Reciprocating compressors	10 to 50HP		
Pumps	3 to 5HP		
Air handling units			
Unit air conditioners	hung		
Fan coil units	hung		
Axial flow fans	10 to 50HP	25	75
Axial flow fans	up to 10HP	30	70
Centrifugal fans	up to 10HP		
Reciprocating compressors	up to 10HP		
Pumps	up to 3HP		
Pipes	hung		
Gas fired boilers (more than 100 000BThU, 25kW)			12 to 20Hz
Oil fired boilers (more than 60 000BThU, 15kW)			12 to 20Hz

controlled because it is the stiffness of the springs which controls the movement. In the second region, the system is said to be mass controlled because here it is the mass which provides the controlling feature.

When the system is stiffness controlled, the effect of the spring stiffness is always to restore the mass to its equilibrium position against the influence of the disturbing force. In other words, the spring stiffness can be thought of as acting inwards, restoring the mass to its base position. When the system is mass controlled, the tendency is for the mass to resist the rapid change of direction of the movement at the extreme end of each stroke. If the mass is moving upwards, in the absence of the disturbing force the mass would tend to continue upwards. In other words, the effect of the mass is an outward one, in that it tends to keep the mass away from its equilibrium position. The stiffness is independent of the frequency, whilst the mass effect increases as the square of the frequency for a given amplitude of movement starting from zero at zero frequency. Therefore as the frequency is increased from zero, passing from the stiffness controlled region to the mass controlled region, there will be an intermediate region where the effects of the stiffness and the mass cancel out and neither factor exercises any restraint on the movement of the mass. Within this region the system will go completely wild unless other factors, such as friction, intervene. The frequency at which the mass and stiffness cancel out exactly is the frequency at which the spring and mass would vibrate if pulled away from their rest position and let go. This is called the natural frequency f_0 of the system. The idealised system that we are considering at this stage has only one natural frequency, although real life systems may have many.

Amplitude If we apply a constant disturbing force at increasing frequency (Fig 3) the movement of the sprung mass at low frequencies will be equal to the magnitude of the disturbing force divided by the spring stiffness. As the frequency is increased, the mass effect will gradually reduce the overall restraining force and the movement will increase. As the frequency increases, therefore, the movement will increase until the disturbing force coincides with the natural frequency, at which point, in an undamped system, the movement will become infinite at resonance. If the frequency is increased further still, the mass effect starts to dominate and the amplitude of motion will decrease until, at a point when the disturbing frequency is $\sqrt{2} \times$ the natural frequency, the amplitude of motion will be reduced to the value that occurred at low frequencies. As the frequency is increased higher still, the increasing effectiveness of the mass decreases the movement below the low frequency level.

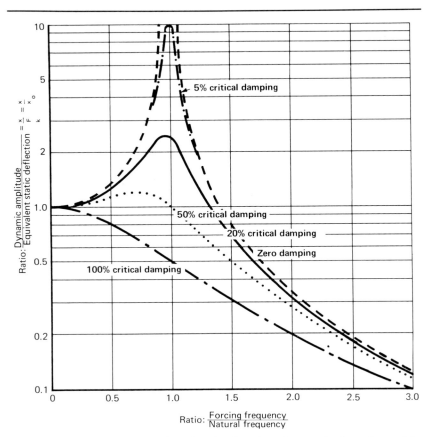

Figure 3. Dynamic amplitude of vibration for an isolated machine when subjected to a constant disturbing force

Transmitted Force The force is transmitted into the structure by the springs and is equal to the product of the spring stiffness and the amplitude of motion. If the motion is large, the transmitted force is large; if the motion is small, the transmitted force is small. Fig 3 can be re-labelled to show the variation of transmitted force with frequency

(Fig 4). Since the object of the exercise is to reduce the transmitted force below the value that we would have in the absence of the springs, we must arrange the system so that the forcing frequency is very much greater than the natural frequency. Until the forcing frequency reaches

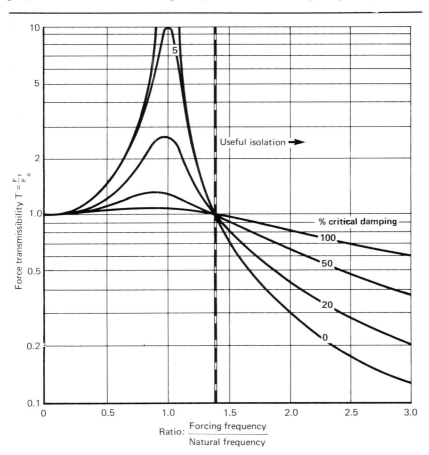

Figure 4. Transmissibility for a viscously damped system

$\sqrt{2}$ × the natural frequency, we get no benefits and possible disadvantages from fitting the springs.

In Fig 5a, we take the case of a machine running at 4-pole speed (50Hz) of 1440rpm. This is equivalent to a forcing frequency of 24Hz.

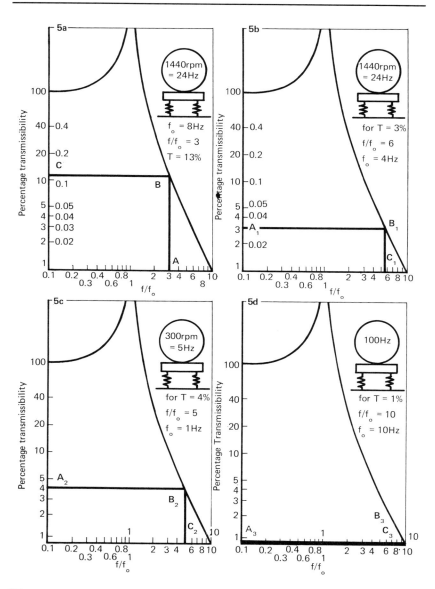

Figure 5.   Examples of natural frequency requirements to produce differing degrees of transmissibility

If we consider the machine on a resilient system with a mounted natural frequency, f_0, of 8Hz, we see that the frequency ratio is 3:1 and we enter the curve at point A, striking the main curve at point B. We see from point C that this gives a transmissibility of 13%.

In Fig 5b, we take the same machine but now require a transmissibility of 3% to be achieved by the mounting system. We enter the transmissibility scale at point A_1 and strike the main curve at point B_1 down to the frequency ratio at point C_1 – indicating a frequency ratio of 6:1. At this point C_1 must be the running speed, 24Hz, this makes the main resonant frequency necessary 4Hz to satisfy the required 6:1 ratio. Hence an unmounted natural frequency, f_0, of 4Hz, is required from the resilient mounting system to ensure a transmissibility of less than 3%.

In Fig 5c, we have taken a machine running at a much lower speed of 300rpm, giving a forcing frequency of 5Hz. Choosing a required transmissibility of 4%, we enter the curve at point A_2 and strike the curve at point B_2, indicating at point C_2 a required frequency ratio of 5:1. As point C_2 is to represent the forcing frequency of 5Hz, the resonant frequency, f_0, becomes 1Hz. Hence the resiliently mounted natural frequency must be 1Hz and we will see later that this is, in fact, an extreme and generally unacceptable selection.

In Fig 5d, we consider an audible problem of mains hum with a forcing frequency of 100Hz. We wish to remount the electric unit with a transmissibility of 1% offering an acoustic noise reduction of 40dB. Entering the chart with a transmissibility of 1% at point A_3 we strike the curve at point B_3^-, indicating that the operational frequency of 100Hz at point C_3^- corresponds to a frequency ratio of 10:1, hence the required resilient mounted natural frequency, f_0, becomes 10Hz. We will see later that this can be readily supplied by a simple rubber resilient mount.

Since it is the opposing effects of the spring stiffness and the mass of the equipment which governs the natural frequency, it is not surprising that the natural frequency can be expressed in those factors alone:

$$f_0 \; \alpha \; \sqrt{\frac{K}{m}}$$

This can be summed up by saying that the natural frequency, and thus the transmissibility, is inversely proportional to the deflection of the springs under the load of the installed equipment regardless of the total mass.

$$f_0 = \frac{15.8}{\sqrt{d}} \text{ Hz } - \text{ d in mm}$$

$$f_0 = \frac{948}{\sqrt{d}} \text{ cycles per minute } - \text{ d in mm}$$

$$f_0 = \frac{3.13}{\sqrt{d}} \text{ Hz } - \text{ d in inches}$$

$$f_0 = \frac{188}{\sqrt{d}} \text{ cycles per minute } - \text{ d in inches}$$

For example, if the deflection of the springs under load was 25mm (1in) the natural frequency f_0 would be about 3 Hz. The relationships between forcing frequency, natural frequency, static deflection and transmissibility can be combined in a single chart (Fig 6).

Considering the four examples cited in Fig 5, we find the corresponding static deflections for simple linear springs would be:

Fig 5a   Mounted natural frequency $f_0 = 8$Hz
         Static deflection d = 4mm
Fig 5b   Mounted natural frequency $f_0 = 4$Hz
         Static deflection d = 16mm
Fig 5c   Mounted natural frequency $f_0 = 1$Hz
         Static deflection d = 250mm
Fig 5d   Mounted natural frequency $f_0 = 10$Hz
         Static deflection d = 2.5mm

One can clearly see that the acoustic problem of mains hum requires only a modest degree of resilience with a deflection of around 2.5mm, whilst for the slow running example at 300rpm, if isolation to 4% were required, a very large deflection of 250mm would have been required.

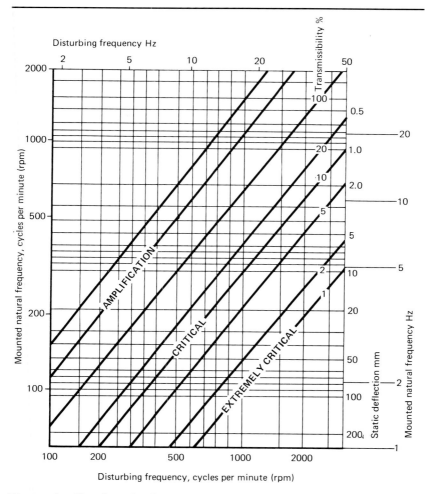

Figure 6. Combined vibration isolator selection chart

The Effect of Damping If there is damping in the spring system, it is equivalent to having a link between the mass and the supporting structure, short circuiting the spring and providing a means of dissipating energy. The damping may take various forms; it may be due to viscous effects in a liquid, internal damping within a material, friction between sliding surfaces, and so on. The damping has the effect of reducing the movement of the system, particularly at resonance when there is nothing else controlling the movement. The damping does, however, reduce the movement at all other frequencies as well (Fig 3). This restriction of the movement of the system is normally a good thing. However, because the damping restricts the movement by short circuiting the spring, the damper increases the force transmitted into the supporting structure. In other words, it increases the transmissibility (Fig 4). It may be necessary in some cases to use a high degree of damping to prevent excessive movement as a system starts up, but in most cases, if the system is designed properly, it is better that there should not be too much damping otherwise vibration isolation is very much reduced.

For a damped system the transmissibility is given by

$$T = \sqrt{\frac{1 + 4D^2\left(\frac{f}{f_0}\right)^2}{\left[\left(\frac{f}{f_0}\right)^2\right]^2 + 4D^2\left(\frac{f}{f_0}\right)^2}}$$

where D is the damping ratio which compares the actual damping present C to that required for critical or dead beat damping C_0. Thus:

$$D = \frac{C}{C_0}$$

The Effects of Spring Stiffness The natural frequency of a simple spring mass system depends only on the static deflection of the spring under the mass. Since, for a given disturbing frequency, the transmissibility depends only on the natural frequency, the transmissibility also depends entirely on the static deflection. A heavy mass that depresses a stiff spring by 25mm will vibrate at the same frequency as a light mass which depresses a soft spring by the same amount – both will vibrate at about 3Hz. For good vibration isolation, we require the disturbing frequency to be greatly in excess of the natural frequency of the system so that the system is operating in its mass controlled condition. Under these circumstances, it is the mass that controls the amount of the movement and not the spring. The amplitude does not depend upon the spring stiffness. However, if we make the spring softer, although

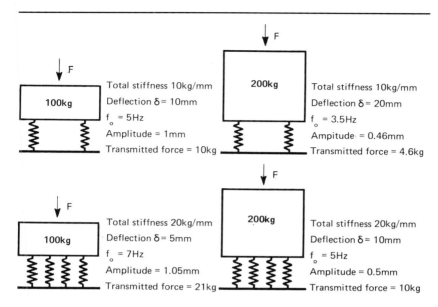

1. Transmitted force depends only on static deflection
2. Increasing mass for the same static deflection reduces movement but not transmitted force
3. Reducing stiffness for the same mass reduces transmitted force and does not increase movement.

Figure 7. The effects of changes of mass and stiffness

the amplitude will be unchanged, the force transmitted into the structure will be reduced (Fig 7).

The Effect of Adding Mass to the Spring System If the mass supported on the spring is increased, the deflection of the springs will also increase. This in turn will decrease the natural frequency and the transmissibility. If, with the increased mass, the spring stiffness is increased to bring the system back to the same static deflection, the natural frequency and the transmissibility will both be restored to the original value. When the system is operating in the mass controlled region, above resonance, the movement will be reduced in proportion to the increase in mass. However, since the spring stiffness has been increased, this reduced movement will still produce the same transmitted force. In other words, increasing the mass of the system whilst keeping f_0 constant reduces the movement, which is a good thing, but has no effect on the transmitted force, contrary to popular belief. Thus the use of an 'inertia base' will not reduce the transmitted vibration but will produce reductions in equipment movement. The provision of inertia bases from this point of view alone is rarely justified. However, they do have far more important functions which will be covered in the chapter on installation.

Differences between Theory and Practice – Running Speed The traditional transmissibility curves show the variation of transmissibility with frequency. What they do not show is that for most normal machines the out-of-balance forces increase as the square of the running speed. Although for zero disturbing frequency the transmissibility is 100%, that is of academic value since at this running speed there is no disturbing force and thus the transmitted force is also zero. As the running speed increases, so the disturbing force also increases, and in due course the system will pass through resonance. When the system is operating in the mass controlled part of its characteristic, the rate at which the out-of-balance force increases with running speed will exactly compensate for the reduction in transmissibility that the same increase in running speed produces. The net result is that the transmitted force settles down to a constant value regardless of the running speed. It is therefore a fallacy to assume that, as equipment runs faster and faster, the transmitted force will fall away towards zero (Fig 8).

Movement in Directions Other Than Vertical The analysis so far assumes that the motion of the system is in one direction, i.e. vertical. In practice most systems can vibrate in any of six possible ways (Fig 9), i.e. movement along each of the three axes and rotation about the same axes. Normally some of these movements will be linked, i.e. translational movement sideways will be associated with a sideways rocking motion. The six natural frequencies associated with these various movements will generally all be different. Some will be at higher frequencies than for the basic up and down movement, whilst others will occur at lower frequencies. If all of these other natural frequencies are lower than that assumed for the vertical movement, a system designed on the simple principles outlined so far will be satisfactory. However, if any of the natural frequencies are significantly higher than vertical natural frequency, they may be close to the frequency of the disturbing force and the transmissibility will be higher than expected. The assumption of purely vertical motion is also unrealistic because with most rotating machinery the out-of-balance forces have as much effect in the sideways direction as up and down. In extreme cases, e.g. a vee twin compressor, the out-of-balance forces may be purely sideways!

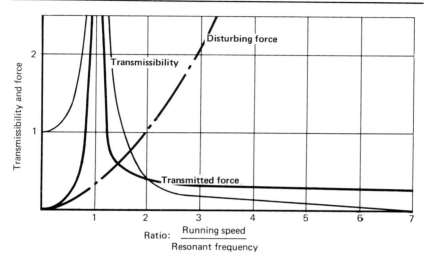

Figure 8. Variation of disturbing force and transmitted force for a rotating machine

Although, providing sufficient is known about the geometry of the system, all of the basic natural frequencies can be calculated, the calculations are tedious and often require information that is not available at the design stage.

Support Stiffness The assumption that the supporting structure is infinitely stiff may be valid for structures built on very conservative lines, but it is being found that, as building techniques become more and more adventurous, it is a less valid assumption. It is very rarely valid for a steel structure, and even with concrete structures situated at ground or basement level there is a possibility that the support springiness will be significant. The effect of the lack of stiffness in the supporting structure is to turn the problem from a simple one of a mass on a spring on a firm base, into one which consists of a mass on a spring on a mass on a spring, which may or may not itself be on a firm base. A system consisting of two masses and two springs has two natural

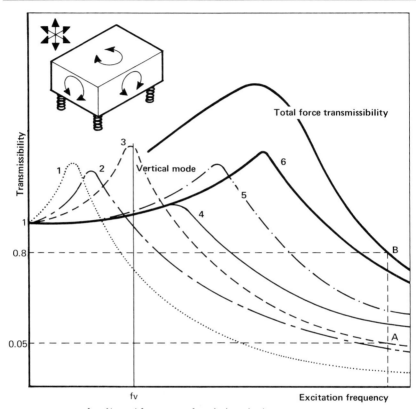

fv = Natural frequency of vertical mode alone
A = Expected transmissibility 5% from pure vertical motion
B = Actual transmissibility 80% from the combined
    coupled motions

Figure 9. The effects of complex motion

frequencies. A low one with the two masses moving in unison, and a higher one where the two masses move in opposition. Depending on the relative stiffness of the two springs and the relative sizes of the masses, these two natural frequencies may be close together or a long

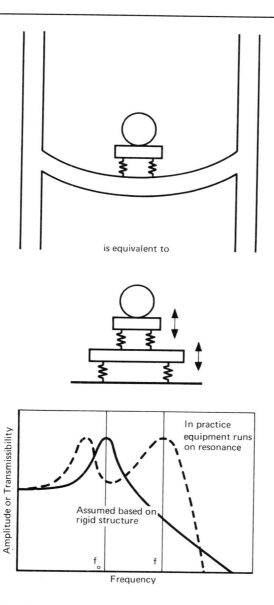

is equivalent to

Figure 10. The effects of flexibility in the support structure

way apart. These two natural frequencies occur one above and one below the natural frequency associated with the top mass upon its spring. If the upper natural frequency is high, it may come close to the disturbing frequency, in which case a resonant situation may occur. Depending on the relative masses of the equipment and the support structure, either the equipment or the structure, or both, may vibrate violently (Fig 10).

Mount Selection by Static Deflection Until fairly recently, the tendency has been in the UK to select vibration isolators on a basis of providing a given transmissibility which is chosen on a rule of thumb basis. Over the last few years, an increasing number of instances have occurred where vibration isolation selected according to the traditional transmissibility criteria has failed to provide adequate isolation, usually as a result of unexpected resonances associated with the lack of stiffness of the building structure. Increasingly, the tendency is to select purely on a static deflection basis where, depending on the type of structure and on the type of equipment being isolated, a static deflection is chosen which is high enough to avoid any possible resonances of the combined equipment and structure, and also to ensure that the natural frequencies for all modes of vibration are well below the disturbing frequency. This method of selection leads to vibration isolators being selected (see Table 3 at end of this chapter) which have a very much higher static deflection than has been normal practice until recently. At first sight it would be thought that the use of such high static deflections would lead to installation and instability problems. However, in practice, it is found that many of the problems associated with high deflection springs are imaginary and most installation problems can be overcome with the appropriate techniques.

Acoustic Isolation Although flexibility is frequently built into a system and described as vibration isolation, it is often intended for acoustic reasons, i.e. to prevent relatively high frequency vibrations which are ultimately radiated as noise. One example of this is in the acoustic enclosure illustrated in Fig 12 of Chapter 12. Comparing the figures, it can be seen that the inclusion of vibration isolators in this machine has produced a marked reduction in the sound pressure levels in the frequencies below 250Hz. This improvement occurs both with and without the acoustic enclosure in place around the machine. Without this vibration isolation, the total sound reduction potential of this enclosure would not have been achieved and the enclosure itself might have been blamed for inadequate performance at low frequencies.

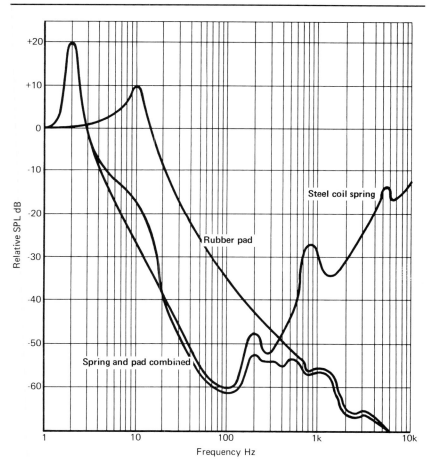

Figure 11. Acoustic transmission of a typical steel coil spring and rubber pad

Hitherto the emphasis on vibration isolation has been centred mainly in the region between 2 and 20Hz. However, the basic theory applied so far continues with reservations into the audible frequency range, as superficially illustrated by our mains hum at 100Hz in Example 5d.

Unfortunately it is not usually possible to achieve the full isolation predicted by this simple means.

The simplicity of the up and down vertical motion of a small rigid body on a light, perfectly elastic spring attached to a stiff base breaks down when moving into the audible frequency range. Individual components can no longer be considered rigid and the mass of the spring becomes significant. The spring itself starts to behave as a series of small masses interlinked by springs which acts as a transmission line. This allows the telegraphing of high frequency sounds, particularly with steel springs, to a degree not expected from simple theory (see Fig 11). This can be overcome by adding a ribbed rubber pad to the basic metal coil. The addition of the rubber has a further merit of adding a small amount of damping to the spring at its 3Hz mounted resonant frequency.

Shock Isolation Shock implies a process which is sudden, probably involving impacts of short duration. Shock operations can be divided into two categories; repetitive, such as with a punch press or cold forming machine, and single impacts, as with a large single action press. With the repetitive process, it is essential that the vibration caused by any impact has died out before the next occurs. If not, there is a possibility that the second impact will add to the movement caused by the first, and a form of resonance will build up with each impact, causing successively larger movements of the machine. This requires the use of isolators which have a natural frequency at least three times higher than the repetition rate of the machine. This, at first sight, seems to contrast with the normal selection where resonant frequency below the operating frequency is selected. In this case, however, one is aiming at isolating the relatively high frequency energy of the individual impacts and not the relatively unimportant repetition rate.

With single impulse machines, there are two distinct cases. In the first, the energy used in performing the operation is derived from energy stored within a machine, usually within a fly-wheel. With a machine of this sort, no external force is applied to the machine and the total momentum of the machine remains zero at all times. This means that the frame of the machine starts to move as the process occurs but at the end of the process the frame comes to rest, albeit at a different position from where it started. In this case, the isolators merely have to cushion the operation and restore the equipment to its original position ready for the next stroke. In the second case, the momentum of the machine is increased by external forces, such as a heavy weight falling under the influence of gravity, and at the end of the operation the whole machine has acquired an increase in momentum. This means that the isolators not only have to restore the machine to its position, but in addition they have to stop it moving and dissipate the stored energy. This requires the isolators to have a considerable damping capability.

Table 3

Type of Equipment		Non-critical Locations		Critical Locations		
		Basement	Ground level and 6m floor span	9m floor span	12m floor span	15m floor span
		For concrete structure only minimum static deflection, mm				
Refrigeration Machines						
Absorption machines		6	6	25	45	70
Centrifugal chillers or	Hermetic	6	6	45	60	90
Heat pumps	Open type	10	10	45	60	90
Reciprocating air or	500 to 750rpm	25	40	60	70	90
Refrigeration compressors	751rpm and higher	25	25	40	60	70
Reciprocating chillers or	500 to 750rpm	25	40	60	70	90
Heat pumps	751rpm and higher	25	25	40	60	70
Packaged boilers		6	6	25	45	70
Pumps						
Close coupled	Up to 5hp	10	10	25	25	25
	7½hp and higher	19	25	40	60	60
Base mounted	Up to 5hp	10	10	40	45	60
	7½hp and higher	20	25	45	60	90
Vent Sets and Low Pressure Packaged AH, AC and H & V Units						
Suspended units	Up to 5hp	20	25	25	25	25
	7½hp and higher					
	175-500rpm	30	30	30	45	60
	501rpm and higher	25	25	25	30	45
Floor mounted units	Up to 5hp	10	25	25	25	25
	7½hp and higher					
	175-500rpm	10	45	45	45	60
	501rpm and higher	10	25	25	40	45
Centrifugal Fans and High Pressure Packaged AH, AC and H & V Units	Up to 20hp					
	175 to 300rpm	10	60	60	90	125
	301 to 500rpm	10	45	45	60	90
	501rpm and higher	10	25	25	45	60
	25hp and higher					
	175 to 300rpm	10	60	90	125	150
	301 to 500rpm	10	45	60	90	125
	501rpm and higher	10	25	45	60	90
Cooling Towers and Evaporative Condensers	Up to 500rpm	10	10	45	60	90
	501rpm and higher	10	10	25	45	60
Internal Combustion Engines and Engine Driven Equipment	Up to 25hp	10	10	45	60	60
	30 to 100hp	10	45	60	90	90
	125hp and higher	10	60	90	125	125

Plate 1. Pumps mounted on special inertia bases with isolating springs to reduce vibration transmission to the floor. Care must also be taken to prevent transmission along the pipework, by the use of the flexible connectors.

7
Basic Sound and Vibration Measuring Systems

SOUND measuring systems use a microphone which transforms the sound pressure variations into their electrical analogue. Vibration measuring systems require an accelerometer to detect vibrations and generate a corresponding electrical signal. The technique for processing these electrical signals is similar, regardless of whether they were produced by vibrations or sound pressure fluctuations. The signal is amplified, conditioned, and measured by electronic instrumentation. In the following sections we will not only consider the transducers but also the amplification, signal processing and display instrumentation. Fig 1 is a schematic representation of the main components in a typical sound or vibration measuring system.

Transducers – Microphones Although there are microphones operating on many different principles, for most acoustic measurements, either condenser, electret, or piezoelectric microphones are used. Table 1 shows the relative merits of each type.

Generally the piezoelectric type is suited to field use. It is more robust, does not require polarisation voltages for operation, and does not suffer from the severe effects of condensation which can affect the condenser type. For laboratory measurements, however, the flatter high frequency response of the condenser microphone is desirable (Fig 2). The piezoelectric or ceramic microphone depends upon movement of a diaphragm being transmitted to a piezoelectric crystal. Fluctuating forces on the crystal generate a charge across the crystal which is connected to the input of a high impedance amplifier.

Condenser microphones consist of a very thin metal diaphragm positioned close to a rigid backplate. A polarisation voltage is applied

Table 1

Factors	Electret	Microphone Type Piezo-electric	Con-denser
Dynamic range	A	A	A
Sensitivity	B	C	B
Low frequency response	A	A	A
Frequency linearity	A	B	A
High frequency response	A	B	A
Dimensions	A	A	A
Need for associated supplies	A	A	C
Long term stability	A	B	A
Range of working temperatures	A	B	A
Influence of temperature	A	A	A
Influence of vibration	A	B	A
Influence of moisture	A	B	C
Influence of magnetic field	A	A	A
Fragility	B/C	B	C
Price	B	A	C

A – most favourable   B – satisfactory   C – not favourable

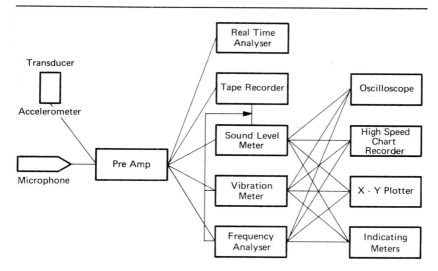

Figure 1. **Basic sound or vibration measuring system**

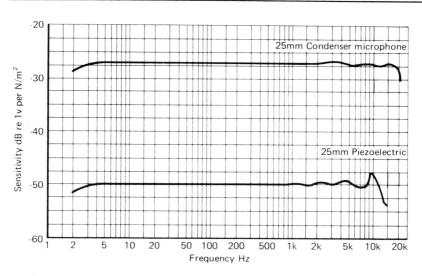

Figure 2. **Typical free field frequency response curves of the 25mm diameter condenser and piezoeletric microphones showing comparitive sensitivities after Bruel & Kjaer**

between these two plates. Fluctuating pressure varies the distance between the two plates causing fluctuations in the capacitance of the assembly. An alternating voltage is generated which is proportional to the sound pressure fluctuations on the diaphragm over a large frequency range. Fig 3 illustrates the basic construction of these microphone types.

Condenser microphone cartridges are available in sizes ranging from ⅛in dia to 1in dia. The smaller the condenser microphone, the better

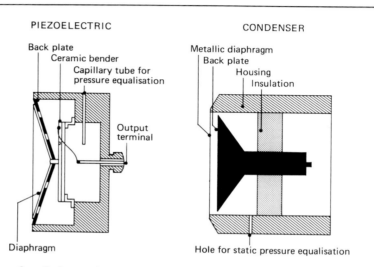

Figure 3. Schematic constructions of piezoelectric and condenser microphones

the high frequency performance becomes. However, this is offset by the reduced overall sensitivity of the smaller microphone.

The electret is a variant of the condenser microphone which uses a plastic diaphragm. It does not require an external polarisation voltage. The great advantage of the electret microphone is that it can operate in high humidity conditions.

The important considerations in selecting a microphone for acoustic measurements are frequency response, sensitivity and dynamic range.

These three factors are usually interrelated and selection will therefore most probably depend on the desired frequency range of measurements.

There is no doubt that the piezoelectric microphone, where appropriate, is much cheaper than the condenser microphone. If, however, measuring precision is of prime importance, then unfortunately it is necessary to bear the additional cost penalty of a condenser microphone and its external polarisation voltage source.

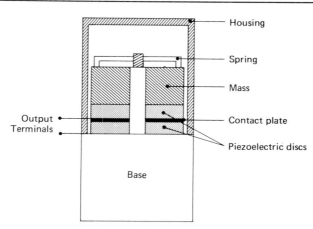

Figure 4.   Construction of a typical piezoelectric accelerometer

Vibration Transducers Vibration can be defined in terms of displacement, velocity or acceleration. There are transducers which can be used to measure each of these directly. Displacement transducers generate an output voltage that is directly proportional to the relative displacement of the pick-up. They usually have poor frequency response and low sensitivity. Velocity transducers generate a voltage that is proportional to the relative displacement of the pick-up, which is proportional to both the displacement and frequency. They are quite large but have high output voltage with a more uniform frequency response than the displacement transducers. An accelerometer produces an output voltage proportional to the acceleration it experiences, which is proportional to the displacement and to (frequency)^2. Fig 4 shows the construction of a typical accelerometer. A mass is clamped against two piezoelectric discs which act as a spring. The whole arrangement is mounted in a metal housing with a substantial base. When the whole assembly is subjected to vibration, the mass exerts a force on the piezoelectric discs which is proportional to the acceleration of the mass. The piezoelectric effect of the discs produces a voltage which is proportional to the applied force, and hence the acceleration to which it is exposed. The voltage produced for a given acceleration will depend upon the transducer sensitivity. Fig 5 shows

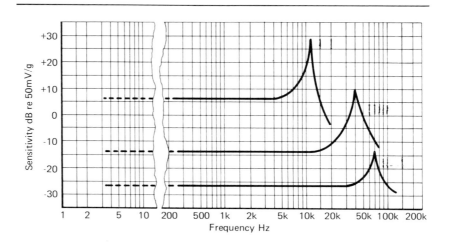

Figure 5. Typical frequency response curves of the accelerometer after Bruel & Kjaer

the variation of transducer sensitivity with frequency for a typical accelerometer. It is desirable to have a constant sensitivity over the operating frequency range.

The frequency response is generally flat up to the 10kHz to 100kHz mark, at which point the resonant frequency of the crystal mass system produces a sharp peak in the response trace. An accelerometer will be sensitive to acceleration in any direction with different frequency responses along its different axes. A well designed unit has a cross sensitivity of less than 5% of the sensitivity to the motion along the principal axis. Fig 6 is a table of accelerometer characteristics for three different sizes. It can be seen that the larger the mass of the accelerometer, the greater its sensitivity but the lower its free resonance frequency, and the greater the effect of its mass on the system being measured. The acoustic sensitivity is a measure of the stray effect of airborne sound fields. The smaller the device the more sensitive it becomes to acoustic fields.

Relative dimensions	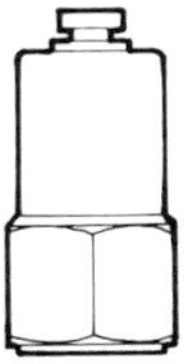	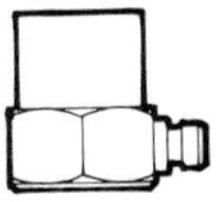	
Height mm	24	20	11
Weight gm	43	11	2
Sensitivity pC/g	98	10	3
Capacitance pF	1200	1200	650
Free resonance kHz	16	42	55
Maximum shock g	2000	20000	25000
Transverse sensitivity %	<4	<4	44
Temperature sensitivity $ms^{-2}/°C$	0.04	0.4	5
Magnetic sensitivity g/K gauss	0.01	0.04	3
Acoustic sensitivity ms^{-2}	0.001	0.01	0.04
Max. acceleration with mounting magnet g	60	150	–

Figure 6. Comparisons of three different sizes of accelerometer after Bruel & Kjaer

Preamplifiers These are used both to amplify the relatively low signal from the transducer and to match the high impedance of the transducer to the relatively low impedance of the signal analysis equipment. They fall into two types – voltage amplifiers and charge amplifiers.

A condenser microphone or piezoelectric device can be regarded as having a constant charge sensitivity so that if the capacity of the system is increased, e.g. by the presence of a long cable between the microphone and the preamplifier, the voltage is reduced. Voltage preamplifiers should therefore be located as close to the microphone as possible to minimise the input capacitance and to avoid reducing the system's sensitivity. Preamplifiers designed for use with condenser microphones incorporate the polarisation voltage supply for the microphone. They can still, however, be used with piezoelectric microphones and accelerometers.

Charge amplifiers are sensitive to charge and so the sensitivity is unaffected by input capacity. The lengths of the cable between the microphone and the amplifier are therefore no longer important. Charge amplifiers are in general more expensive than voltage amplifiers and, as a result, are less common.

Integrators An accelerometer produces an output proportional to acceleration. However, the output of an accelerometer may be modified using a device known as an integrator. This is a filter which makes the output frequency sensitive. By providing the right filter slopes, an output proportional to velocity or displacement can be produced. This enables velocity or displacement information to be obtained directly from an accelerometer.

Signal Conditioning Devices – Amplifiers Amplifiers receive a signal transmitted by cable from the transducer preamplifier. The whole signal is first processed by an amplifier designed to have a wide frequency response. It is usually of a high gain and high stability characteristic. It produces a strong, relatively low impedance, electrical output which precisely reproduces the amplitude-time sequence measured at the transducer. The output of this amplifier is therefore in a suitable form for the application of electronic frequency weighting or for more detailed frequency or other analysis of the signal.

Signal Processing The commonest form of signal processing is filtering where only the signal within a limited frequency is accepted. This enables the original noise to be separated into frequency components.

Frequency analysis is carried out using either a tunable filter or a selection of fixed frequency filters which can be switched in as required. Filtering with filters having an octave band width is the simplest common procedure. This involves using filters having an upper frequency limit which is equal to twice the lower limiting frequency. The upper frequency is $\sqrt{2} \times$ the nominal filter frequency

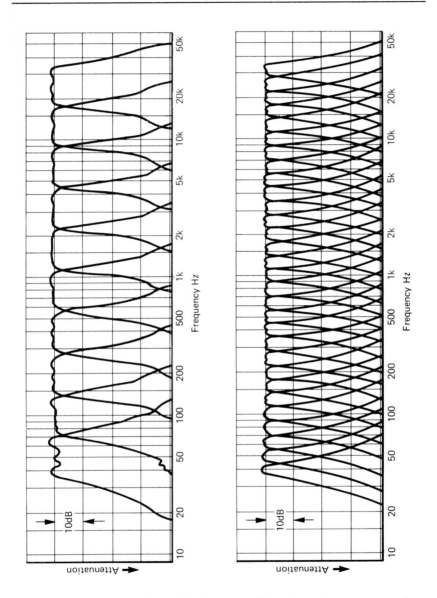

Figure 7.   Octave and one third octave filters in a frequency analyser
after Bruel & Kjaer

and the lower frequency is $\frac{1}{\sqrt{2}} \times$ the nominal frequency, e.g. the 1kHz filter covers the range from approximately 707Hz to 1414Hz. A set of octave fixed filters typically consists of filters having nominal frequencies of 31.5, 63, 125, 250, 500, 1k, 2k, 4k and 8kHz (Fig 7).

When a more detailed breakdown is required, filters having a band width of ⅓ octave can be used. When tunable filters are used, these have a band width expressed as a certain percentage of the nominal

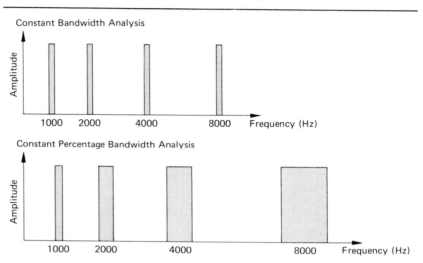

Figure 8. Frequency analysis of sound or vibration data

frequency, e.g. 2% (an octave filter has a band width of approximately 70% and a ⅓ octave one of 23%). There are constant band width analysers available which have a fixed band width, say 5Hz, regardless of centre frequency (Fig 8). These employ a fixed filter and a heterodyne process which modifies the frequency of the signal being processed. In general these are not really suitable for general noise work. For most applications, especially those involving rotating machines, the constant percentage band width device is to be preferred.

Signal Display Devices Finally the signal, filtered if required, is passed to an output device. There are several different ways of describing the level of an AC signal. The simplest is the arithmetic average of the rectified value. Occasionally the peak value of the signal is of interest, particularly in some vibration and shock phenomena measurements. However, the 'root-mean square' (RMS) value, which gives a measure of the physical effect of the signal, is generally the form in which the output is displayed (e.g. domestic electricity supplies in the UK are at 240v RMS). The simplest signal display device therefore is a meter which displays the RMS value of the analyser output. Meters do not always lend themselves to ease of reading nor can they provide a

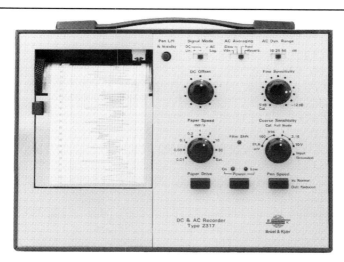

Figure 9. High speed level recorder

permanent record. They are however relatively inexpensive. For acoustic measurements they are normally graduated directly in sound pressure level, but for vibration measurements they can be graduated in terms of voltage, acceleration, velocity or displacement.

High Speed Level Recorder An alternative to the meter is the high speed level recorder. One such device is shown in Fig 9. This is a chart recorder which responds to the RMS value of an applied signal. The recorder can either follow rapid variations of RMS level or be damped to provide average values and give a permanent record of the measurement. Although expensive, they have the advantage that they can be operated for long periods of time unattended, and therefore provide a continuous monitoring of noise or vibration signals, providing a comprehensive history of the applied signal. Because of their high speed capability, they can be used to measure transient phenomena such as rapidly varying noise levels or reverberation time decays.

Oscilloscopes Display meters or high level recorders can only provide an averaged level of the input signal. They cannot provide information about the wave form itself. Often it is useful to be able to observe the wave form of the signal, either as a check on the operation of the measuring equipment or as an aid to understanding a noise generating mechanism. This can best be done with an oscilloscope.

Magnetic Tape Recorders Magnetic tape recorders are not display devices but are merely a storage facility. They can be used as an intermediate device between the transducer system and the final display devices. A tape recorder enables a single event to be replayed at a later date, many times if necessary. The main use of this is to enable a single event to be analysed in more than one way (e.g. a single pistol shot used to determine reverberation time may be analysed in several octave bands) or for a short sample of data to be replayed many times to enable a long analysis procedure to be carried out.

For most problems involving noise affecting people, a good quality 'hi fi' tape recorder is adequate. It is only infrequently that the higher capability of the quality instrument recorder is required.

All conventional tape recorders have a limit to the lower end of their frequency response. However, a frequency modulated carrier system can be used to extend the performance down to zero frequency, at the price of a restricted high frequency performance or very high tape speed.

Complete Sound and Vibration Measuring Systems – Sound Level Meters. The simplest combination of the basic sound and vibration measuring systems outlined in Section 1 is the sound level meter. Fig 10a shows a block diagram of a typical instrument in which a sensitive electronic voltmeter is used to measure the electrical output generated by a microphone. The electrical signal from the transducer is amplified and filtered such that, after rectification to direct current, it can be used to drive an indicating meter. An output socket is usually provided to enable the amplified signal to be taken to other instruments for further

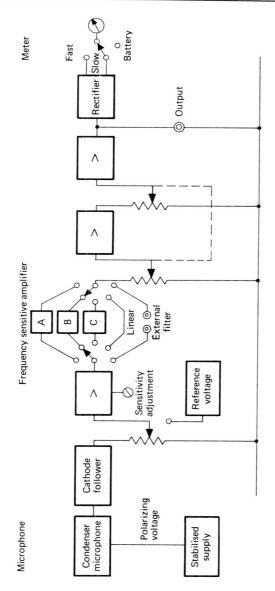

Figure 10a. Block diagram of sound level meter using a condenser microphone

processing if necessary. The attenuator networks control the total amplification of the instrument, whilst the signal conditioning is controlled by the weighting networks. The photograph in Fig 10b shows a typical instrument together with an octave filter network. The instrument is entirely selfcontained although the microphone can be used remotely with an interconnecting cable if required.

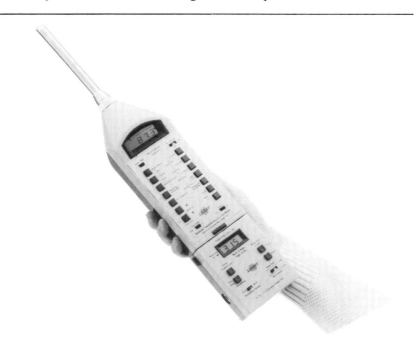

Figure 10b. A sound level meter and filter set for acoustic measurements

The microphones fitted are usually more or less omnidirectional, although random incidence correctors are available to improve the omnidirectional response of the microphone cartridge, which is designed to have a flat frequency response in free field sound measurements. Windshields and nose cones are available as optional extras to protect the microphone from the effect of wind noise when measurements are being taken out of doors or in moving air streams. In meters where there are separate attenuation switches for the amplifiers before and after the weighting network filters, it is essential that these are operated in the correct order, otherwise either the full capabilities of the equipment will not be achieved or overloading may occur. Either way, incorrect readings may result. The maker's handbook will give full details for the correct method of operation.

Most sound level meters are capable of displaying the linear sound level together with an 'A' weighted sound level. The meter rectifier circuit providing the RMS is equipped with two standardised damping rates – 'fast' and 'slow'. More expensive meters are able to measure the peak value of the signal as well as its RMS value. Where an operator might require to measure loud but short duration noises, a hold facility can be obtained. This enables the instrument to record the maximum level and hold the indicating meter needle at that point until manually reset by the operator. Further facilities available include the ability to measure impulsive sound and vibration phenomena. Impulse type noises such as those produced by punch presses or drop hammers can only be properly measured with sound level meters containing an impulse detector response with fast rise time and slow decay rate.

Some sound level meters are provided with detachable octave or ⅓ octave filter sets. Other instruments have the filter analysis networks integral within the body of the sound level meter. Fig 10b shows the bolt-on type octave filter set, electrical connections being made to the sound level meter via the bridging strap.

Precision Grade and Industrial Grade Sound Level Meters The British Standard referring to sound level meters, BS 5969 (IEC 651) specifies four degrees of precision. These are designated Types 0, 1, 2, 3 for the measurement of certain frequency and time weighted sound pressure levels. The major differences are the tolerance limits to which each instrument must conform and the frequency response and directional characteristics of the microphone. Fig 11 shows the permitted measurement tolerances in the context of the 'A' frequency weighting curve. Unfortunately, since the standards were originally set it has been found that for most industrial applications it is necessary to use a meter which is much better than the minimum standards set by Type 3 but not necessarily attaining the near perfection (and consequent high cost) of the Type 1 meter. There are some relatively cheap meters available which come close to the Type 1 meters but can only be classified as Type 2 meters these are most suited to general industrial use. Equally there are some meters which only just meet the Type 3 standard. These are best avoided for serious use.

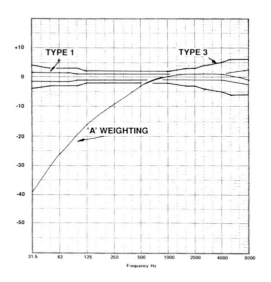

Figure 11. Measurement tolerances for sound level meters with reference to 'A' frequency weighting curve.

Vibration Meters Although the sound level meter may be used for vibration measurements, the combination of accelerometer and sound level meter calibrated in dB with respect to a reference sound pressure does not provide an immediate measure of acceleration. A calculation process is required to convert from the indicated sound pressure level to the RMS value of the acceleration, usually using a purpose designed slide rule and based on the sensitivity of the accelerometer used. Purpose made vibration meters comparable with the sound level meter directly suited to the measurements of vibrations are available. They normally use a wide frequency range piezoelectric type vibration pick-up operating from 2Hz to 20kHz, together with an integrator to provide a direct readout in displacement velocity and acceleration as required. Detection offered includes RMS and peak-to-peak. The peak-to-peak detection is generally used in shock measurement. Like the sound level meter, a hold facility may be provided which operates in both modes of detection. This is of value where transient vibrations are being investigated.

Real Time Analysers The normal procedure for frequency analysis is to use preset band width filters in order to investigate a particular section of the total signal at any one time. It is not possible to take an

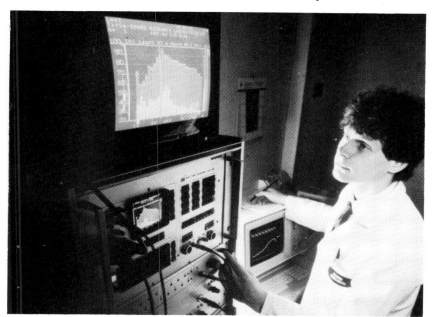

Figure 12. A real time analyser and computer terminal

instantaneous reading in any filter band. Depending on the band width, it is necessary to average the signal over a period of time in order to obtain a meaningful value. The finer the band width, the greater the averaging time that is required for each reading. For very detailed analysis, the total time taken becomes immense. Real time analysers have been designed and built to minimise the time for complete analysis of a signal. This is done by having a bank of parallel filters covering the whole frequency range of interest. The signal is passed through all of these simultaneously and the output of each filter is continuously averaged. A rapid scanning device then reads out the average values which can be recorded as required or displayed on a CRT to give a graphical display. This way the analysis time is limited to the time required for the narrowest filter and not the total time for all of the filters. This gives a theoretical time saving of 5:1 and in practice much greater savings are usually achieved. Commercially available real time analysers generally provide a continuous bank of as many as 30 one third octave filters ranging from 25Hz to 20kHz. The equipment can generally be programmed by digital signals and can output the information in digital form, so it lends itself readily to combination with a computer to provide an on-line facility to record and process results automatically. Fig 12 shows one such system.

Statistical Distribution Analyser This consists of a set of 12 contacts which is mounted on the arm of a level recorder and scanned by a contact on the pen. Each contact is connected to a counter. The counters register the time that the pen spends within each sound pressure level range. At the completion of a given time period, the total count registered on each counter then permits a histogram of the noise to be plotted. From this mean and percentile levels may be estimated. An estimate of the proportion of time for which a particular noise level is exceeded may be made and the 'equivalent continuous noise level' (L_{eq}) or the noise level corresponding to the American OSHA regulations can be calculated. Sound level meters are now available which give direct readouts of statistical noise parameters including L_{eq}, L_{10}, L_{90} etc.

Noise Average Meters and Noise Dose Meters For assessment of hearing damage, L_{eq} values are frequently required for rapidly varying noise levels. These can be obtained using a statistical distribution analyser in conjunction with a high speed pen recorder as above, but noise average meters have been developed to measure L_{eq} directly.

Where it is necessary to monitor one individual's exposure to noise, this can be done by equipping them with an instrument designed to monitor continuously the sound field in which they are working. The noise dose meter, or noise exposure meter, as it is sometimes known, has been developed to satisfy this requirement in a midget instrument that can be worn by an operator going about his normal daily activities. Some are selfcontained and produce a direct readout; others require interrogation by a central processing device. Care must be taken in the selection of dose meters for, although most instruments are designed to satisfy the requirements of the International Standards Organisation (which has adopted the fundamental premise that a 3dBA increase in sound level requires half the duration to give the same noise dose), some dose meters operate on the American OSHA system. In the normal ISO system, as used in the United Kingdom, an exposure to 93dBA for four hours or 96dBA for two hours is equivalent to 90dBA for eight hours – a relationship based on an equal energy dose. On the other hand, the American Occupational Safety and Health Act system operates on the basis that a 5dBA increase in sound level is required to halve the duration for the same noise dose. In this case, for a 90dBA eight hour exposure, the equivalent exposure for four hours would be 95dBA or 100dBA for two hours. Some instruments can be converted from one system to the other.

Calibration of Sound and Vibration Measuring Instruments Unless the instruments described in the previous sections have been accurately calibrated for acoustic or vibration measurements, using known calibration signal sources, it is unrealistic to expect to get the maximum measurement accuracy from the system. Accurate calibration is also essential if the repeatability of measurement is to be guaranteed.

Sound Measuring Instrument Calibration Calibration of the microphone and analysis equipment is essential before and after the start of a series of measurements. The accepted procedure for providing this calibration is by the use of a reference sound source. Given the known sound pressure generated at the microphone it remains a simple problem to adjust the otherwise fixed gains of the analyser amplifying devices such that the RMS value indicated on the meter agrees with the reference sound pressure source. Pistonphones, electronically generated sound sources and falling ball calibrators may all be used for this purpose (Fig 13). The pistonphone is a battery operated device with two small reciprocating pistons driven by a cam to produce a constant sound pressure level at a fixed frequency within a void of predetermined dimensions. The void is tailored to fit around the microphone cartridge. To ensure a good seal, a rubber O ring is housed in the wall of the void. The accuracy of commercial pistonphones is about ±0.2dB. It is small, easy to use and generates a relatively high sound pressure at the microphone which lends itself well to calibration in noisy environments. A serious limitation, however, is that the reference sound pressure is generated at one frequency only.

Figure 13. Sound and vibration calibrators

In an attempt to overcome the limitation of single frequency calibration, there are now available electronic calibrators which generate known sound pressure levels at several different frequencies, usually pure tones at octave intervals from 125Hz to 2000Hz. These provide an additional check on the frequency response of the sound measuring system.

Falling ball calibrators are used less frequently and even then only for field work. They depend on the action of a collection of small shot pellets falling on a diaphragm. The absolute accuracy of these instruments may change with much use. This can be overcome if the calibrators are regularly checked and recalibrated against a master source.

It is possible to carry out a form of calibration without using a reference sound source. Most manufacturers provide calibration data for their microphone cartridges which is in conjunction with an internal reference signal in the measuring equipment. This system, however, assumes that the microphone calibration is absolute. Unfortunately the microphone is the most vulnerable part of the system, so this method, although convenient for a running check in conjunction with an acoustic calibrator, should not be relied on alone.

Vibration Calibration   Vibration measuring equipment is either calibrated by subjecting the transducer to a known vibration level or on a basis of the nominal sensitivity of the transducer. When the accelerometer is being excited at a known level, it is simply a matter of adjusting amplifier gains within the vibration measuring instrument to ensure that the final meter reading indicates the known input signal level. The accuracy of such calibration used properly will be better than $\pm 2\%$.

A less accurate form of calibration can be carried out without using reference acceleration levels. This presupposes that a calibration chart is available with the vibration transducer. From this, the overall sensitivity of the system can be calculated. This method is not expected to produce calibration accuracies of much better than $\pm 10\%$.

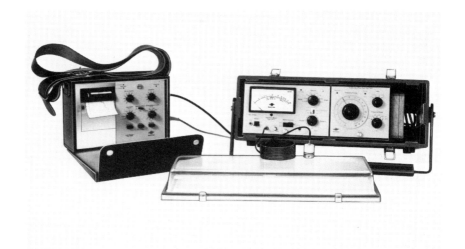

Plate 1. A typical portable vibration analysis equipment. The accelerometer output feeds a vibration meter via a tunable narrow band filter which is also synchronised with a chart recorder for production of frequency spectra 'hard copy'

8
Measurements and Measuring Techniques

SOUND level meters and vibration meters measure the sound pressure level or vibration level at a particular location. For these measurements to be meaningful, they must be both accurate and relevant. The first part of this chapter covers factors which affect the accuracy, whilst the second part covers the question of relevance.

Accuracy – Calibration Sound level meters are delicate items of equipment and must be calibrated by means of an acoustic calibration device at regular intervals, preferably before and after each time they are used. Reliance upon an internal calibration facility in the sound level meter itself is not satisfactory, as this does not check the most vulnerable part of the system, i.e. the microphone. Unfortunately, even acoustic calibrators are not 100% reliable and it is good practice to carry out a calibration using both the calibrator and the internal calibration signal. These should cross-check. If they do, the calibration can be relied upon with reasonable confidence since the probability of identical errors in both systems is extremely remote. If the two calibrators do not correspond, the reasons for the discrepancy must be investigated.

Malfunction of a measuring system will normally be spotted relatively quickly by someone who is familiar with the equipment whereas a stranger may not notice it for a considerable time. Practice should be obtained with equipment in familiar surroundings and experience gained about its normal behaviour so that unusual behaviour can be recognised.

Accurate measurements depend on the correct operation of the equipment. In particular on some sound level meters the operation of the attenuator switches for changing ranges is important. Incorrect operation of these can lead to overloading of the electrical circuits, which in turn can lead to readings either higher or lower than the correct values. Briefly, the normal procedure is to start with the instrument operating in the linear mode and to increase the gain of the first amplifier stage until a reading is obtained within the operational range. The instrument can then be switched to the desired weighting or filter setting, after which all further gain increases must be made using the second stage amplifier. This procedure and other precautions are normally covered in the manufacturer's handbook. This should be studied before use. Not all equipment is quite as obvious as it looks!

The normal microphone supplied with most sound level meters is designed for optimum response when directly facing a sound source in free field conditions. This approximates reasonably to the conditions which exist when equipment noise is being measured with a microphone relatively close to the equipment. In theory, when measurements are being made in reverberant surroundings where sound waves are approaching the microphone from all directions, a truly omnidirectional microphone is required. Many of the microphone manufacturers supply 'random incidence correctors' which can be fitted to the microphone in place of the normal protective grid to give the desired characteristics. In practice, however, the effects are normally negligible below about 4kHz, which normally covers the major regions of interest. The normal acoustic calibrator cannot be used with the random incidence corrector in place, so that if a random incidence corrector is used it has to be removed for calibration. This exposes the very vulnerable diaphragm of the microphone. For a lot of general purpose work the risk of damage to the microphone that is inherent in the use of the random incidence corrector is not justified by the increased accuracy at high frequencies.

The microphone samples the sound pressure level over a small area but whether the sound pressure level at the microphone is representative of the surroundings will depend on many factors. Many sound level meters are shaped so as to minimise the shielding effect of the body of the instrument, and of an observer behind the instrument. Where precision measurements at high frequencies are required, it is preferable to move the microphone at least 1m away from the observer, either by the use of an extension for the microphone or by placing the equipment on the tripod so that it can be read from a distance.

In reverberant surroundings the sound pressure level averaged over a region does not vary markedly from region to region. However, at any particular point there may be quite substantial departures from the mean. It is therefore necessary to take a sample of readings, randomly spaced through the area under investigation, and a mean value obtained from these. Reliance on a single point value can lead to quite considerable errors, especially at low frequencies.

Relevance Acoustic measurements are normally made for one or more of the following reasons:
1. To find out whether a noise problem exists or is likely to exist
2. To obtain product data
3. To solve a noise problem

The measuring techniques used will depend on the reasons. Common sense ultimately must be the guide as to how measurements are carried out; an excessive number of measurements cannot make up for insufficient forethought. Where there are standard procedures in existence, e.g. BS4142, which detail measurement procedures, these should be complied with and any departures, and the reasons for them, noted.

The simplest measurements are usually those to determine whether or not a problem exists and, since most advisory standards are based on measurements in dBA, the measuring procedures are usually fairly simple.

External Noise Problems The assessment of most external noise problems will be made against the background of BS4142 or similar standards (see Chapter 18). Under ideal circumstances the standard is simple to follow but the following points should be borne in mind.

Night-time Problems If the potential problem is a night-time one, it is usually necessary that a survey be carried out at the appropriate time of night. Experience has shown that it is difficult to predict the night-time situation from observations of the site during daytime. Night-time conditions often differ from what would legitimately be expected from daytime observations, in some most surprising ways. Unusual road traffic movements and unexpected night-time operations, sometimes a considerable distance from the site of interest, can greatly affect the problem.

A very common example of this is found in some of the old areas of
terraced housing which are mixed up with areas of heavy industry.
Where there is no night-time working, and also no through traffic,
some of these areas are incredibly quiet at night with the result that a
surprisingly quiet plant noise can produce severe problems. The situation is often complicated because the inhabitants of such areas are
often elderly and very sensitive to noise at night.

Varying Noise Levels With external noise problems, it is very rare for
either the noise itself or the background to remain constant. It is
therefore often necessary to make tape recordings and to play these
back on a pen recorder so that the variation in noise levels and
extraneous noises like barking dogs can be accounted for. Direct
readings from a sound level meter are often difficult to interpret in
these circumstances.

Weather The weather has three effects on outside noise measurements. Wind and rain can affect the sounds present; wind by causing
noise in trees, etc., whilst rain changes the type of noise from vehicles.

Wind has a secondary effect by directly affecting the microphone of the
meter and causing high readings. This is equivalent to the noise that
you hear in your ears when you stand in a high wind. 'A' weighted
readings are less sensitive to this problem than individual octave band
readings which are badly affected at low frequencies. If you plug
headphones into the output socket of the sound level meter you can
listen to the sounds registered by the meter and tell whether or not you
have problems. Using a windshield over the microphone helps to a
limited extent and you can sometimes minimise the problem by choosing a sheltered measurement position.

Rain falling on the microphone usually renders sensible readings
impossible, even if it does not damage the microphone.

The third effect of weather is to affect the transmission of sound over
long distances, creating variations in noise level of as much as 20dB at
distances over 1km. Due to refraction effects, sound travels better
down wind than up wind, especially in temperature inversion conditions (typically clear nights with a very light wind). Ultimately common
sense and experience enable reasonable deductions to be made about

the effect of weather conditions and whether or not the measurements are likely to be typical.

Whenever you carry out an external noise survey some distance from the noise source, you will always be told by the complainant that 'you should have heard it last night. It was much worse then'. If it is practicable, an unannounced visit the night before the official survey is a useful exercise.

Internal Factory Noise Problems   These will normally involve measurements in accordance with requirements of the Noise at Work Regulations 1989 and the associated Guidance Notes published by The Health and Safety Executive.   Measurements normally fall into the categories of general work area levels, determining worst level, and personnel exposure.

When covering general work areas, there is always the problem of how many measurements to make and what sort of spacing to adopt. For preference, carry out a relatively low number of measurements initially, and based on these and on subjective observations add additional measuring points if necessary. If the noise level judged both by the meter and by ear does not vary significantly over large areas, there is no need for a large number of measurements. The time is better spent in areas where more marked variations make additional measurements necessary. In most cases, to obtain representative noise levels, one avoids measurements close to reflecting surfaces, i.e. within 1m of any object with dimensions of more than a few centimetres. Close to reflecting surfaces the noise levels may be either higher or lower than in the general spaces. Measurements in such places are therefore likely to be unrepresentative of the area as a whole. However, when one is interested in measuring the exposure of a particular person, one must measure at locations corresponding to the position of his head. If he normally works with his head nearly touching a large surface, this is where the measurements should be taken. The conditions may not be typical of the general workshop area but they are typical of that person's exposure.

Product Data   Measurements may be needed to provide data about a product to satisfy tender requirements, for use as a sales aid, or to provide data for design calculations. Ideally, where the requirement is to satisfy a tender, the specification should be compiled with exactly.

Unfortunately, many specifications are still worded loosely or sometimes in a way which demands the impossible. If snags in the specification can be resolved by negotiation in advance, the results are likely to
be more satisfactory in the long run. A submission of unqualified
measurements not in accordance with the specification requirements
may result in the loss of a sale in the short term, or involvement in
expensive contractual arguments over performance at a later stage.

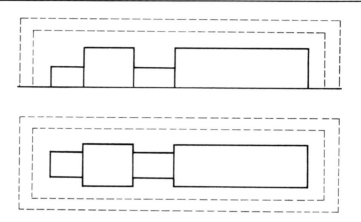

*Figure 1. Microphone location diagram for measurement of sound
pressure levels of a large machine for calculation of sound power levels
by the two-surface method after G M Diehl*

Where data is going to be used as a sales aid, a knowledgeable potential
purchaser will be more impressed with measurements carried out in
accordance with recognised standards than with purely arbitrary figures which may be regarded with suspicion.

Although there may be no standards that apply directly to the product
in question, the ones that do exist can often be used as models. Most of
these are based either on sound power estimations which are independent of the surroundings, or on sound pressure measurements at
specific locations and under specific conditions. The Oil Companies
Materials Association recommendations, which are typical of many,
are very comprehensive and give measurement methods that are usable in most circumstances.

If possible, measurements should be carried out either in conditions which are as near free field as possible or as reverberant as possible. In the former case, which usually only applies out of doors or for small equipment items inside very large spaces, the surroundings have no effect on the sound pressure levels measured, the levels depending entirely on the measuring position. It is then easy to convert from sound pressure measurements to sound power. On the other hand, in highly reverberant surroundings the measuring position is unimportant, the level being determined entirely by the surroundings. If the properties of the surroundings can be measured in terms of room size and reverberant time, the calculation is again simple using the charts in Chapter 4. Problems tend to arise when conditions fall between these two extremes and neither assumption is reasonable. Under these conditions the two surfaces method of sound power level measurement is useful. The principle of the method, set out below, is to measure the sound pressure level over two surfaces (Fig 1) surrounding the machine and by comparing the measured differences between the two results and the theoretical differences to correct for the effects of the surroundings, using the relationship:

$$SWL = \overline{SPL_1} + 10 \log S_1 - C$$

where C is obtained from Fig 2.

Source Identification When it is necessary to cure a noise problem rather than merely to identify that it exists, the measurement procedures become more complicated. Whereas, if identifying whether a problem exists, measurements in dBA terms are usually adequate, where remedial action is to be taken, it is necessary to have information about the frequency content of the noise. Usually at least octave band information is needed and this normally forms a good starting point, although more detailed information may be needed later.

The most important step in noise control is correct source identification. If noise sources are not accurately identified, money spent on noise control measures may be completely wasted.

Sources are normally identified by one or more of the following methods:
1. Running sources more or less independently
2. Sound power assessment
3. By identifying frequency components
4. By cross-correlation and similar techniques

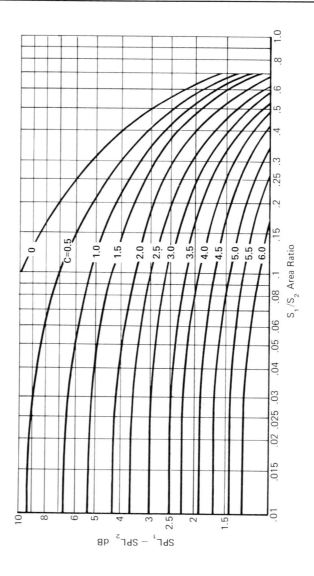

Figure 2. Environment correction factors for calculating sound power levels by the two-surface method after G M Diehl

Running Sources Independently If the suspect sound source can be operated truly independently of other equipment, switching it off is one of the most reliable methods of source identification. If, when all the plant is operating normally, there is a noise problem and switching off one plant item removes the problem, it is usually a reasonably safe deduction that the item switched off is the cause of the problem. The snags with this procedure arise not with the acoustics but with the plant operation. In some cases the plants are not truly independent and shutting down one item affects the running and thus the noise production of other items. For instance, shutting down one fan in a ventilation system may cause the load on other fans to change, thus affecting the noise level. One should also beware of plant items which are interlinked in hidden ways. Sometimes when a major piece of equipment is started, auxilliary items start automatically at the same time, which can confuse the issue. One instance of this involved some large refrigeration compressors which were suspected of causing noise problems at neighbouring houses. What had passed unnoticed was that, whenever the compressors were started, fan condenser units started at the same time. Separation of these items showed that it was the condensers that caused the problems and not the compressors.

When it is not possible to run plant continuously in isolation, it is often possible to run it under abnormal conditions for a short time, which, although not enough in itself for full measurements, will be sufficient to enable brief tape recordings to be made for detailed analysis later.

When shutting down a single plant item produces the required reduction in noise level, the problem is simple. More often it will be found that shutting down no single item has the required effect. As a general rule, if shutting down any single item produces an audible or measurable effect, then that item is contributing significantly to the total. This follows from the rules of addition in Chapter 1. For example, if two equal sound sources are producing a sound, shutting down either item, which contributes half the energy, only produces a barely audible 3dB reduction. When the contribution in energy terms is less than 50%, the reduction will be even smaller. For example, if we consider the following four items:

Item A which produces 68dBA   Item C which produces 65dBA
Item B which produces 68dBA   Item D which produces 55dBA

These will produce a total noise level of 72.1dBA. Shutting down each item in turn will produce levels from the other three items of 69.9, 69.9, 71.1 and 72dBA respectively. The drop of 2dBA shows that the first two sources are significant. The smaller reduction obtained when shutting the others down does not enable them to be ruled out.

When measurements have to be carried out over any distance, the variable effects due to weather can often mask the small changes that

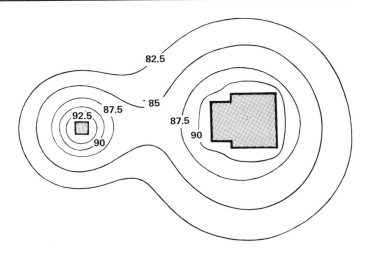

Figure 3.   Comparing sound powers by contour method

are being sought. In such conditions it is absolutely essential that very good communications are maintained to co-ordinate the various starting and stopping operations. The ideal is to have two-way radio communication available; even the use of a very carefully kept log always seems to raise doubts and lead to possible wrong conclusions.

Sound Power Estimation   When it is impossible to identify sources by running them independently, it may be necessary to predict their contributions by sound power measurements. The fact that they cannot be run independently probably precludes the measurement methods given in the previous section for obtaining product data. In these circumstances there are two possible approaches. The first is to plot noise contours around the various plant items, in which case the sound power is proportional to the area around each item which is above a given noise level (Fig 3). The alternative method is to carry out measurements very close, i.e. 25mm from the surface of the items concerned, to obtain an average sound pressure level over the surface and then to combine this with the surface area of the items to compute the sound power, using the relationship $SWL = SPL + 10logA$ where A is in m^2 ($SWL = SPL + 10logA - 10dB$ when A is in ft^2). Although there are theoretical objections to this procedure, it is a procedure that is usable when others fail. Usually the problem is that small intense sound sources tend to mask ones that are larger in size and, because of their large size, are less intense. A large piece of equipment like a boiler may have a very low power density in watts per square metre, but the large number of square metres may mean that the total power produced is greater than for a much smaller source having greater intensity. Unfortunately our ears react to the greater intensity and large sources may go unnoticed. An example of such a situation is shown below and in Fig 4.

Rootes Blower
Surface area = $2m^2$ ∴ 10logA   =   3dB
Mean SPL   = 85dB
Equivalent SWL   = 88dB

Heat Exchanger
Surface area = $25m^2$ ∴ 10logA   = 14dB
Mean SPL   = 80dB
Equivalent SWL   = 94dB

Identification of Frequency Components When one is dealing with pieces of equipment that produce sounds at discrete frequencies, a comparison of the spectrum of the suspected source and the noise at the position of interest may enable these suspicions to be confirmed or rejected. Unfortunately such straightforward cases tend to be rare and too often one is faced with a large number of plant items, all of which would be expected to produce the same or nearly the same frequencies. Once the frequencies fall within 2-3% of each other, a very high standard of frequency analysis is required to separate them reliably and it is necessary to resort to correlation techniques.

Cross-correlation and Similar Techniques In theory it is possible to identify whether the noise is coming from a particular sound source by simultaneously recording the sound signal close to the source and at the point of interest and by multiplying the two together with an appropriate time shift. The common parts of the signal combine to give a finite answer, whereas the unrelated parts should cancel out over a

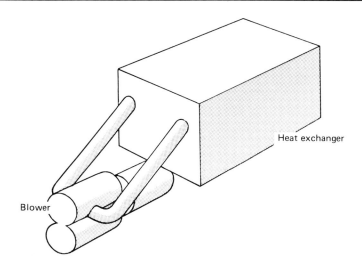

Figure 4. Which is the major noise source, the small blower or the large heat exchanger?

period of time. In practice it has been found that, although there are many examples where such techniques can be used, these are often more easily solved by less sophisticated techniques, and in situations where the simple methods fail, the correlation techniques also fail or are not physically practical.

Conclusion Ultimately noise measurement is 50% acoustics and 50% common sense and observation. Lack of either ingredient can spell disaster.

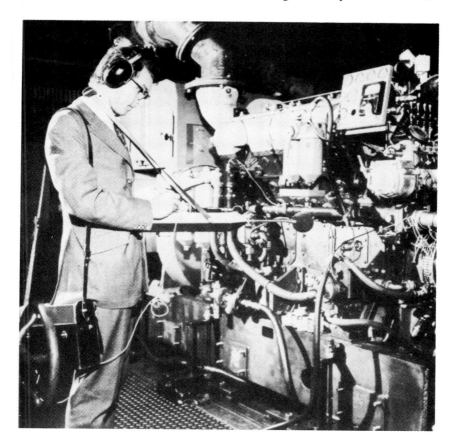

Plate 1.   Close-up of airborne sound level measurements being made in the direct field of a diesel generator. The portable tape recorder may be used to record data for detailed analysis in the laboratory.

Plate 2. It is essential to control noise emission from mobile generator sets, particularly when operating in residential areas.

9
Planning for Noise Control

Introduction Noise is often conveniently defined as sound which is unwanted by the recipient. Consequently, if the degree of 'unwanted-ness' can be defined it will provide a starting point for any calculations for the control of noise. Sound may be 'unwanted' for a variety of reasons and Table 1 summarises some of the causes for justifiable complaint due to noise.

In industrial surroundings, the primary cause for complaint due to noise is nearly always linked to excessive sound levels, either within or external to industrial premises. Such problems may be compounded by the presence of 'character' (hiss, screech, whine, etc) or a variability in noise exposure.

Any problem involving the avoidance of unwanted sound may be tackled by a systematic approach since all sound transfer systems break down very simply into three elements:
1. Source
2. Transmission path
3. Receiver

Sound control procedures can be applied at all points in this sound transfer chain in order that the desired end result shall be obtained. Subsequent sections of this chapter will be devoted to preferred methods of achieving this desired end. First, however, it is necessary that the terms used here shall be clearly defined and understood.

Noise Control Noise control is activity directed towards modification of a perceived sound field such that it shall conform to the desired targets set down for the recipient. In this context, it should be noted that noise control does not necessarily entail the reduction or elimination of a sound. No noise is not good noise, and for most receivers of noise or vibration excitation there will be established maximum and

Table 1

Dominant feature of noise environment	Location	Subjective reaction
Excessive sound pressure level	Internal or external near field	Hazard to hearing
Excessive sound pressure level	External far field	Noise pollution/ discomfort
Detectable character	Internal or external sound field	Irritant
Variable sound level (noise climate)	Internal or external sound fields	Fatigue
Intermittency or impulsiveness	Internal or external sound fields	Startle
Audible speech	Internal far field	Lack of acoustic privacy

minimum limits that it is desirable to obtain (see later section entitled 'Receiver'). It is a useful analogy to liken noise control to speed control. The latter is obtained not by constant use of a brake but rather by use of a governor which eliminates the variability element and

ensures a predetermined constant output. Noise and vibration control could involve any or all of the following procedures:
Reduction of sound power level of source
Reduction of vibration levels of source
Modification of spectral content of noise
Modification of wave forms of impulsive sounds
Modification of environmental noise climate
Introduction of masking sound
Change of sound exposure as experienced by a recipient

Source The source of any sound or vibration excitation will normally be identified as the point of origin of the noise which is deemed to be offensive. In large industrial complexes – an oil refinery for example – there could be several hundred potential sources of intrusive noise. Where such a complex distribution of sources exists, it is necessary that each one shall be individually controlled such that the total acoustic output from the entire installation does not cause the resultant sound field at the receiver to exceed the design target. It should also be noted that a single sound-generating unit may be capable of further subdivision into several sound sources which may take differing forms of acoustic treatment. A boiler installation, for example, could radiate noise both from the burner assembly and the flue discharge. In such circumstances each point of origin should be considered as a separate sound source and an independent analysis conducted for each in order to ascertain the most effective forms of control.

Transmission Path The second stage of the chain – the transmission path – is identified as all wave transmission media which communicate the sound and vibration excitation of the source to the recipient. It could be comprised of any or all of the following:
Direct airborne sound transmission
Reflected airborne sound transmission
Reverberant sound fields
Duct-borne noise
Ground-borne vibration
Liquid-borne sound and vibration
Structure-borne sound

Receiver The final part of the chain – the receiver – is identified as the occupant of the location most critically affected by any noise nuisance. In most cases it will be a single individual, either the operator of a noisy machine or the occupant of the nearest property to a noisy activity. However, in certain circumstances, the receiver may be a group of persons or even an entire community. In fact the critical receiver in the sound transmission chain may not even be human. Certain precision instruments, such as electron microscopes or high-resolution photographic equipment, could be more critical than their operators in their need for low levels of ambient noise and vibration. However, irrespective of the identity of the receiver, it should be possible to quantify the permissible noise and vibration exposure in order that optimum conditions can be ensured. Such targets are usually stated as maximum and minimum advisable sound levels, together with an advised sound spectrum.

In certain isolated cases, an *increase* in noise level at the receiver may be required in order to provide adequate environmental conditions. As an example of this latter procedure, consider the case of two adjacent offices where it is required to provide good speech privacy. In the absence of any other background sound, speech might be heard clearly through the adjoining partition, but if additional broad band characterless noise (sound conditioning) was introduced at levels which did not of themselves constitute a noise nuisance, the perceptibility of speech sounds would be diminished and the privacy of the room occupants improved.

As inferred above, noise control can be applied at any point along the sound transmission chain. It is a cardinal rule that, where possible, the modification of sound should occur at the source. In this way the exposure of all potential complainants is controlled equally. If this procedure is impracticable, noise control at a point along the sound transmission path should be considered. This is seldom as cost-effective as treatment at source and, in certain circumstances, can create further difficulties. For example, a screen interposed between a source and complainant may effectively control sound transmission along the primary transmission path, but reflected sound might cause reinforcement of a sound field at some other point.

Sound control at the receiver can be considered cost-effective in certain circumstances but it is seldom a convenient procedure. An example would be the use of personal hearing protection for the occupants of a noisy process area. This would ensure that the risk of hearing damage was minimised while doing nothing about the primary sound source. If, however, the principal complainant was the occupant of premises adjoining the installation in question, there would be little that could be done other than providing additional sound insulation for his living accommodation. Although this procedure could reduce noise levels inside the house, it does nothing towards improving environmental conditions and the consequent enjoyment of the gardens and grounds surrounding such buildings.

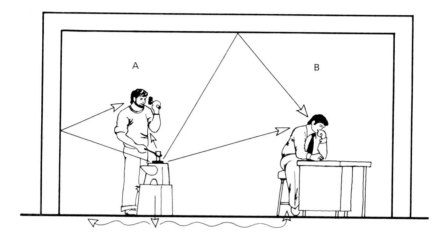

Figure 1.   Simple noise transfer from source to receiver

In order to clarify the discussion that follow, the following definitions are inferred:

Noise control at source infers modifications to the structure or configuration of a noise emitting unit, or its mode of operation. Such treatment will also be deemed to include supplementary attachments to the sound source (such as silencers of enclosures) provided that they are located close to the machine within the 'near field'.

Noise control along the transmission path embraces any changes, modifications or supplementary noise controlling elements introduced at any point between the vicinity of the sound source and the recipient. Noise control at the receiver will be deemed to include any treatment which is applied directly to the complainant or the immediate surroundings. For cases of alleged neighbourhood noise nuisance, this treatment will be considered to include any structural changes made to the complainant's housing but not necessarily any screening at the boundaries of his property. The latter point is considered as part of the noise transmission path.

Systematic Analysis for Noise Control (Example 1) Fig 1 represents an extremely simple noise transfer situation which breaks down into

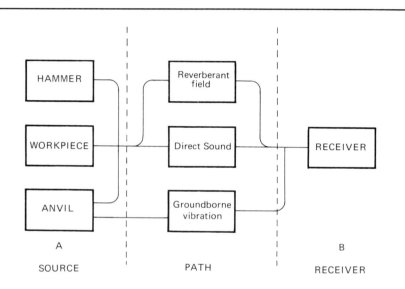

Figure 2. Equivalent block diagram of situation shown in Figure 1

the block diagram shown in Fig 2. It will be noted that the source consists of three individual components, as does the path. Two sound receivers are indicated for which differing criteria may be considered. The man at point A will require simple hearing protection, whereas the other at point B may require a more stringent control of the noise in order to ensure comfort conditions. Before pre-judging such a situation, it is a useful exercise to set down all of the potential controls that could be applied to the situation. As an example, consider the following lists:

Control at Source:
Modify or change work process to reduce noise output
Apply local sound damping treatment to hammer to control ringing
Apply local sound damping treatment to anvil
Mount workpiece on sound damping pad
Apply detachable vibration damping material to workpiece
Locate work activity in total enclosure
Arrange hood over work area
Modify work schedule to reduce total daily acoustic output
Mount anvil on vibration isolator

Control along Sound Transmission Path:
Reduce direct components of sound field by locating receiver B further from source
Change orientation of work activity with respect to receiver B
Control reverberant sound field by introducing sound absorbent roof and wall linings
Reduce structureborne sound by vibration-isolating discontinuity in slab foundations

Control at Receiver A:
Reduce daily noise exposure by changing the operator at set intervals (the remainder of his work period being spent at a quieter activity)
Issue personal hearing protection

Control at Receiver B:
Provide sound isolating enclosure
Provide personal hearing protection
Reduce time duration of periods spent in high level sound fields
Provide vibration isolating flooring
Provide local screening
Provide local sound absorbency
Introduce broad band masking sound to correct noise climate

Fig 3 illustrates various noise control procedures that suggest themselves from the foregoing breakdown of the problem. Yet more ideas may suggest themselves to the reader. Having completed the initial study, the next step is to consider the improvement in acoustic conditions that is required. The main object is to determine the most cost-effective method of providing precisely the right amount of noise control at both critical points – over-attenuation might represent a waste of money. However, in addition to the strictly economic considerations, other conditions also apply. It is necessary that the introduced noise control equipment should be convenient in use, should not reduce the efficiency of the process, and should not down-grade other comfort standards while improving the acoustic environment.

Example 2 This represents a very typical example of noise intrusion into private premises which often results in legal action being taken against the owner of the alleged noise source. Fig 4 represents in diagrammatic form a situation where a generator unit is installed at the

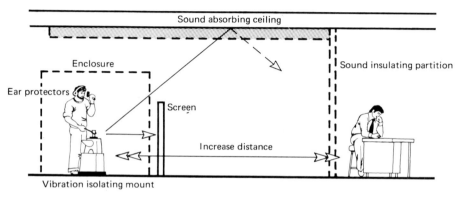

Figure 3. Typical noise control procedures

rear of factory premises, and which could give rise to high levels of perceived noise inside and external to adjacent housing. Fig 5 represents in block diagram form the key features of the sound transfer system and suitable forms of treatment which could be considered for noise control. The objective of the noise control exercise will be to ensure that perceived noise levels immediately external to the house comply with advisory standards – either derived from British Standard 4142 or in accordance with pre-existing by-laws or Codes of Practice affecting the industry and the local community. Each of the noise controlling procedures inferred in Fig 5 is capable of making a contribution to the reduction of environmental noise levels. It should be noted, however, that in many cases the application of one procedure is dependent on other treatments having been similarly or previously applied. For example, the use of a sound limiting enclosure around the machine will reduce noise radiation from the main body of the unit by up to 20dB. However, this reduction will not be of any value if high levels of noise are still radiated from an unsilenced exhaust. Virtually

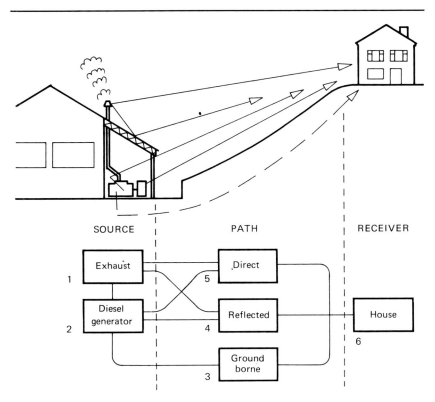

Figure 4.   Neighbourhood noise control analysis

every plan for noise control is unique. Each type or method of applica- tion of noise control procedure will result in either a major or minor reduction of sound and vibration, depending on the specific details describing the unit. Thus, if the large number of potential treatments of any problem are considered, and if the variability of the potential change resulting from each is taken into account, there will be seen to be a virtually limitless combination of procedures worth considering, all of which could achieve the desired target. It will be appreciated that there is therefore virtually no single 'best buy' for noise control and the following guidelines are put forward to assist anyone contemplating using data contained in other chapters of this book in a plan for noise control.

Noise Control by Redesign of the Source Irrespective of the type of machine or installation to be studied for a noise control programme, whether it is a saw mill or a ventilating fan, some of the energy input invariably materialises as noise. The proportion generally ranges from about 0.01% to 2% of the input and obviously depends upon the type of machine. A 200HP diesel engine is obviously a lot noisier than a

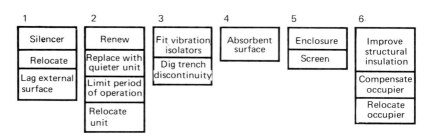

Figure 5. Block diagram – forms of treatment

200HP electric motor. In all cases the acoustical energy output will be a small part of the power delivered by the shaft and too insignificant to make the recovery of the acoustical energy worthwhile. Nevertheless, the noise is generally such a closely related part of the total energy output that it is difficult to conceive a way to eliminate the noise at the source without stopping the machine.

The fundamental noise source will be sited at that part of the machine where the vibrational energy input originates. The vibration usually results from cyclic or impulsive acceleration or deceleration forces which excite resonances of parts of the machine and thus radiate noise over selected frequency bands. As stated above, the best way to eliminate noise is to prevent it occurring, i.e. to modify the moving parts which give rise to the vibrations. These moving parts are usually found to do one or more of the following: rotate with an eccentric (out-of balance) load, oscillate in translation or rotation, move with intermittent or varying speeds, or impact against other parts. A brief consideration of an internal combustion engine will reveal that all of the above sources are present either singly or together in the gear trains, bearings, piston movements, valve movements and cooling fan.

Control of Sound Radiation Noise produced by vibrating components of machines can be controlled by reducing the amplitude of vibration, the area of the vibrating part, or, where feasible, the frequency of vibration. Amplitude reduction is the most important consideration. This is done by minimising acceleration or deceleration forces between moving parts and other components of the system.

The surfaces of sliding or rolling parts should be as smooth as is economically feasible and well lubricated.

The mass of accelerating parts should be kept to the absolute minimum and all rotating parts dynamically balanced.

The rate of change of velocity of any moving part should be reduced and vibration levels will be reduced by making use of the maximum time available to bring about any necessary velocity changes.

Jerky noise-producing motions associated with peak accelerations will be reduced by holding the acceleration of a component as constant as possible while any velocity change takes place. By reducing the area of the vibrating component or by decoupling any source of vibration from large radiating surfaces, the noise emission of a machine can be significantly reduced.

Because of the relative insensitivity of the human ear to the low frequency end of the spectrum, a frequency reduction will assist in reducing noise. If it is possible to lower the cyclic speed of a vibrating action the resulting change in the character of the sound will be interpreted as an extremely beneficial reduction in noise, although the net acoustic power output need not have changed.

Where a machine includes impacting sources such as cams or gears, a significant improvement may be obtained by eliminating any metal-to-metal contact by the introduction of plastic or other flexible surfaces possessing the requisite resistance to wear and abrasion. Adequate lubrication is always essential at contact points and careful attention must be paid to manufacturing tolerances, since poorly fitting parts can cause impacts which thereby generate noise. Similar considerations apply to the control of noise generation at bearings, where unavoidable surface irregularities can exist in ball, roller or journal bearings.

The use of a lubricant creating a film thicker than the surface irregularities will improve the quiet running properties of any rotating or sliding component. In practice, bearings in good condition seldom radiate a great deal of noise since they are such relatively small components of a machine, unless they are directly coupled to larger radiating surfaces such as the casing of a gear box or to the bell housing of an electric motor.

Control of Aerodynamic Sound Another type of noise source often encountered in process machinery, and which does not necessarily involve the vibration of a solid surface, is classed as an aerodynamic source. Such sources generate broad band noise at disturbances caused by turbulent or vortical motions in gases. Typical examples are the noise of flames, jets, valves, fans and flow noise in pipework. In these cases the generated noise usually has a wide band spectrum and will be related to the turbulence intensity. Turbulence intensities are usually a function of the speed of the fluid medium, whether liquid or gaseous, and therefore it is advisable that all flow velocities be kept to a minimum in piped and ducted services by increasing their cross-sectional area. Also, the generation of intense turbulence by sharp changes of direction can be avoided by ensuring that right-angled bends and constrictions are eliminated from the design of process equipment before it is assembled. The noise of air jets or machine exhausts discharging to atmosphere is easily controlled by the use of conventional dissipative or reactive silencers, and transient explosive aerodynamic sources, such as those associated with air blast circuit breakers, can be controlled to a certain degree by incorporating suitable expansion chambers and resistive elements into the path of propagation of the generated shock wave.

Noise Control along the Transmission Path – Enclosures Having exhausted all the possibilities of introducing noise control at the source, the acoustic engineer is forced to switch to the second line of attack – that of controlling noise radiation along its transmission path.

Where the problem merely involves the radiation of airborne sound from a machine, the most effective means of obtaining the requisite attenuation would be to totally enclose the machine by a noise reducing enclosure. Such solutions, however, although attractive, are almost invariably unacceptable to the operators of the equipment since they can seriously impede the product throughput, ease of operation and maintenance on the enclosed unit.

When such a solution can be considered, it is necessary to ensure that adequate access is provided for operations and maintenance by means of sound resistant doors and hatches, and controls, gauges, and ancillary services may require relocation at some new operating position.

The cladding should be so constructed that no resonances of the enveloping structure occur. This can be ensured by the use of bracing members to stiffen the structure, together with the application of vibration damping compounds.

Since all industrial processes tend to generate heat, acoustic enclosures may require ventilating to prevent overheating which could damage the equipment, since a temperature increase could lower the viscosity of lubricants and thereby accelerate wear at moving points or cause a breakdown in the insulating materials of electric motors.

The supplementary ventilation system must obviously be acoustically attenuated in order to prevent sound leakage via the ventilating airways and, in the same way, where raw materials require to be fed to the machine and the resultant product discharged, acoustically treated ducts will have to be built to permit these movements, while controlling noise emission.

Sound Resistant Screens When total enclosure of a machine is inadmissible, a partial solution to the problem may be obtained by the use of sound resistant screens placed at carefully selected points between the operator and the noise source. However, screens have a reduced effectiveness in highly reverberant surroundings, when the noise field is able to 'flank' the screens by reflection and re-reflection at the internal surfaces of the building where the machine and its operator are located. Consequently, any treatment that can reduce such a build-up of the reverberant sound field, such as the application of sound absorbent linings to walls and ceilings, will reduce the perceived noise levels at all locations and improve the efficiency of screens.

In absolute terms, the measured background noise will drop by 3dB in the reverberant far field when the reverberation time of the building is halved, and by a further 3dB for each further halving of the reverberation time.

A screen placed near the operator and separating him from the noise source can provide a further 10 to 15dB reduction of mid-frequency noise depending on the dimensions of the source and the screen, and their location with respect to the recipient of the noise.

Vibration Isolators If noise or vibration originating at a machine has been sensed via groundborne vibration, then a major reduction can be effected by mounting the machine on vibration isolators. These units normally consist of rubber or steel springs which are selected to give their maximum isolation at the forcing frequencies associated with the machine operation. They are small, relatively cheap, and can represent the most dramatic noise-reducing equipment in the acoustical engineer's armoury.

The reduction in structural vibration that can be brought about by correctly specified vibration isolators can sometimes provide the requisite reduction in noise without any other process having to be considered.

When a machine is mounted on compliant mountings, it is mandatory that all other connections to it, such as ductwork, piping, electrical connections, structural members, etc. incorporate compliant links to prevent vibrational energy from being short-circuited to the structure from which the machine itself has been isolated.

Noise Control at the Receiver When all other approaches to noise control at a machine or in its vicinity have failed, and only then, a programme of noise control at the receiver should be undertaken.

Although the tolerances of vibration-sensitive devices such as electron microscopes may be specified in absolute terms, the response of human beings, either singly or in a group, is obviously a statistical problem. No one individual is likely to exhibit the same reaction to a noise stimulus on two successive days and in larger samplings of people there will always be those who, by either their hypersensitivity to noise or total insensitivity, disagree with the preferences of the majority as to the acceptability of a given noise environment.

The problems of noise in industrial surroundings usually involve a few people who are normally located within a short distance of the noise generating process. For these personnel a limited choice of procedures is available which will provide an improved acoustic environment. They may be isolated from the noise field by means of suitable sound-proof enclosures, they may be issued with hearing protection in the form of ear defenders, or ear plugs, or their work schedules may be reorganised to ensure that they are not exposed to high level noise fields for periods longer than is advisable for the conservation of hearing.

The final step in drawing up specifications for the control of noise and vibration will be to assess the contribution that can be made to the desired result at each of the three primary variables of the total system in the context of its cost, time taken to accomplish the modifications, delivery time of new components and the possible reactions of the operators from the safety and productivity standpoints. It is obvious that absolute criteria cannot be applied to all of the variables referred to, and the final configuration of a successful procedure for noise control, whether utilising one or many of the available control measures discussed here, will represent the best optimisation of the many economic and human factors involved.

Plate 1. Noise reducing enclosure round a standby diesel generator adjoining the garage of a large private house. Note the sound resistant door and acoustic louvres designed for attenuated inlet and outlet

10
Noise Control by Planning and Maintenance

NOISE control by planning is probably the most neglected form of noise control. It is the avoidance of noise control problems at the planning stage so that the requirement for noise control by other means is eliminated or reduced. As a consultant, it is very frustrating to be confronted by noise problems which need never have occurred, or which are rendered to all intents and purposes insoluble by lack of thought at the planning stage. In the noise control field, prevention is usually very much better than cure.

Noise control by planning can be divided into three sections:
1. Selection of quiet processes
2. Layout
3. Making provision in advance for noise control procedures

Selection of Quiet Processes   In many cases no feasible alternatives have been found for common and important noise processes, in which case the question may not arise. However, there are cases when there is a choice of method or process, in which case the noise factor should be included with the others at an early stage. Clearly noise is not the only factor but must be given due consideration. If the choice of one process is going to result in an expensive noise control bill at a later stage, this should be included when an initial cost comparison is made. This may show that an apparently more expensive but quieter process may turn out to be cheaper in the long run.

It is gradually becoming easier to obtain noise data about machines and processes from their vendors. As more prospective purchasers press for this information, so it will become more readily available.

Where information cannot be provided by the vendor, a visit to see the machinery in operation is informative – often about factors in addition to noise. Even if the circumstances and surroundings are very different from the ones in which the equipment will eventually be operated, an approximate idea of the end result can be obtained.

The charts presented in Chapter 4 for estimating noise levels within a room can be used in reverse to estimate the sound power output from machines. The sound power data can then be used as a starting point to predict the likely general area noise levels. The levels close to machines, where operators are likely to be, are relatively unaffected by surroundings, except in the extreme case of a large number of machines in highly reverberant surroundings.

Layout   The most important part of noise control by planning concerns layout. This involves the use of not only distance to reduce noise levels but also psychology. Layout can be important both inside a plant and outside. The latter case will be discussed first.

When a new plant is built, the immediate neighbours often regard it with mixed feelings, quite regardless of whether or not it is likely to make a noise. Neighbouring residents often see the rear or side view of the plant, rather than the front. Unfortunately, the front, which is often well separated from residential properties, gets the most attention. This usually has a neat and pleasing appearance, while the rear is where all the essential services are located, often looking as though they have been put in as an afterthought (Fig 1). As a result, unless an unusual amount of forethought has been exercised, air compressors, condensor units and ventilation fans that frequently run all night are in full view of sleepless residents, and are probably floodlit into the bargain! If such equipment had been sited so that it was screened from the gaze of neighbours, not only would the noise level have been reduced by the screening effect of the intervening building, but there would have been psychological screening as well, to further reduce the effective noise level. Where screening by building structures is not practicable, the use of screening walls or even acoustic louvres can produce a similar effect – hiding the source of sound both from the eyes and ears.

Large fan outlets are quite directional so where possible these should be arranged so they do not point directly at the nearest resident.

Reductions of noise levels by careful planning of outlets may reduce noise levels by 10dB or more – an improvement that would be expensive to obtain by other means.

Inside the plant itself, or even within the office buildings, similar rules apply. One should not make noise problems more difficult by siting noisy areas close to noise sensitive ones. Ultimately it will probably be production considerations which will settle the final layout, but it is still

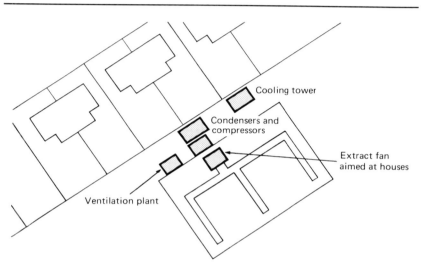

Figure 1. Services located at the rear of the factory – just outside bedrooms windows

often possible to effect great improvements in the noise situation. Noisy operations can be grouped together. This reduces the area requiring noise control treatment and provides automatic noise control by virtue of distance for the other employees. Dead areas like stores and holding areas can be used as buffer zones between noisy and quiet areas. Often spectacular improvements can be made provided they are considered early enough. It is a good idea if, at the very earliest layout stages, noisy items are marked in red on the sketch layout and noise sensitive areas in green. This highlights the possibilities, gives guidance to where changes can be made and spotlights potential problems.

Planning Ahead for Noise Control   The final aspect of planning is to plan for noise control at the beginning, rather than introducing it reluctantly as an afterthought at a later stage. There are two aspects to this; the first is that noise control problems should be predictable at an early stage, and the second is that the solution is almost certainly easier if it has been planned ahead.

If you can avoid annoying the neighbours in the first place, they will probably accept higher noise levels than they will once their anger has been aroused. Once their attention has been drawn to a noise, they are likely to campaign for a reduction to lower noise levels than would

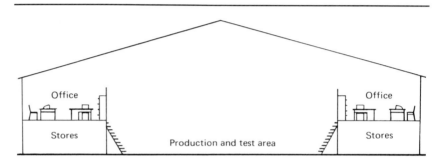

Figure 2.   Open topped offices provide no protection against noise in an enclosed space

have been necessary to satisfy them in the first place. It is often said that people will get used to any noise in time. Some people will, but others will become more and more worked up about it the longer the noise continues. It is these people who will complain to the council. The fact that 95% of the population will have learned to live with the noise is of no help when 5% are bringing an injunction to close the plant.

With all noise control problems it is almost invariably cheaper to incorporate quietening measures from the start rather than later. One simple case is shown in Fig. 2.

Design offices were separated from a main workshop area by metal and glass partitions. The author was asked to advise on better partitions to reduce the unacceptably high levels of noise in the offices.

Measurements showed that the noise level in the office was only 1 to 2dB lower than in the workshop, although the existing partitions had a potential insulating capability of 25dBA. The trouble was not that the partitions were inadequate but that the offices had no roof. The sound was coming over the top of the partitions. The cure would have been to fit ceilings to the offices, which would have enabled the full performance of the partitions to be realised. Unfortunately the arrangements of services and the structure made it impossible to make such a change at that late stage without very considerable cost.

Frequently the reduction in noise from an existing dust extract system will involve a complete redesign of the system and of part of the building. On the other hand, if noise had been considered at the design stage, the problem would not have arisen and the total cost of the system would probably have been no greater.

Noise control by planning is probably the least spectacular form of noise control but in many cases it is the form which is most effective.

Maintenance   After noise control by planning, noise control by maintenance is probably the next most neglected area. Almost without exception all machinery and equipment runs quieter when it is in good condition and proper adjustment than when it is in a bad state. In many cases the difference may be as much as 10 to 20dB. Frequently we have been asked to comment on the noise level in a workshop. A quick investigation has shown that one plant item is responsible for a high level over a relatively wide area. Switching off this one item of plant produces a very considerable reduction.

Frequently the plant item is one of several apparently identical machines, the others operating quietly. Further investigation often reveals that the quiet machines have been overhauled recently, or have had defective components replaced. In cases like this, either reducing the maintenance interval or checking the state of health of the machines if the noise levels become high represents a cheaper way of reducing noise than the use of expensive and possibly inconvenient enclosures.

Increasing noise levels or vibration levels from machines can be used as a guide to the condition of the machine and should be interpreted as warning signs of impending trouble. It may well be false economy to ignore these warning signs. There is little point in calling a noise consultant to advise on quietening a noisy machine when his recommendation is going to be 'overhaul it'!

Plate 1. A specially quiet fan-cooled condenser set chosen for a critical residential location. It is essential in such cases to select plant equipment carefully at the design stage since noisy systems can often be difficult later to attenuate effectively

11
Noise Control at Source

Experience throughout a wide range of manufacturing and processing industries has shown that perhaps the single most common cause of excessive noise is due directly or indirectly to poor maintenance. Relatively simple, low-cost treatment almost invariably produces rewarding results and while this confirms the need for improving standards of maintenance, it also demonstrates the value of noise control at source. There are two major virtues of controlling noise at its source: first, the results will be appreciated everywhere and not just along one path or for one receiver. Second, the need to examine the mechanism by which the noise is being created and will need treating often leads to improvements in the machine process or method of working.

In general, the important noise sources are relatively few in type:

a)   Impacts, eg hammers, gear noise, etc
b)   Out-of balance forces
c)   Stick-slip friction, eg brake squeal from honing processes
d)   Magnetostrictive effects, eg transformer or motor hum
e)   Hydraulic noise, eg noise from hydraulic power units
f)   Aerodynamic and pneumatic noise

Essentially all of these processes are capable of producing fluctuating forces which can set machine components into vibration, thus causing them to radiate noise directly or indirectly. In case f), aerodynamic flow variations can themselves radiate noise without necessarily setting mechanical components in motion. Frequently the source itself is insignificant as a noise producer in its own right but, because of its effects on other components which are effective radiators of sound, a great deal of noise is produced. A common example of this is an alarm clock that when held in the hand is quite quiet but has an intolerable tick when standing on a bedside table. Similarly, while the level of vibration produced by a precision gearbox is low, poor mounting of the machine structure often results in substantial structure-radiated noise.

In the context of this chapter, controlling noise at source consists of reducing the energy produced by the source, breaking the path between the source and the radiating surface, preventing the surface radiating, or a combination of all three. The reduction of radiated noise is covered in Chapter 12 and will not be repeated here.

The Energy Sources
Impacts Impacts include not only the obvious examples where hammer blows or other collisions occur, but also less obvious cases like gear noise where each tooth causes an impact as it meshes with its partner. Sharp impacts between hard surfaces produce exciting resonances in a wide range of components. When the impacting surfaces are cushioned, not only is the energy involved usually less but it is confined to the lower frequency ranges which cause less of a problem. Further, the cushioning will often reduce mechanical wear or damage, thus improving machine life. Removing or reducing the effects of impacts can be achieved in several ways.

Substituting other Quieter Processes This can take the form of either a complete change of process or more subtle forms of change. One example of the former was substituting a milling process for weld preparation on diesel engine cylinder blocks. The work had formerly been done with a pneumatic chisel which produced noise levels of 125dBA at the operator's ear. This change involved considerable modification to the manufacturing process and, as is so often the case, was brought about by the desire to improve production methods rather than to reduce noise. Having made that point, it is important to appreciate that the two often go hand in hand.

Other examples of substituting quieter processes are the use of microswitches instead of mechanical limit stops, squeeze riveting instead of percussion riveting, and the use of inert gas electric welding techniques which do not create slag, thus obviating the need for chipping to remove the slag.

Reducing the Impact Reducing the force of the impact can be achieved by modification of the motion of the contacting surfaces, by changing the shape of the surfaces, or by providing a softer surface. Modification to cam profiles to avoid step changes in acceleration is an example of the first process. Not only will this reduce noise and wear between the cam and its follower, but also at any other links in the process. The change from spur gears to helical gears, or from straight tooth milling cutters to helical cutters are examples of modifying the shape to provide a reduced impact. The noise of gear teeth can be partially reduced by improved production methods, although a lot depends on the gear form and loading. At a later stage noise can be reduced by careful lubrication and higher maintenance standards.

One point to note for anyone trying to identify the source of noise in a gearbox is that the subject is relatively complex. Noise peaks do not occur just at the frequency corresponding to tooth meshing. Harmonics of the meshing frequency are normal, while complex "side–band" patterns of tonal noise can result from gear eccentricity and other geometric errors. Other frequencies are often determined by

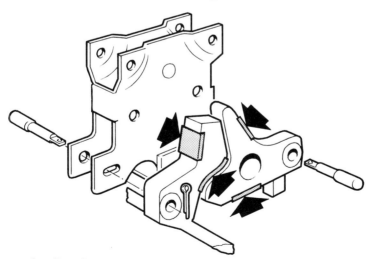

Figure 1. Resilient pads to avoid metal-to-metal contact in latch unit for overhead conveyor

resonances in the gear wheels or the gearbox casing which are excited by broad band noise. Larger gear wheels can have their resonance damped by multiple part construction or by the use of damping materials.

The use of plastic gears to reduce noise is well known and is an example of using a soft material on the impacting surface to reduce the impact. For many cases where soft impacting surfaces are desirable, the problem of life and durability is raised as an argument against such a step. Ironically enough, in many of the cases where this has occurred soft materials have been found in the same circumstances to reduce wear. This includes the lining of dump trucks, vibratory screens in quarrying, chutes and tumbler barrels where the use of specialised lining materials not only reduces noise but also damage by abrasion. In cases where soft striking surfaces are not admissable an improvement can be achieved by using a steel striking surface mounted on a soft insert. The modification made to an overhead conveyor latch mechanism shown in Figure 1 reduced the noise level by 12dBA.

Out-of-balance Forces The degree of out-of-balance in most machines is controlled by design, quality of construction or manufacture. Apart from selection of a different machine or process with less out-of-balance, noise control is normally limited to quality control and maintenance. In other words, ensuring that a machine does not initially have a sub-standard performance and maintaining that performance.

Stick-Slip Friction Here the noise is produced by alternate sliding and sticking of the two surfaces in contact, setting the structure ringing. In many cases lubrication of the process, which is the simplest way of reducing the noise, is not an acceptable solution. For example, it is clearly not practicable for braking devices! However, modification of the the leading edges of brake shoes and changing rake angles on cutting tools can produce spectacular reductions in noise level with no undesirable effects. In most cases the ideal form can only be found by trial and error. Again, with cutting tools, reducing the period between re-grinding or using better quality tools, such as tungsten-carbide tipped saws may be cheaper than having to take noise control procedures to deal with the noise produced by the blunt tool.

Magnetostrictive Effects These are covered in detail in Chapter 19 and will not be dealt with here.

Hydraulic Effects Noise from hydraulic effects is associated with the design of the motors, pumps, valves and other components in the system. In general it can be said that what is good design in terms of component reliability is usually also good design for noise. With hydraulic systems the forces or pressures are so great that sharp pressure pulses caused either by sharp valve cut-off or by flow oscillations are not only noisy but also destructive. Good design of systems to prevent vibration problems also pay dividends from the noise point of view. Further, it is possible to use silencers or pulsation dampers in a hydraulic system much as one would use an attenuator in an engine exhaust or ducted air system.

Aerodynamics Aerodynamic noise can be divided into two sections. The first is purely aerodynamic noise, where high speed jets mix with the low speed air surrounding them and produce noise through turbulence. The commonest industrial example of this is at the exhaust of a pneumatic valve or airline. In the former case the noise can be controlled by the use of porous plastic silencers, while an example of quiet airline nozzles are shown in Figure 2.

Other aerodynamic noise problems come from the interaction of airflow and a solid surface. If the airflow was truly steady, the forces on the solid surfaces, ie the lift or drag, would be constant and the pressure distribution across the surface would also be constant. In practice, due to turbulence or the presence of moving obstructions, the flow is never steady. This results in changes in the force on the structure and changing pressure distribution over the surface. The noise can result either from the force vibrating the structure, or from the region of changing pressure on the surface which radiates directly into the air like an inflating and deflating balloon. This effect can be demonstrated simply with a desk top fan. If a ruler is held close upstream or downstream of the fan, the noise of the fan will appear to increase considerably. This is the result of the airflow fluctuations over the fan blades or ruler as it passes through the wakes caused by the other component. In general, good aerodynamic design – providing a uniform air distribution upstream of a fan, or providing smooth low pressure loss ductwork – all helps to reduce noise from this cause. Noise control by improving the aerodynamics upstream of the fan has

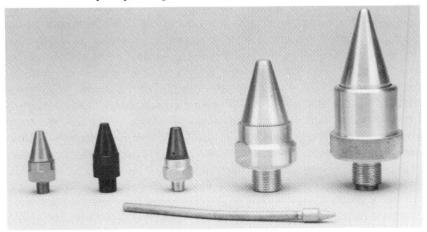

Figure 2 Examples of silencers for a pneumatic airline

been used with beneficial effect on fan installations ranging from fractional horsepower to many thousands of horsepower.

Transmission from the Source   As mentioned previously, the sources themselves are often ineffective at radiating noise in their own right and rely on surrounding structures to complete the transmission chain. In most cases the noise is transmitted to the structure by mechanical means.   These cases can be divided into two classes; those where the source excites resonances in the structure, and those where it is forcing the structure to vibrate at a frequency off resonance.   In the former case, which occurs when the source makes the structure vibrate at the frequencies at which it would vibrate if struck at a suitable point with a hammer, the effective means of control is to supply some means of damping.   This is the only form of control which is effective in a resonance situation if the source is producing energy over a wide frequency range because damping is effective over that range.

Excitation of Resonance   When the problem results from the unfortunate coincidence of a specific source frequency matching a natural frequency, there is scope for de-tuning the system by changing the mass or stiffness.   If the noise source is broad band, however, changing the stiffness or mass will only change the frequency of the problem. Damping removes the resonance condition regardless of frequency. The damping can be introduced by the use of different materials, 'stick-on' treatments or the incorporation of frictional joints. Bronze, aluminium and steel are materials with relatively low damping. This is why bronze is used for bells. Cast iron and some special copper-manganese alloys, however, have comparatively high internal damping. This is one reason why some of our modern machine tools with light alloy castings have more noise problems than their cast iron forerunners. Where light structures are concerned, coating with bitumen or rubber type materials can provide sufficient damping to make useful noise reductions. Suitable materials are either proprietary damping compound or car undersealing materials. This form of treatment is only practical when it is feasible to apply a layer of material which is comparable in weight to the structure and is in practice limited to 3mm. The use of this treatment, which is referred to as unconstrained layer damping, is not effective on heavier components. Where it is possible to incorporate a layer of damping as a sandwich between two parts of the component, preferably at a location where shear will occur as a result of the vibration process, the technique can be effective for rather more massive components, say up to 6mm. This is known as constrained layer damping. Sandwich steels are now available making use of this principle. Although there are still limitations on their use, these are gradually being overcome and are proving particularly effective for chutes.

Excitation Away from Resonance Where the problem is one of vibration from the source forcing the associated structure to vibrate at a frequency not corresponding to resonance, the process can be controlled either by inserting a soft link between the source and the surface or by stiffening or adding mass to the surface itself. Unfortunately, in many cases the structure is very light and, for an intermediate link to be effective, it would have to be unacceptably soft. Adding weight to the structure in this case is not usually acceptable, so the approach has to be to stiffen the structure. Figure 3 shows the general arrangements of a refrigeration compressor in a small room air conditioner unit. The compressor was mounted on the light base plate shown. Vibration of the compressor, despite the fact that it was on rubber mounts, was sufficient to bend the base plate, which in turn distorted the rest of the structures so that all panels were radiating

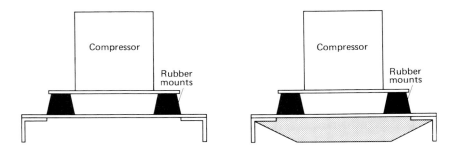

Figure 3. Stiffening of air conditioner base to prevent bending

sound. The solution in this case was very simple. Two braces were fitted under the panel to increase its stiffness and to bridge across the frame mounts. This reduced what had been a serious noise problem to a level where it was undetectable.

When separation of the source from the radiating surface is being considered as a form of noise control, it is often worth trying complete separation, even on a temporary basis (in the case mentioned above the compressor was held by hand to achieve this), before embarking on extensive modifications. If complete separation is not effective, any separation that can be achieved by practicable means will be similarly ineffective. The principles of separation are covered in Chapter 6. In many cases of 'rogue' machines which are abnormally noisy compared with other nominally identical machines, the trouble will be found to be due to bridging of isolation devices. This is often due to accidental displacement of isolated components possibly during transit.

12
Enclosures, Barriers and Cladding

ONE of the cardinal rules in planning for noise control is to reduce the noise at its source by modification of the noise emitter, changing its operating conditions, or any other appropriate treatment. When such approaches are impractical, or if it is necessary to supplement small reductions achieved by modifications of the source, other means of controlling emitted sound at some point along its path to the receiver must be considered. An airborne sound field (as distinct from ground-borne, duct-borne or structure-borne sounds), once established, can only be modified by reflection, diffraction, insulation or dissipation. In other words, it will be necessary to use some form of solid object to either destroy part of the sound energy by absorption, or to redirect part of the sound energy by wave reflection. The use of sound absorbents to modify semi-reverberant sound fields will be dealt with in Chapter 15. The concept of sound control by insulating media will be developed in succeeding sections of this chapter. Three forms of total or partial containment of a sound field are recognised and will be termed 'enclosures', 'barriers' and 'cladding'.

Enclosures are sound insulating structures designed for the total containment or exclusion of a sound field. They may also incorporate sound absorbents to further modify the internal sound field. Their primary function will be to provide a form of encapsulation which has a high sound insulating performance around a noise source. Alternatively, they may be required to provide a quiet enclosure within a high intensity sound field. The design of acoustic enclosures will often entail a basic understanding of structural engineering and building technology. They may be permanent structures fabricated from conventional building materials, or small hoods made from specialist modular sound insulating panels. Large enclosures usually function acoustically in accordance with the standard laws relating to room acoustics and sound insulation and include such applications as engine test cells, mechanical equipment rooms, quiet refuges, etc.

Small enclosures which function as sound insulating shells around a noise source do not always conform to the laws governing sound in rooms, and in general provide significantly less sound attenuation than would be expected from the standard sound insulation data. Among this class of enclosure will be booths and hoods for unitary machines, and the specialist sound insulating casings and panels such as are used to construct modular air handling plant.

In the following discussions, the word 'barriers' will be used as a generic term to imply either partial enclosures or acoustic screens, canopies or baffles. Since they cannot provide encapsulation of a sound field, barriers can only be expected to provide relatively low values of sound attenuation in certain directions by wave screening effects and by sound dissipation at acoustically absorbent linings.

Sound insulating cladding will be considered as a form of composite treatment for the control of sound emission from a surface. It functions by a combination of sound insulation, sound absorption and vibration damping. A typical example is the external treatment which is often applied to control noise radiated from pipes and ducts. This normally takes the form of a compliant wrapping of mineral fibre mat or plastic foam overlaid with one or more sound insulation layers. The frictional constraint so applied to the sound radiating surface serves to damp its vibration amplitude and thus directly reduces the radiated sound levels. The external insulating jacket further reduces the radiated sound and the fibrous layer serves to dissipate some of the acoustic energy transmitted through it.

Barriers Acoustic barriers or screens placed in the path of free field sound radiation will block part of the sound energy and create a relatively quiet zone in the acoustic 'shadow'. However, when screens are used in semi-reverberant surroundings, where sound is reflected and re-reflected from all internal surfaces, noise will be transmitted to the shadow area by the reverberant component of the sound field and the effectiveness of the screen will be seriously diminished. Consequently the effective use of barriers can only be considered out of doors or in non-reverberanr surroundings. In particularly favourable circumstances they may be able to provide as much as 15dBA sound reduction. However, it is unrealistic to expect better than 10dBA and for many cases it will be found that the net sound reduction by a screen scarcely justifies the cost.

The screening of a sound source is not analogous to the sharp edged shadow that is created from a light source. Because the wavelength of

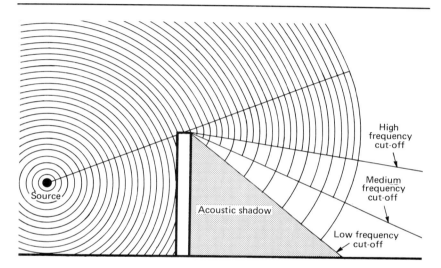

Figure 1. Acoustic screening

low frequency sound is often equal to or greater than the dimensions of the screen, much of this low frequency will be diffracted around the panel. However, high frequency radiation is better controlled by screening and a more pronounced cut-off will be detected on the quiet side of the barrier. (Fig 1)

Size is not the only dimension which affects screening. Studies by Maekawa have shown that the distances from the screen to the sound source and the observer also affect the measured noise reduction. The three significant dimensions defining a screening situation can conveniently be combined to form the 'path difference', δ (see Fig 2), this being the difference between the straight line path connecting the source and receiver and the shortest two-leg path over the intervening barrier. It can be found that the insertion loss of a barrier will be a function of the Fresnel number $(2.\delta/\lambda)$ and the relationship between screening effect and path difference is illustrated in Fig 2. This relationship has been expressed in a more convenient form by the chart in Fig 3 which displays the octave band spectra of screening attenuation

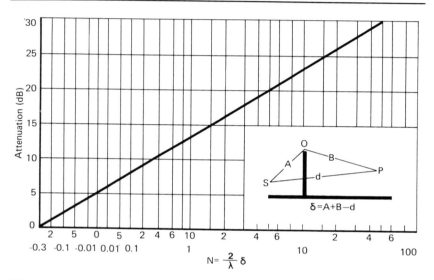

Figure 2. *Sound attenuation by a semi-infinite screen in free space after Maekewa*

for a range of both positive and negative values of δ. Also shown are the three configurations of screening elements which are most frequently met in practice.

In Fig 3a, δ is positive, i.e. there is no direct line of sight between the source and the observer. In this case, the source has been taken as a louvre and the screening effect has been accomplished by means of a parapet on the edge of the building. In Fig 3b, δ is shown in the negative sense, e.g. when a cooling tower fan is radiating into the air and there is a wall alongside the cooling tower which, although it does not apparently screen the source, does give rise to a measurable effect

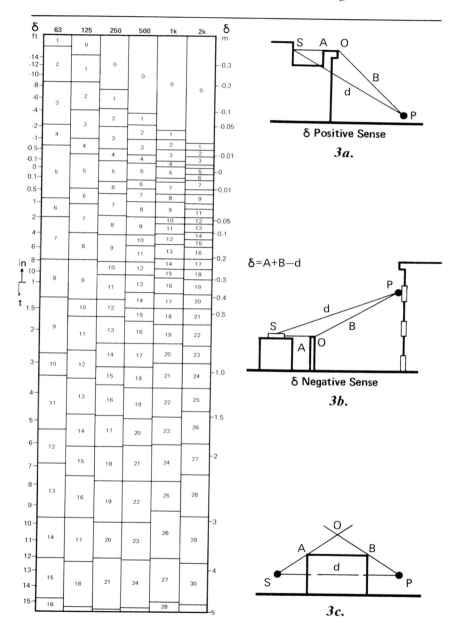

Figure 3. Attenuation due to screening

at the observer. In this case, the general effects are minimal at high frequency, but it can add a useful degree of low frequency attenuation. Fig 3c shows the effect of a thick barrier or earth mound. For such cases the shortest two-leg path over the barrier will be determined by the two straight lines that graze the barrier and intersect above it. Fig 4 shows a barrier of finite width and height – a free standing wall, for example – which shields the observer from a noise source but is flanked by sound radiation around three sides. It will thus be apparent that the sound energy reaching the observer will be the sum of the total energy received along these three paths.

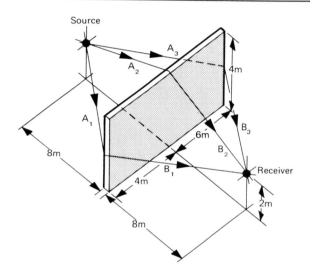

Figure 4.   Acoustic screening – worked example

Worked Example (see Fig 4)
A 4m×10m screen is interposed midway between a small sound source and an observer which are 16m apart and 2m above the ground plane. If the centre line of the screen is offset by 1m from the line connecting the source and observer, what is the resultant screening effect?
Length of path A_1+B_1 = 17.88m
Length of path A_2+B_2 = 16.492m
Length of path A_3+B_3 = 20m
δ_1 =1.88m δ_2 = 0.492m δ_3 = 4m

Frequency	125	250	500	1000	2000	4000	Hz
Path 1	15	17	20	23	26	29	dB
Path 2	10	12	15	18	21	24	dB
Path 3	18	21	24	27	30	33	dB
Effective attenuation	9	11	14	17	20	23	dB

Note: The individual attenuation values have to be combined by considering the energy transmitted, e.g. if, in the absence of the screen, the level would have been 80dB, the level resulting from the individual paths would have been 65, 70 and 62 which, using the rule of thumb in Chapter 1, total 71dB, i.e. giving an effective attenuation of 9dB. The same result can be obtained by using the rule of thumb in a negative sense, e.g. -18 and -15 combine to give -13, -13 and -10 combine to give -9dB.

From the foregoing worked example, several salient points concerning the effectiveness of screens will become apparent. Firstly, it will be seen that the shortest path difference will be the critical one and it is generally appropriate to consider the screening effect for the shortest path difference only in a situation such as the one illustrated here. However, if all the flanking path lengths are fairly similar, it will still be necessary to separately compute the individual screening effects and determine the total screening attenuation by summation.

Most sound sources to be screened will have finite dimensions and, in computing the lengths of the various path differences, the points of origin of the sound should be considered to be the outermost edges of the sound source.

If the sound source is, for example, a grille set in a wall, it is possible that the screen could reflect sound back to the wall and thence on to the observer. In a situation such as this, or whenever it is necessary to control sound reflected off a screening structure, it will be necessary to consider the use of acoustically absorbent treatment on the side of the screen exposed to the sound field.

In the previous example, it will be noted that the screen provided an average attentuation in the region of 15dB. By reference to the acoustic Mass Law chart for sound insulation, it will be noted that this is equivalent to the performance of a sound insulating structure which, if it entirely enclosed the sound source, would need to have a superficial weight of approximately 1kg/m^2 ($\simeq 0.2 \text{lb/ft}^2$). This is comparable with the performance of a sheet of thick card. Hence, if the sound insulating performance of a barrier exceeds its screening attenuation by 5dB or more, it can be assumed that any sound reaching the observer will have been transmitted around the screen and not through it. Thus, for the above example, it will only be necessary to provide a screen constructed from 8mm plywood. In fact, as noted previously, the realistic limit for screening attenuation will be in the region of 15dB in which case there is virtually no requirement for a screening structure to provide better than 20 to 25dB average sound insulation. Thus the point emerges that external screens do not have to be massive structures. They must, however, be impermeable, stable enough to withstand wind loads, strong enough to stand up to accidental damage, and must resist weathering. To meet these conditions, most screens will be fabricated from standard building components, e.g. sheet metals, timber, brick or blockwork, asbestos or glass-reinforced cement board, etc. Barriers made of such materials virtually cannot fail to meet the acoustic insulation target.

If a screen is required to have a sound absorbing surface, it should be noted that such materials are much more susceptible to damage, either by weathering or normal wear and tear. Most sound absorbent materials are spongy and hence tend to retain water, which on freezing can damage the cellular structure of the absorbent. A more rugged form of sound absorbent which is frequently used for outdoor screening purposes is woodwool cement. Slabs of this material, when rendered on one side only, provide very effective screening modules with an acceptably high sound absorbent surface.

So far this discussion of screens has been limited to the case of barriers in free field, i.e. open air surroundings. In semi-reverberant surroundings, say a large workshop, much of the sound will reach the observer behind a screen by reflection from the internal building surfaces. This can result in the screen being largely by-passed, particularly when the observer is some way from the sound source. Consequently the use of screening for effective noise control will normally be limited to cases where the direct component of the sound field is dominant. In other

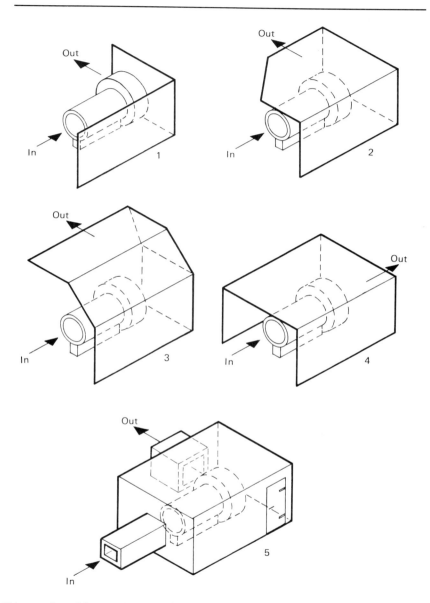

Figure 5.   Alternative configurations of partial acoustic enclosures for production machinery

Figure 6.   An example of an acoustic curtain

words, in relatively 'dead' surroundings where the barrier can be placed as close as possible to and around the source or the receiver. Fig 5 illustrates some of the configurations that typical barriers and partial enclosures can take. They are all designed to maximise the screening effect around a machine, while at the same time allowing easy access for the operator and for the supply of raw materials and the discharge of a finished product.

Although it was inferred above that screens will require to be constructed of rigid sound insulating media, this does not preclude the use of alternative sound attenuating materials. Acoustic louvres which have airways lined with sound absorbent materials can have a transmission loss which at middle and high frequencies reaches 15dB or more. Consequently, for screening applications where an uninterrupted airflow is required (for example around cooling towers or engine installations), this type of structure will provide a useful alternative to impermeable panels. Similarly, in industrial surroundings it is often more convenient to use curtains fabricated from heavy sound barrier mats rather than rigid panels around production areas. Fig 6 displays this type of screened enclosure.

To summarise, the performance of any acoustic barrier can be shown to be dependent on the parameters listed in the following table. In order to achieve maximum screening performance, it is desirable that the optimised conditions noted here should be achieved. Failure to take account of one or more of these aspects of barrier design could result in an ineffective barrier.

Parameters affecting Acoustic Screen Performance

Design Parameter	Optimum Condition
Size	Very large with respect to size of source and wavelength of lowest significant frequency
Location	As close as possible to the source or observer
Form	Barrier should wrap around the source or observer
Local reflecting surfaces	Keep as remote as possible, or treat with sound absorbing materials
Reverberation time of surroundings	Keep as low as possible

Design Parameter	*Optimum Condition*
Transmission loss of barrier	Should exceed screening insertion loss by at least 5dB
Permeability of structure	Eliminate all holes or apertures or use acoustically lined louvres or splitter attenuator modules
Sound absorbency	Surface exposed to incident sound should be treated with a high efficiency sound absorber

Cladding Sound radiated from the surfaces of pipes and ducts can become a significant component of the external sound field when the diameter of the pipe or the equivalent dimension of rectangular duct-work exceeds 200mm. For smaller sections, sound radiated from the metal surfaces is only likely to be a problem in extremely quiet surroundings. Most so called pipe-borne noise arises not from direct radiation of the pipe surface but from pipe-borne vibration being coupled to the support structures by stiff hangers and clamps. In this way a small diameter pipe having a limited surface area can be coupled to a large partition which effectively acts as a sounding board.

For the case where high levels of sound are radiated from the surface of a large pipe, by wrapping this pipe with a sound absorbent layer only, it is possible to achieve a noticeable reduction at the high frequency end of the noise spectrum (frequencies in excess of 1000Hz). This is partly due to some vibration damping being provided by friction at the interface between the pipe surface and the fibrous layer, and also to the dissipation of acoustic energy that occurs when sound propagates through a high performance sound absorber. At these high frequencies the cladding, even if only a lightweight fibre blanket, will have sufficient inertia to remain stationary while the air molecules displaced by the passage of sound waves move in it. However, at low frequencies, the light cladding will not have sufficient inertia to resist the applied forces due to the motion of the underlying surface. The resultant periodic displacement of the outer surface of the cladding will result in low frequency sound being radiated with virtually no reduction in amplitude.

If the fibrous blanket is now wrapped by a limp impermeable layer, there will be a change in the levels of sound radiated. At high frequencies, in addition to losses already noted due to damping and absorption, the normal incidence transmission loss of the external membrane may be added to the insertion loss attributable to the absorbent layer only. However, at low frequencies, there may even be an increase in sound radiated due to resonances arising from the mass of the external membrane and the springiness of the layer of air enclosed under the external layer of casing. The resonant frequency will be given by:

$$f_0 = \frac{42}{\sqrt{Md}} \text{ Hz}$$

where M = surface mass of membrane (kg/m²)
and   d = thickness of absorbent blanket (m)
or

$$f_0 = \frac{34.4}{\sqrt{Md}}$$

where M and d are in lb/ft² and ft respectively

For example, if a sound barrier mat having a weight of 5kg/m² (1lb/ft²) is applied to pipework over a 25mm glass fibre mat, the resonant frequency of this cladding will be 118Hz.
Up to frequencies of 1.5× f_0, the insertion loss of external cladding will be effectively nil and it may even have a small negative value at certain frequencies. Thus, great care should be taken in the selection of suitable claddings for noise control. Good control at high frequencies may be offset by an increase in low frequency noise. In general any external blanket will have to provide thermal insulation as well as acoustical absorbency. This will tend to limit the choice to various glass or mineral fibre blankets or comparable fire resistant foams or felts. The external limp casing may be comprised of a variety of treatments. Proprietary sound barrier mats consisting of dense mineral or lead-loaded PVC sheet may be used. These have weights which range from 5 to 15kg/m² (1 to 3lb/ft²). Sheet lead foil can also be used despite the high intrinsic cost of lead, as it can be used in the form of very thin foils.

Where appropriate, materials can be obtained to meet BS476 Class 1 Surface Spread of Flame. Limp barrier mats should be overlapped by at least 100mm at all joints and the overlaps bonded with manufacturer's recommended adhesive. Plastic, fibre or metal banding may also be necessary on large cross-sectional ducts. For example, a sheet weighing 5kg/m² (1lb/ft²) will have a thickness of less than ½mm and will be significantly cheaper than the equivalent weight of proprietary sound barrier mat. However, lead foil has little mechanical strength and may require further external protection by banding, or an external wire mesh. Irrespective of the type of material used for cladding, whether limp or rigid, all joints should be made airtight by sealing strips or adhesive compounds.

Multiple layers of cladding, provided that the weights and thicknesses of the materials used are chosen to give dissimilar resonance frequencies, can give high performance of sound insulation. Fig 7 shows acoustic lagging which was applied to natural gas pipework on the discharge side of a turbine compressor. The treatment, working from the external casing inwards, was as follows:

1mm galvanised steel jacket for weather and vermin protection
Waterproof PVC membrane
25mm (1in) mineral wool (120kg/m³ – 7.5lb/ft³)
2mm (0.08 in) lead sheet
50mm (2in) mineral wool (120kg/m³ – 7.5lb/ft³)

Resonance frequency for outer jacket = 100Hz
Resonance frequency for inner jacket = 40Hz

On test, the treatment was found to give an effective noise reduction of 18dBA with the following octave band insertion loss:

Frequency	63	125	250	500	1k	2k	4k	8k	Hz
Insertion loss	5	7	10	12	14	18	23	31	dB

Fig 8 illustrates two methods of applying sheet lead cladding to sheet metal ductwork. Wired timber battens are used to prevent the lower surface from sagging under wide ducts. Typical results obtained for a 600×750mm rectangular duct clad with 50mm semi-rigid glass fibre mat, and 10kg/m² (2lb/ft²) lead foil are represented by the following reductions in octave band noise breakout:

Frequency	63	125	250	500	1k	2k	4k	8k	Hz
Insertion loss	2	3	9	12	12	15	18	18	dB

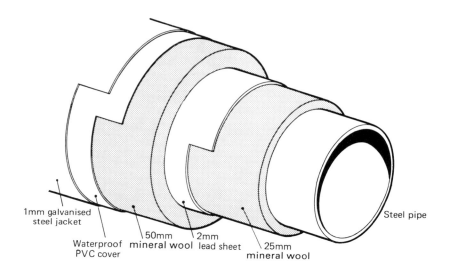

1mm galvanised
steel jacket

Steel pipe

Waterproof   50mm   2mm
PVC cover   mineral wool lead sheet   25mm
                              mineral wool

Figure 7.   Compound sound resistant cladding for noise radiating steel pipe

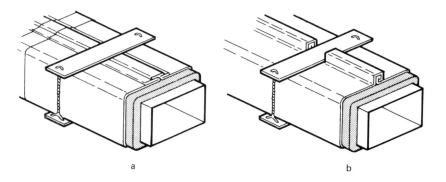

a   b

Figure 8.   Duct cladding using sound barrier matt applied over fibrous semi-rigid slab

Enclosures An acoustically insulating enclosure can provide a high degree of sound reduction. Relatively light-weight units can provide noise reduction of 20dBA and specialist complex erections can provide better than 50dBA. Such enclosures can be used for noise containment or noise exclusion – in other words they can be used either to surround a noisy machine, or to provide a quiet refuge for the observer. The former procedure is obviously preferable, as noise control treatment applied near the source of sound will benefit all occupants of the surrounding area. However, where the scale of the problem precludes the use of individual enclosures, or where a few operators tend a large number of machines, the obvious solution is to provide sound-insulating personnel shelters.

The noise reduction achieved by the use of such an enclosure will be highly dependent upon its size. For large enclosures having dimensions in excess of 2.5m (8ft) and which are large in relation to the size of the contained machinery (plant rooms and test cells for example), the sound reduction through the various elements comprising the structure will be predictable from standard architectural acoustics theory. Such enclosures will be large enough to have a conventional and measureable reverberation time which be will be amenable to treatment by the standard procedures of applying sound absorbent materials to the inner wall surfaces or by hanging functional absorbers within the enclosed space. Each halving of reverberation time will result in a reduction of 3dB in the internal reverberant sound level and consequently the level of sound breaking out through the enclosure structure can be reduced by 5-8dB by the appropriate choice of internal treatment.

For many applications, the use of large and massive enclosure structures is impracticable. On ships and other vehicles the enclosures might be as light as possible, and where space is at a premium, they must be made as small as possible. This brings in the concept of using close-fitting tailor-made hoods around machines – a treatment which is particularly appropriate for modern industrial situations where operators do not need constant physical contact with production units, but rather require to observe, monitor and occasionally adjust the process.

The acoustic performance of small enclosures departs significantly from that of larger units fabricated from the same materials. In general the acoustic insertion loss of small machine hoods is very much less than that of a full-scale unit. This arises from the fact that the contained source is generally large with respect to the outer casing, and the air trapped between the sound source and the enclosure forms a mass-spring system which resonates at some low audio frequency. To reduce this resonant frequency out of the working range, either the mass per unit area of the enclosure or the spacing between the enclosure and the sound source must be increased. However, if it is required to increase the attenuation at low frequencies by increasing the resonant frequency for a casing of given weight, the mechanical stiffness of the casing must be increased. Furthermore, to reduce the amplitude at any resonance frequency requires that the external casing be adequately damped, either by correct choice of basic materials, or the application of a damping compound. At the higher frequencies, particularly those where the air space within the enclosure is an integral number of half wavelengths of sound in air, standing wave resonances can occur which tend to reduce high frequency noise control. These resonances can only be suppressed by the use of sound absorbent linings. For example consider the following data, which compares the airborne sound insulation of 16g sheet steel measured first of all under random-incidence conditions in accordance with BS2750 and then measured as an insertion loss for a small air-tight enclosure over a sound source.

Frequency	63	125	250	500	1k	2k	4k	Hz
Airborne sound insulation	10	14	21	27	32	37	37	dB
Enclosure insertion loss	10	14	16	15	18	23	26	dB

Practical Sound Resistant Enclosures Commercial suppliers of sound resistant enclosures have adopted the practice of supplying standard modular panels which can be combined to form an infinite variety of enclosures of any size or shape. Although timber and glass or asbestos-reinforced cement panels are sometimes encountered, the most popular method of enclosure fabrication uses sheet steel in thickness ranging from 10g to 20g for the external insulation surface. This is normally lined with up to 50mm (2in) non-flammable absorbent (for example rockwool or glassfibre) contained by a permeable internal facing which is strong enough to resist damage. Wire mesh or perforated metal having an open area of at least 20% is normally used. Acoustic performances vary, but a typical construction consisting of

16g steel plate lined by 50mm (2in) glass fibre will, as a result of the combined sound insulation and absorption, give the following net sound reduction when used as a small enclosure:

Frequency	63	125	250	500	1k	2k	4k	Hz
Insertion Loss	10	14	23	33	40	43	44	dB

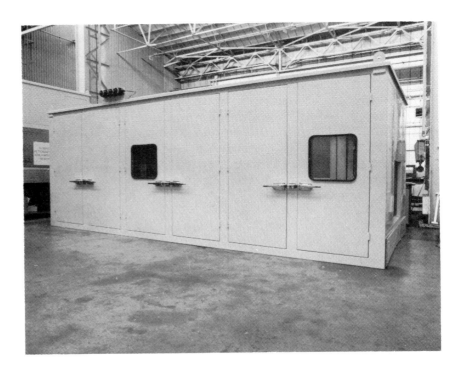

Figure 9. Machine enclosure fabricated from modular panel units

Figures 9 and 10 show typical installations involving this type of modular construction. The panel modules are capable of an infinite variety of uses as acoustic screens, partial enclosures, hoods or even large weather resistant buildings. Figure 11 shows an example of the last-named application. Each sound resistant enclosure will to some extent be unique and consequently various practical details will need to be borne in mind in designing these units. The following paragraphs

Figure 10. Partial enclosure

indicate some of the points that may have to be considered. At all times the cardinal rule should apply that an acoustic enclosure should allow no apertures for sound leakage. Sound is like water and the presence of any gap, no matter how small, will down-grade the eventual performance.

Figure 11. Acoustic enclosure for a generator

Absorbent Linings Flammable materials should never be used for sound absorbing or vibration damping treatments. If liquid fuels, cutting oils, solvents or other flammable liquids are present as part of the process to be enclosed, it should be noted that even inert fibrous linings are likely to act as wicks, and contribute to a potential fire hazard. In these circumstances it is preferable that no sound absorbent linings should be used, but the sound insulating properties of the enclosure increased to ensure that the design insertion loss is achieved. Non-flammable liquids and dust can clog sound absorbent surfaces and seriously reduce their efficiency. Consequently, where water sprays are encountered, the internal lining should be chosen for its ability to resist water penetration (a thin film of plastic should protect the panel infill or a waterproof material should be used in self-draining panels). In dusty environments such as mineral screening or wood-working equipment, arrangements should be made for the enclosure surfaces to be cleaned at set intervals.

Ventilation Virtually all mechanical processes involve an output of heat and thus the use of a total enclosure with its relatively high thermal insulation could result in a temperature build-up which could accelerate failure of the machine by the break-down of lubricants, electrical insulation, or uncompensated thermal expansion, etc. Consequently most machine enclosures will require ventilation. Occasionally natural ventilation will suffice and acoustically-lined attenuating air inlets and discharges may admit sufficient cooling air while at the same time limiting noise breakout from these apertures. More complex installations may involve the use of forced ventilation. This will entail the provision of one or more fans or blowers which supply the requisite number of air changes to limit thermal build-up. Such cooling air inlets and discharges must be attenuated (see Chapter 13). It should also be noted that cooling fans may themselves be an additional source of noise. Therefore, all attenuators should be placed on the atmosphere side of any fan (whether used as supply or exhaust) in order to control both fan noise and process noise break-out along these paths.

Windows It is not usually necessary to provide large windows in machine enclosures. Small vision ports will be needed to allow inspection of certain aspects of the process and internal artificial light should be provided to aid this activity. As long as these vision ports only comprise a small percentage of the total area of the enclosure, they may be fabricated from single thick sections of shatter-proof plate glass or plastic. It is only when the enclosure is used to form a quiet refuge that large windows may be needed to provide natural light and all round vision. In such circumstances it may be necessary to resort to double glazing if high values of sound exclusion are desired.

Doors All enclosures will require doors and access hatches. These should be fabricated in the same way as the fixed panel elements in order to give comparable sound insulating performance. Efficient seals should be provided around the entire periphery of all hinged elements.

Rubber or plastic compression seals provide the best results when closing of the door gives progressive compression of the seals by cam-action fasteners or espagnolette bolts. Alternatively, 'refrigerator type' flexible magnetic strips set in plastic extrusions, can be utilised for the door seals – a procedure which often doubles as the latching mechanism of the door. Both the foregoing systems are destroyed by heat and if such risks are likely to be encountered it is recommended that specialist seals made of woven asbestos fabric be used in their place.

Other apertures Many services connections will have to be made through enclosure walls. These will include electrical cables, fuel lines, water pipes, exhaust pipes, shafts and control rods, to mention a few. In each and every case it will be necessary to ensure that the connection passes through the wall of the enclosure without creating a point of potential sound leakage while at the same time decoupling any inherent vibrational energy, which if it contacted the external surface of the enclosure could cause it to radiate sound. It is therefore recommended that all such connections be led through oversized holes in the sound resistant casing, which are then packed with sound resistant and vibration-decoupling grommets or glands. Flexible links such as electrical power cables do not require any detailed attention. Neither do small diameter pipes such as fuel lines which can be fabricated from flexible hose or metal piping incorporating a few helical turns. Hot pipework such as exhaust pipes will require to be wrapped by asbestos rope or similar, and led through an oversized annular tube let in the enclosure casing. Rotating shafts can be arranged to pass through a specially designed bearing seal, or along an acoustically lined sleeve. Shafts having short axial motions such as control rods, may also be fed through sliding seals or acoustically lined sleeves, or a "gaiter-type" concertina seal can be arranged to be directly fixed both to the sliding rod and to the point at which it emerges from the enclosure.

Stock Feed and Discharge Possibly the first difficult point to provide good sound attenuation on many machines is where the raw stock is fed to the process and the finished product removed. There is no single simple universal treatment and the final solution must be individually worked out for each installation. Where small components are involved or the feed stock consists of a dispersed medium, the use of sealed hoppers suggests itself. In this way noise would only be radiated

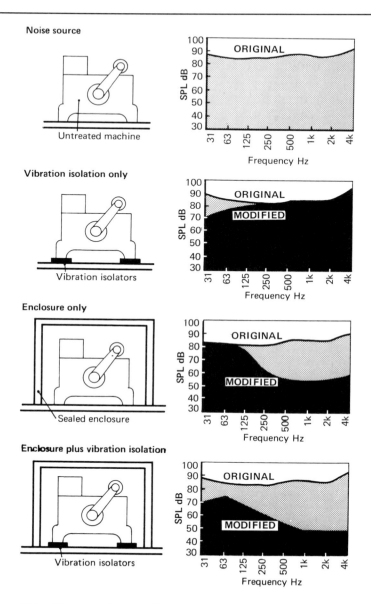

Figure 12. *Noise reduction by configurations of acoustic enclosure and vibration isolating mounts after Bolt and Ingard*

for short periods when the materials in question were added or removed. Larger single elements can be made to transit through self-sealing apertures consisting of flexible flap-type doors. Continuous processes may be fed through acoustically-lined tunnels. The list is endless and the solutions are only limited by the ingenuity of the designer!

Conclusion Designs for sound control along the transmission path from the source to the receiver can involve application of virtually every known application of sound control technology. It is therefore

Plate 1.   Acoustic screens used to reduce noise transfer from noisy plastic granulators to other factory areas. Also shown here is vibration damping treatment to the sheet metal inlet chute of the granulator

essential that the designer should have a full understanding of all of the principles involved. The results obtainable from differing techniques are highly variable and in consequence the basic guiding principle must be the cost-effectiveness of any procedure that may be considered. The variability of the results that can be achieved are graphically illustrated in Figure 12. This series of charts, based on work by Bolt and Ingard originally published in 'Handbook of Noise Control' (C M Harris, ed.) aptly summarises the results that are likely to be achieved for the many approaches that can be adoped in a noise control programme.

Plate 2. A sound resistant enclosure around noisy production equipment. Efficient internal lighting and observation windows give good visibility for monitoring the plant and equipment

Plate 3.   A sound resistant control room enclosure designed to protect operators from high levels of factory generated noise. Enclosures can have a high insulating performance and may be found in such applications as engine test cells, mechanical equipment rooms, quiet refuges etc

13
Silencers, Mufflers and Sound Attenuators

THERE are many areas of noise control where air or other gases must be transferred from one location to another, whilst limiting the transfer of noise. In order to satisfy this requirement, some sort of acoustic device is required which will permit the passage of airflow but minimise the flow of acoustic energy. Perhaps the most commonly encountered example of this problem is the need to discharge the exhaust gases from an internal combustion engine to atmosphere without the high noise levels associated with this process. A similar problem occurs at the air inlet. Both of these can be dealt with using an acoustic filter.

Air conditioning systems employ fans, which are characteristically noisy, and if a room is to be successfully ventilated without exposing its occupants to unacceptably high noise levels then some sort of sound attenuator will be required between the fan and the conditioned area. When applied to combustion engines and compressors, the filters are usually called 'silencers' (or 'mufflers' in the USA). For ventilation systems the term 'attenuator' is more common; although for widely differing applications, the requirements of the acoustic devices in the above examples are similar in principle.

The statement of the acoustic problem is relatively simple. An acoustic filter is required to minimise the transfer of sound waves whilst allowing the steady flow of air through it. This is a 'low pass' acoustic filter.

Sound attenuators, silencers and filters may be divided into two types. The first, the 'reactive' type, relies on a tuned element, where the second, the 'dissipative' type, is an untuned frictional device converting acoustic energy into heat. Attenuators working in the first way tend to be more effective at low frequency absorption than the second type. Dissipative attenuators depend for their operation upon material which physically absorbs acoustic energy from the airflow by frictional means. Many real life silencers or attenuators are hybrid devices combining both principles.

Reactive Attenuators Purely reactive attenuators are in general of more use for fixed speed machinery producing pure tones. Because they are essentially tuned devices, there will be some frequencies at which they are very effective and others at which they have no beneficial effect and may make matters worse. For this reason, most so-called reactive silencers also incorporate a dissipative element which is not so highly frequency dependent.

Conical Connectors Before dealing with more sophisticated devices, it is worth mentioning in passing the simplest of all forms of reactive attenuator. This is the coned connection between two ducts of different cross-sectional areas. Fig 1 relates the transmission loss, $10\log_{10}E_1/E_2$ (where E_1 and E_2 are the incident and transmitted

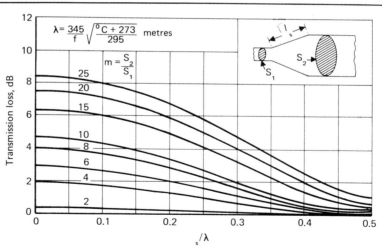

Figure 1. TL of conical connectors, the units of l_s must be the same as those for λ after Franken

energies respectively), to the ratio of the duct areas and the length of the connecting wall. The maximum attenuation occurs when the ratio of duct cross-sectional areas is as large as possible and the change from one area to the next occurs instantaneously.

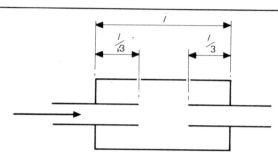

Figure 2. Simple reactive attenuator suitable for high speed machines after EEUA

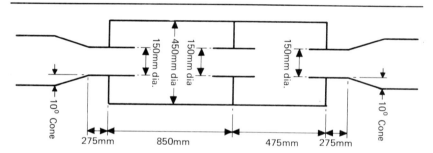

Figure 3.   An acoustic filter that relies on the interference of reflections produced at various changes in section within the silencer body after EEUA

High Speed Machines Fig 2 shows a typical arrangement of a simple form of silencing element suited to high speed machines. It has a single expansion chamber. Fig 3 is a more advanced design using two expansion chambers.

The following is a simple design method for such attenuators. Using Fig 4 and knowing the ratio of the outside pipe area to the inside pipe area, it is possible to derive the maximum attenuation in dB per section. From Fig 5, .the ratio of the cut-off frequency (f_c) to the

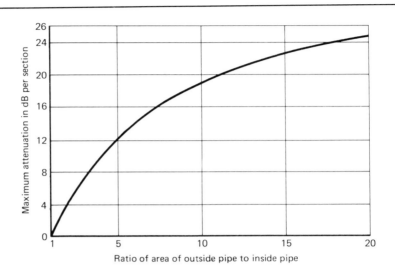

Figure 4. Maximum attenuation for acoustic filter of type shown in Figures 2 and 3 after EEUA

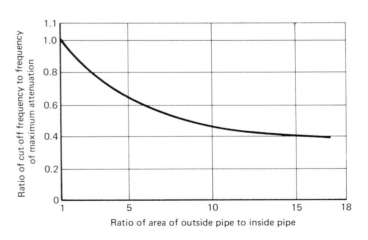

Figure 5. Ratio of cut-off frequency to frequency for maximum attenuation, with an acoustic filter after EEUA

frequency at which maximum attenuation will occur (f_m) may also be calculated. The maximum attenuation occurs when the length L_s of the section is equal to a quarter of a wavelength. From this, the frequency for maximum attenuation f_m will be given from:

$$f_m = \frac{c}{4L_s} \tag{1}$$

where c = velocity of sound
$\quad L_s$ = length of section in consistent units

For example, a silencer having a length L of 1m and inner and outer diameters of 50 and 150mm respectively will give a maximum attenuation of about 18dB at 85Hz and have a cut-off frequency of 42.5Hz.

This form of reactive attenuator will not attenuate frequencies below the cut-off frequency f_c. By virtue of its design, the filter will also have pass bands which are to be found at even multiples of the frequency f_m. However, by having more than one section in series, the total attenuation may be increased. Furthermore, by making the lengths of the two sections unequal and by varying the proportions of the pipe lengths and chamber lengths, it is possible to design the compound attenuator such that the various sections interact favourably. Computer programmes are available to optimise the design for a given engine or blower, based on its measured unsilenced noise output.

In order to estimate the aerodynamic resistance of this type of attenuator, it is usual to adopt the conventional methods of predicting pressure loss as if a steady flow is passing through the attenuator, although this may be over-optimistic.

Attenuators for Low Speed Machinery The design method above gives unacceptably long designs when used for silencing low speed reciprocating machines. To overcome this difficulty, the design shown in Fig 6 can be used. This uses the capacity of the chamber and the mass of the air in the interconnecting pipes in an analogous manner to the capacitance and inductance of an electrical circuit.

This type of silencer, frequency used for air intakes, is normally designed to have a cut-off frequency (f_c) of 0.7×the lowest frequency for which the attenuator is designed to operate. f_c is the frequency at which the expansion chambers resonate.

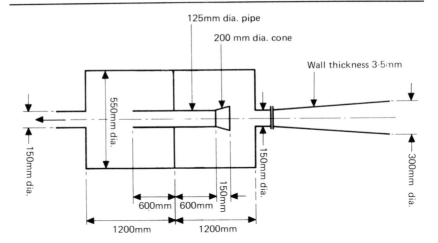

Figure 6. Reactive attenuator suitable for low speed machinery air intakes

The cut-off frequency may be derived from the following expression:

$$f_c = \frac{c}{2\pi} \sqrt{\frac{2A}{L_pV}} \qquad (2)$$

where A = the cross-section of the connecting pipe
    L_p = the length of the connecting pipe
    V = the volume of each expansion chamber
    c = the velocity of sound in the medium
    (all in consistent units)

As a guide, the attenuation to be expected from such attenuators may be calculated from the following equation:

$$\text{Attenuation} = 20 \log_{10} (1 - 2\beta^2) \text{ dB} \qquad (3)$$

where β = the ratio of cut-off frequency to the lowest frequency. Higher frequency performance prediction for such attenuators requires a detailed analysis of the signal applied to the attenuator. It will however have a maximum value which is a function of the area ratio of the connection pipe between the two expansion chambers and the pipe containing those expansion chambers.

Fig 7a shows a cut-away section of a commercially available reactive exhaust attenuator. This clearly shows how the acoustic energy and gas has to flow through several changes of cross-section each producing energy reflections.

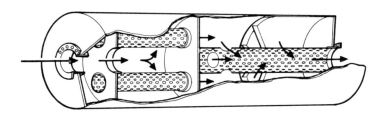

Figure 7a. Exhaust gas attenuator after Nelson-Burgess

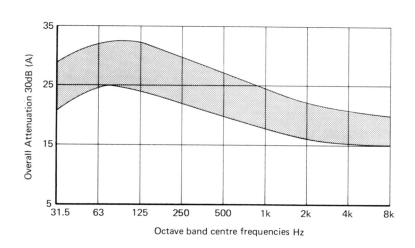

Octave band centre frequencies Hz

Figure 7b. Typical acoustic performances associated with the attenuator in Figure 7a after Nelson-Burgess

Fig 7b gives typical attenuation characteristics of such an attenuator. Clearly the optimum performance is found in the 63Hz and 125Hz octave band widths, becoming less effective at the higher frequencies.

Side Branch Attenuators In the devices dealt with so far, the main gas flow has always been through the various baffles and chambers. This sometimes results in an unacceptable pressure loss. This can be overcome by using side branch resonators, which can take the form of either Helmholtz resonators or tuned stub pipes. In these devices the resonant device communicates with the main gas flow line via a branch connection. Fig 8 shows one such method of achieving this. In this case the main duct has been perforated by a series of holes of diameter D_0.

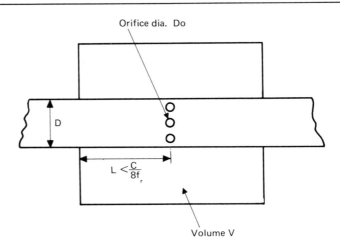

Figure 8. Helmholtz resonator type of attenuator consisting of a chamber connected to the main duct through branch holes after EEUA

The resonant device may either be a Helmholtz resonator which relies on the mass and volume of the enclosed air to provide the tuned system, or a tuned pipe length where the time taken for a sound wave to travel along the pipe provides the tuning.

For the Helmholtz resonator, the attenuator transmission loss may be calculated using the formula:

$$\text{T.L.} = 10 \log_{10} \left[1 + \left(\frac{2\sqrt{CV}}{\pi D^2} \left[\frac{f}{f_r} - \frac{f_r}{f} \right]^{-1} \right)^2 \right] \text{ dB} \qquad (4)$$

where C = the conductivity of connecting orifices = $\dfrac{nS}{t + 0.8\sqrt{S}}$ (5)

  V = the volume
  D = the main duct diameter
  c = the velocity of sound in gas at the operating
      temperature
  n = the number of orifices
  S = the area of each orifice
  t = the length of each orifice
  D_0 = the diameter of each orifice
  f^0 = the frequency to be damped (Hz)
  f_r = the resonant frequency of the silencer (Hz)
  (in consistent units)

$$f_r = \frac{c}{2\pi}\sqrt{\frac{C}{V}}\ \text{Hz} \tag{6}$$

Fig 9 is a graph of the attenuation plotted against the ratio of frequency to resonant frequency for a side branch resonator. It can be seen when $\dfrac{f}{f_r}$ approaches 1 then extremely large values of attentuation may be realised. These equations only hold if all of the volume V is less than ⅛

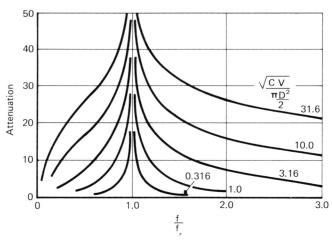

Figure 9. Attenuation values for side branch resonators

of a wavelength from the connector openings. If this condition is not fulfilled, the air does not behave as a single volume.

Tuned Pipe Side Branch Resonators These use a tuned pipe instead of a Helmholtz resonator. They can provide extremely high performance for certain frequencies related to their dimensions but only over a very narrow frequency range. This occurs for any frequency where the tube length corresponds to an odd number of quarter wavelengths.

Dissipative Attenuators Unlike reactive attenuators, dissipative attenuators have the ability to filter out acoustic energies over a wide range of frequencies. Consequently, dissipative attenuators are usually associated with continuous wide band noise sources such as fans, jet engines and other gas moving and regulating devices, although they can be used for discrete frequency sources as well, especially where the frequency is likely to vary over a wide range. In its simplest form, the dissipative attenuator consists of sound absorbing materials such as mineral wool or glass fibre installed along the inside of rectangular or cylindrical ducts, whilst still leaving a free passage for the air to pass through the attenuator. Some of the many ways in which this can be achieved are shown in Fig 10. The sound absorbing materials are selected such that they have a high absorption coefficient over a wide range of frequencies and a smooth surface to minimise frictional losses in the air flowing over the face of the sound absorbing materials. This is in addition to the non-acoustic requirements of withstanding wear and tear in operation and the other hazards such as fire, rot, etc. In many industrial applications the sound absorbent lining must be resistant to contamination by oil, grease and dust. In these cases a special non-porous membrane is frequently bonded to the porous absorptive material. Although this adversely affects the performance of the sound absorbing material at the middle and higher frequencies, the use of this membrane frequently improves the low frequency performance of the material.

In the following sections we will consider lined duct attenuators, packaged cylindrical and rectangular attenuators, acoustic louvres, and lined plenum chambers, all as dissipative attenuators. Typical acoustic performances will be presented and reference will also be made to the operating problems in selecting an attenuator not only to

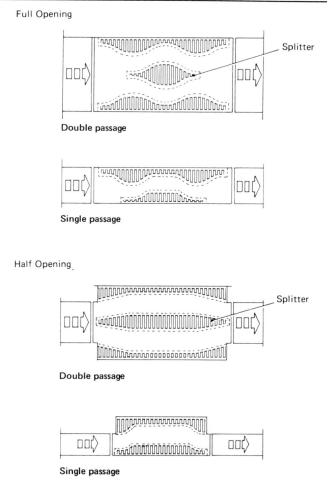

Figure 10. Packaged dissipative attenuators, for air or gas handling ductwork

satisfy a desired acoustic performance but to maintain minimum aerodynamic penalty.

Lined Ducts and Bends The simplest form of dissipative attenuator is produced by lining the inside walls of a duct with sound absorbing material. The material may be either bonded to the duct wall or held in place using special fasteners. This is more appropriate to an attenuator required for handling limited quantities of air or gas in relatively small cross-sectional area ducts. The 'straight through' silencers used on private cars usually consist of a cylindrical duct with a sound absorbent lining around its inside face, although these normally have a partially reactive effect in addition to their dissipative action. The attenuation can be computed from:

$$\text{Attenuation} = 4.2 \, \alpha^{1.4} \, \frac{\text{Length (L)}}{\text{diameter (d)}} \tag{7}$$

where α is the absorptive coefficient of the lining material. For rectangular ducts $d = 4 \left(\dfrac{\text{sectional area}}{\text{perimeter}} \right)$

Although this type of attenuator offers reasonably acceptable acoustic performance for ducts with small cross-sectional areas, its effect on a typical ventilation duct which might be $1m^2$ will be relatively low, unless very thick linings are used. In its favour, however, is the minimal resistance to airflow that a thin acoustic lining on the inside faces of the large duct will cause.

The need for better insertion loss performance has led to the development of the various forms of cylindrical and rectangular splitter attenuators.

Rectangular and Cylindrical Attenuators These have evolved as a method of obtaining similar insertion loss performances to long lengths of lined ducts but within a restricted length. This is obtained by the addition of splitters (see Fig 10) constructed from sound absorbing material, which provide an increase in the ratio of the perimeter to the cross-sectional area as in equation (7). Fig 11 shows the attenuation that might be achieved from the rectangular attenuator design shown. One such packaged rectangular attenuator is shown in Fig 12. The splitter element is being inserted into the prefabricated duct to provide a symmetrical arrangement of 100mm airways alternating with 200mm wide splitters. The side of the duct is lined with half splitters as the duct wall acts as a mirror, doubling the effective width of the outside element. It also shows a facing material that has been applied to the glass fibre sound absorbing material prior to assembly of the splitters. This material is bonded using a specially selected adhesive, such that in operation all the glass fibres are securely retained behind the porous facing material. Great care is required in the application of this adhesive if the attenuator is to give its optimum performance. Too much adhesive can degrade the high frequency performance significantly and too little will allow the facing to pull away from the glass fibre and ultimately result in erosion of the sound absorbing material by the airflow.

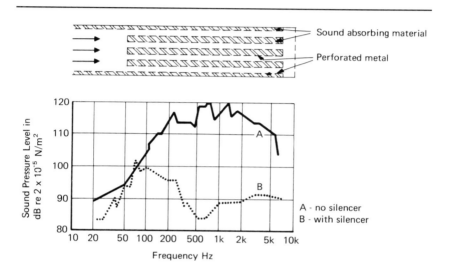

Figure 11. Packaged rectangular attenuator and influence on typical noise spectrum.

Attenuators required for operation in heavy duty conditions require a sheet of perforated metal plate placed in front of the sound absorbing material to protect it from erosion by high air or gas velocities. The optimum attenuator performance can only be realised by carefully selecting the percentage open area of the perforate.

It has been shown that the addition of splitters into an airway can greatly improve the static insertion loss performance of an attenuator, but this is only achieved at the expense of a greater pressure drop. Normally manufacturers publish not only the acoustic performance data but also detailed aerodynamic performance data for packaged units. Like most fixed geometry pressure loss devices, the resistance is proportional to the square of the passage velocity. This means that if, for example, an attenuator had a pressure drop of 50N/m² (0.2in wg) at a passage velocity of 10m/sec (2000ft/min approx), then doubling the passage velocity to 20m/sec (4000ft/min approx) would result in a quadrupling of the pressure drop to 200N/m² (0.8in wg). The bulk of the pressure loss occurs as a result of the sudden expansion at the outlet

Figure 12.   Rectangular attenuator

of the attenuator. Only a minimal loss occurs because of friction over the face of the splitters. In an attempt to minimise this loss and therefore reduce the overall pressure loss of the attenuator, some manufacturers offer low pressure loss attenuators with tapered airways which permit the air in the passageways to decelerate more gradually to the mean velocity of the full duct. A further saving is achieved by having rounded inlets to the attenuator passageways instead of the abrupt entry shown in Fig 12. Cylindrical attenuators follow a similar principle, however, in this case the splitter consisting of a cylindrical

Figure 13. Cylindrical attenuator

pod in the middle of a lined cylindrical duct. One of the problems with this form of device is the difficulty of making circular components from the sound absorbing materials, which are normally produced in rectangular slabs. Fig 13 shows an attenuator which overcomes this problem by using circular moulded inserts which can simply be inserted into the appropriate casing, thus giving a uniform filling without unintentional spaces. A further advantage of this method is that the facing material can be bonded to the glass fibre during the moulding process.

As for rectangular attenuators, heavy duty applications will require a more robust facing and this is usually provided using either pre-shaped perforated galvanised plate or expanded metal.

Cylindrical attenuators without a pod have negligible resistance to airflow. For design purposes, the resistance may be considered to be the same as that of an equivalent length of matching galvanised ducting. A podded cylindrical attenuator, however, does have a significant resistance to airflow. In an attempt to minimise this resistance, many manufacturers make rounded ends to the pod so that the change in passage velocity is more gradual than it would be with an abrupt change of cross-section. Many cylindrical attenuators with pods are installed immediately adjacent to an axial fan. In this case the problem of pressure loss is reduced by virtue of the fact that the pod is situated in the wake of the hub of the fan.

Attenuators, whether rectangular or cylindrical, will not only attenuate noise but they will create noise as a result of air flowing through them. This 'regenerated' noise is a function of the speed at which the air is passing through the airways of the attenuator. Attenuator manufacturers normally publish this information in terms of 'regenerated sound power levels in duct'. It is essential that the prospective user is aware of this problem. If too small an attenuator is used the 'regenerated' noise may mean that the net result of adding an attenuator will not be a decrease in the overall noise level but an increase!

Attenuator selection is based therefore on the static insertion loss performance, the aerodynamic resistance or pressure drop, and the regenerated sound power levels. Manufacturers will readily advise on the most appropriate combination of splitter width, airway width and attenuator length to achieve the desired attenuation within an acceptable pressure loss and without creating any unwanted side effects from the regenerated noise of the attenuator.

Most attenuator performance data has been measured in accordance with BS4718: Method of Measurement of Attenuator Performance. In this way, standardised performance data can be obtained and it is therefore easier for prospective buyers to make comparison of one manufacturer's equipment with another's. He should however be aware that these tests are carried out under ideal conditions which are not always representative of conditions under which attenuators are used in practice. It is essential therefore that the user should consult with the manufacturer to ensure himself that the attenuator he has selected will not only satisfy his design requirements in ideal conditions but also satisfy them in his own actual operating conditions.

Acoustic Louvres There are many applications in industry where large quantities of air must be drawn from the atmosphere. The equipment handling the air is frequently noisy and it is necessary to provide some attenuation between the air moving device and the exterior. We have already seen that this can be done with lined ducts, cylindrical or rectangular packaged attenuators. However, in certain conditions it is more appropriate to use an acoustic louvre which is a combination of a normal louvre, as associated with air inlets to buildings, and a dissipative attenuator. They are frequently installed in the facades of buildings where they are architecturally acceptable and yet provide an adequate amount of attenuation to prevent creating unacceptably high noise levels outside. Effectively, an acoustic louvre is a very short attenuator with a very large cross-sectional area, so it is appropriate where length is restricted but face area is not.

The acoustic performance for an acoustic louvre is usually measured in terms of transmission loss. This enables a direct comparison to be made between the performance of the louvre and a solid wall which it probably replaces. Acoustic louvres as well as packaged attenuators are frequently used in acoustic enclosures where a requirement for ventilation exists. A very common example of this is the diesel or gas turbine generator set which not only requires an acoustic enclosure to minimise noise transfer to the exterior, but also needs relatively high volumes of cooling air passing through the enclosure to prevent build-up of heat from the engine. The device used to admit air to the enclosure and subsequently exhaust the air must have an acoustic performance compatible with that of the enclosure itself.

Lined Plenum Chambers It is arguable whether this type of attenuator is dependent upon a reactive principle, and indeed we have already dealt with expansion chambers in the section on reactive attenuators. However, the lining of the plenum chamber is stressed here and so the attenuator will be dealt with as a dissipative device although it is acknowledged that part of its performance depends upon reactive principles. Another significant difference between the reactive plenum chamber type attenuators dealt with earlier and dissipative lined plenum is that the entrance in the dissipative device is not necessarily in the direct line of sight from the discharge. Fig 14 is a sketch of a high transmission loss plenum which clearly shows that

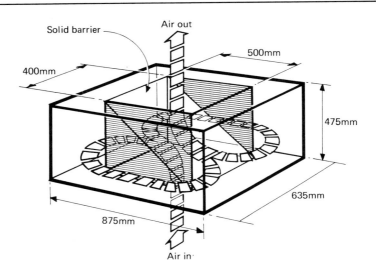

Figure 14. Sketch of a high TL plenum after Wells

there is no line of sight between inlet and exit, indeed for sound to pass through the device it must be reflected at least three times. Fig 15 indicates the difference between sound power entering the device and sound power leaving the device for a bare walled plenum and also with the addition of various acoustic treatments. The unlined plenum does not offer sufficient transmission loss performance to justify the cost penalty of incorporating such a relatively complex device in the system. However, simply treating only the walls of the plenum creates a significant and desirable improvement in performance at all frequencies. There are further returns to be obtained by treating all internal surfaces in addition to the four walls. At the highest frequency this results in a quadrupling of the transmission loss performance. It is also clear from Fig 15 that lined plenum chambers are not the solution to large low frequency attenuation requirements. It should also be borne in mind that the pressure drop penalty may be even greater than for the equivalent rectangular or cylindrical attenuator.

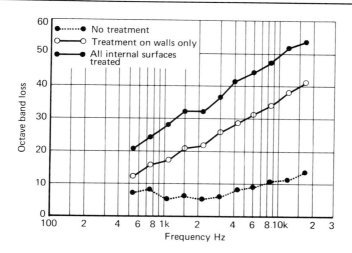

Figure 15. Measured TL for plenum in Figure 14 with no absorptive lining and for various partial treatments after Wells

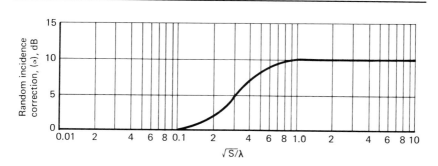

Figure 16. Correction 'a' to be added to plane axial-wave SIL of a duct to obtain the SIL for a random incidence input S =open area of duct, λ =wavelength of sound

Hints on Applications

Temperature Effects Most attenuator manufacturers provide performance data for their equipment assuming they are operating at or about ambient temperatures and pressures. Care is required therefore if the application involves operation with gases at much higher temperatures. It will be remembered that the speed of sound increases with temperature, in accordance with the following relationship:

$$C = K \sqrt{T} \tag{8}$$

where T is the absolute temperature

Knowing also that the wavelength of the sound is proportional to the velocity it follows therefore that, as the gas temperature increases, the wavelength for a particular frequency increases. Unfortunately many of the devices discussed are wavelength dependent. It is quite possible therefore that, if the absolute temperature is quadrupled, the dissipative attenuator, which previously had an attenuation at 200Hz of 20dB and an attenuation at 100Hz of 10dB will now only have an attenuation of 10dB at 200Hz. Similarly, the performance at all other frequencies will be downgraded by approximately an octave.

Influence of Sound Incidence Conditions Normally attenuators are tested under plane wave incidence conditions, i.e. with waves running straight along the duct like sea waves running up a river entrance. It does not follow that the same performance will be achieved when these incidence conditions are varied. Indeed the graph in Fig 16 shows that a correction can be added to the attenuator when operating under conditions of random incidence. The frequency at which this correction becomes significant is a function of both the air passage width and the height of the airway. When the open area of the duct is equal to the square of the wavelength, the increase in performance reaches 10dB.

Attenuator Position It is essential in locating a high performance dissipative attenuator to ensure that its high insertion loss performance is not short-circuited by other paths. An example of this problem occurs when an attenuator is situated immediately next to a fan in a noisy plantroom. This can create a situation where the low noise levels in the duct downstream of the attenuator are then supplemented by much higher levels of noise breaking in through the relatively thin duct walls from the noisy plantroom. This problem could be avoided by locating the attenuator outside the high noise area or, better still, positioning it such that half the attenuator is in the high noise area and half the attenuator is outside the high noise area. Alternatively, if this is not possible, it is then necessary to prevent the breaking in of the high noise levels downstream of the attenuator. This would normally be done by lagging the downstream ductwork to provide a higher transmission loss barrier to the high noise levels.

Attenuators are frequently connected to air moving devices using a flexible duct connector. This is to minimise the transfer of vibrations from the air mover into the attenuator and subsequent ductwork. Whilst this rarely presents problems, in the case of rectangular attenuators connected to centrifugal fans care must be taken in connecting axial fans to attenuators. The use of a flexible duct connector between a cylindrical attenuator and axial flow fan is undesirable. Sagging flexible connectors can impede the airflow into the fan and result in increased fan noise levels. To avoid this problem it is always advisable to bolt the fan and attenuators rigidly together and then use a flexible connector after the attenuator to prevent duct-borne vibration being propagated throughout the system. A danger here, of course, is that the axial fans are frequently suspended from spring hangers and cannot be bolted directly to attenuators which are rigidly supported from the ceiling. In this case it is better that the complete fan and attenuator combination is isolated from the structure.

Air Inlet Conditions Space limitations on site often make it necessary to install attenuators immediately before or after sharp changes in direction. In this case it would be wrong to expect to achieve equal passage velocities across the width of the attenuator. Air has the natural tendency to follow the outside of bends and, in this case, if it then has to pass through an attenuator, it is only reasonable to expect that more of the air will try to go down the passageways near the outside of the duct than down those near the inside. The pressure drop across the attenuators and the noise generated will depend on the maximum velocity rather than on the mean value. Providing one is anticipating this problem, the necessary corrections can be made both for the increased resultant pressure loss of the attenuator and also the increased self noise that it will make. In critical applications, these entry conditions should be avoided at all costs.

Attenuator Contamination Attenuators used in extract systems handling dust, corrosive gases, oil vapours and diesel and gas turbine
exhaust gases, must be selected with care. Certain requirements such
as fume handling equipment will need attenuators manufactured from
non-corrosive materials. Whilst being the same in every other way as
the dissipative attenuator manufactured from galvanised sheet steel,
these are usually manufactured from PVC or glass reinforced plastics.
For some applications it may be acceptable to use standard attenuators
manufactured from metal that have been treated with non-corrosive
paints.

Given that the correct attenuator has been selected, it is also necessary
in design to make provision for occasional cleaning. This may be done
either by the complete removal of an attenuator, perhaps even its
replacement, or ensuring that sufficient access is available for steam
cleaning. It may be necessary to provide drain plugs in the attenuator
or adjoining ductwork to prevent the condensed steam from damaging
the attenuator.

Attenuators operating at high temperature, under intense sound pressures or with high passage velocities, require careful specification,
otherwise rapid and complete disintegration of the infill will occur.

Plate 1. Dissipative attenuators for silencing Rolls Royce Olympus gas turbine installations on a frigate. Great care must be taken to ensure that the mechanical construction of these attenuators will withstand the rigours of their environment

14
Vibration Control Practice

THE design of a complete vibration isolation system can be divided up into the following stages:
1. The selection of the required transmissibility or static deflection for the vibration isolators
2. Selection of the appropriate form of mounting
3. Selection of the location for the vibration isolators and determination of the loads of each one
4. The selection of suitable isolators to correspond with the previous three points
5. The treatment of the various service connections to ensure that these do not cancel out the effect of the vibration isolators

Selection of the Required Static Deflection The selection of the required static deflection is covered in Chapter 6 and will normally be based on one or other of the selection methods given in Tables 1, 2 and 3 in that chapter.

Selection of the Form of Mounting There are normally three possible ways of mounting equipment. The first is to attach vibration isolators direct to the existing mounting feet of the equipment. The second method is to mount the equipment on a steel frame base and to attach the vibrations isolators to this, while the third possibility is to mount the equipment on a concrete 'inertia' base.

The first method of mounting is only applicable when the equipment is rigid and is not liable to distortion when supported individually by its existing feet. This only applies to small machine tools, monoblock pumps and similar compact items.

Steel Bases   Where equipment consists of more than one item, or if it is of significant size, it may rely on being bolted to a rigid floor to provide a significant part of its structural strength. If the equipment is mounted on vibration isolators, the structural effect of the floor is removed and must be replaced in some other form. This is frequently done by mounting equipment on a steel subframe which is made sufficiently strong to provide the necessary support. In many cases, equipment is built on a lightweight subframe for mounting on a rigid concrete floor but the lightweight frame is only adequate to hold the components in their correct relative positions and relies on the floor for rigidity. A frame like this is not adequate when the equipment is mounted on vibration isolators. Typically, a steel base for vibration isolation purposes will be constructed out of channel or 'I' section steel, and the depth of the sections will be at least 8% of the overall length. If the structural base does not have sufficient rigidity, severe vibration problems can occur, particularly on coupled items such as belt or gear driven installations or fans when the equipment may move relative to the driving motor. The provision of the steel base has the further advantage of modifying the position of the vibration isolators, enabling them to be fitted to the extreme corners of the equipment instead of at the positions of the mounting feet, which may be inconveniently placed. Steel bases can also be used to provide a wide base, enabling the vibration isolators to be placed further apart to increase the machine stability. This is particularly important for tall equipment with a high centre of gravity.

Inertia Blocks   These are usually made of concrete poured into a structural steel frame with reinforcing bars, brackets for the attachment of vibration isolators and mounting bolts for the equipment. Although they are generally referred to as inertia blocks and are nominally installed to reduce the movement of the mounted equipment, in most cases they are used for other reasons. These are:
1. To give more stability to the system
2. To lower the centre of gravity of the system
3. To give a more even weight distribution
4. To minimise the effect of external forces
5. To add rigidity to the equipment
6. To reduce problems due to coupled modes
7. To minimise the effects of errors in the position of the estimated centre of gravity of the equipment
8. To act as a local acoustic barrier

It should be noted that reduction of the transmissibility is not listed as a reason for installing an inertia block. This is because, as discussed in Chapter 6, the transmissibility is determined by the static deflection of the vibration isolators, regardless of the presence or absence of an inertia base. The effect on the vibration process on the inertia block is to reduce the amplitude of motion in proportion to the increase in mass, i.e. if the mass of the equipment is doubled by the addition of the block, the movement will be reduced to one half. In practice, it is found that the other uses of an inertia base are frequently more important:

1. To increase the stability of the system. With many machines the mounting locations originally intended for attachment to a rigid concrete slab are too close together to provide adequate stability when the equipment is mounted on vibration isolators. The concrete inertia base provides a means of widening the support and a more stable geometry. (This can of course be achieved with a steel structural base.)

2. Lowering the centre of gravity. Mounting equipment on a substantial concrete base has the effect of lowering the centre of gravity of the complete assembly. This adds to the improvement of the stability provided by extending the width of the base, and also has the effect of reducing the likelihood of rocking motion.

3. To give a more even weight distribution. In many cases, equipment items are very much heavier at one end than the other. This means that, if they are mounted directly on vibration isolators, very different arrangements are needed at opposite ends of the equipment to cope with the uneven weight distribution. If the equipment is mounted on a concrete block, the weight distribution will be more even and, providing the block is heavy enough, it may enable a symmetrical mounting block to be used.

4. To minimise the effect of external forces. Although the use of an inertia block does not improve the transmissibility for a given static deflection, it does mean that very much stiffer isolators can be used for the same static deflection, i.e. if the mass of the equipment is doubled, the stiffness of the isolators necessary to support it is also doubled. This means that the equipment is far less susceptible to the effects of external forces such as fan reaction pressures and transient torques due to changes in speed or load.

5. *To provide or replace rigidity.* An inertia base can be used to provide rigidity for the mounted equipment in the same way that a steel base is used.

6. *To reduce problems due to coupled modes.* The higher of the two rocking sideways coupled movements for a tall item of equipment may occur at two to three times the frequency of the basic vertical frequency. This can lead to resonance problems. Adding an inertia base has the effect of lowering the rocking natural frequency which helps to avoid the problem.

7. *To minimise the effects of errors in estimated positions in the equipment's centre of gravity.* When vibration isolators are being selected, it is necessary to calculate the total load on each isolator so that the appropriate isolator can be chosen. This normally has to be done before the equipment is available and estimated positions of the centres of gravity of each item have to be used. If this information is inaccurate, the estimated loads may be considerably different from the ones which occur in practice. This may lead to vibration isolators being grossly under- or overloaded, or to the equipment sitting at an unacceptable tilt. The latter problem becomes increasingly likely as vibration isolators with high static deflections are used. If a concrete inertia base is used, the centre of gravity of this is normally known accurately and, if the mass of the base is comparable with the mass of the rest of the equipment, it means that, even if the equipment information is not accurate, the possible inaccuracies in the final estimated centre of gravity are small. This reduces the possible errors in isolator loading and reduces the likelihood of a tilted installation. The probability of a tilted installation is also further reduced because of the stiffer springs that will be used to carry the additional weight of the inertia base.

8. *To act as a local acoustic barrier.* When very noisy equipment is mounted directly on the floor of an equipment room, the floor immediately under the equipment may be subject to very high sound pressure levels in the immediate vicinity of the equipment. This local area where the floor is exposed to these high levels may cause problems of noise transmission into the room below. A concrete inertia base can act as an effective barrier, protecting the vulnerable areas of the floor.

Isolator Location There are two approaches to isolator location. The first consists of choosing convenient fixing points such as the four corners of the base frame and then selecting isolators, possibly of different ratings, to carry loads that occur at those points. Alternatively, positions can be chosen so that all of the isolators are evenly loaded. Each technique has its advantages and disadvantages. The equal loading approach simplifies installation on site because it removes the possibility of isolators being fitted in the wrong place. However, there are often problems in that the necessary mounting locations are inconvenient and the mathematics of the solution are sometimes complicated. The use of an inertia base simplifies the situation in that often similar isolators can be used at locations chosen for their convenience.

Four isolator Installation This is the simplest arrangement normally used. When the centre of gravity is obviously at the geometric centre of the four mounting points, each isolator is simply selected to carry a quarter of the total weight. If, as is more likely, the machine is not symmetrical, the loading is uneven but can be estimated by taking moments, or using the simple calculation procedure presented in a later section.

Symmetrical Six Isolator System Many situations exist in which the centre of gravity is on the centre line of the base in one direction, but off centre in the other. In this case the four isolators can be supplemented with a pair of intermediates so that each one will support one sixth of the total weight.

With long items of equipment with the centre of gravity on the longitudinal axis, it may be appropriate to use many pairs of isolators equally loaded to provide even support along the length.

With more complicated systems, it is not usually feasible to arrange for equal isolator loading. It is better to attach the mounts at convenient places and estimate the appropriate loads, but in general the simpler the arrangement the better.

Quick Selection Methods – Four Isolator System When the isolators are arranged at the corners of a rectangle, as is usually the case with a steel frame base or concrete inertia base, a quick graphical solution can be used instead of taking moments in the two directions. This makes use of the chart in Fig 1. Here we have a matrix of dots which marks the possible positions for centres of gravity of each component. Around each dot are grouped four numbers which represent, the percentage of the weight centred at that point to be distributed at each of the four corners. To calculate loads on the isolators for an equipment assembly, each component is taken in turn and its total weight is divided between

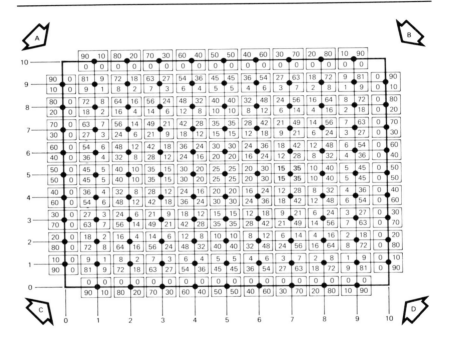

Figure 1. Matrix chart for distributing loads between four isolators

the four corners, as indicated by the dot which is closest to the centre of gravity of the item concerned. The individual contributions are added for each corner to give the total load on each isolator. The chart is best used in conjunction with a sketch of the base, which is divided into ten equal parts in each direction. The locations of the centres of gravity are then compared with the standard matrix and the percentage weight contributions read off the chart. It is however, necessary to interpolate, but this is easily done within the accuracy required. The table below shows the method in use based on the installation shown in Fig 2.

Component	Weight kg	Weight distribution on each isolator kg A	B	C	D
Machine	500	35%=175	15%= 75	35%=175	15%= 75
Motor	200	4%= 8	16%= 32	16%= 32	64%=128
Base	1640	25%=410	25%=410	25%=410	25%=410
Total	2340	593	517	617	613

It will be seen that the four selected isolator duties are: 593kg, 517kg, 617kg and 613kg.

Bearing in mind that commercially available isolators have to cover a wide range of duties and are not individually tailored to a specific load, it would probably be feasible to use the same isolator for each corner, choosing one with a working range of 500 to 650kg.

It is interesting to note what would have happened in the case of, instead of a concrete base, a steel base being chosen with a weight of

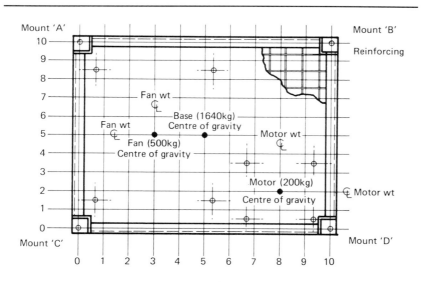

Figure 2. Worked example employing the technique of distributing loads shown in figure 1

164kg. In this case the loads on the individual isolators would have been: 224kg, 148kg, 248kg and 244kg.

Whilst three isolators are similar in duty, the load on the fourth would probably need a smaller size unit than the other three. This immediately introduces the possibility of the special isolator being installed at the wrong corner of the equipment.

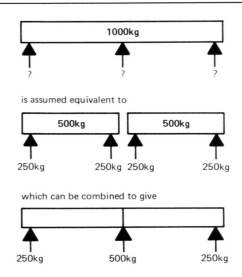

Figure 3.   The distribution of load between six isolators based on split base method

Six Isolator System When six isolators are used, there is no unique solution. Different solutions are possible depending on the proportion of the load carried by the centre two. One solution is to divide the system through the centre isolators into two imaginary four isolator systems, resulting in an apparent solution of eight isolators. The centre loads are then combined in two pairs to be handled by one isolator each. This method of solution means that, with a symmetrical system, the centre isolators carry twice the weight of the outer ones. Although this may appear odd, it is the solution that imposes the least bending strain on the base (Fig 3).

Vibration Isolator Types

Vibration isolators can conveniently be divided into the following types:

1. Solid materials
2. Rubber mounts and pads which are deformed in shear and compression
3. Preformed glass fibre pads and isolators
4. Steel springs
5. Air springs

1. Solid Materials These work in pure compression and normally have the highest resonant frequency due to their small deflection under load. They are relatively cheap and are capable of carrying very high loads, but their application is limited to audio frequency isolation and cushioning of impacts.

2. Rubber in Shear and Compression This category includes the vast majority of rubber or neoprene isolators and preformed sheets and pads in which the material is free to bulge sideways or to distort in shear when it is loaded. Depending on the arrangement, these are capable of providing natural frequencies down to about 5Hz. They are relatively cheap and have the advantage that their performance is maintained at high frequencies. This makes them suitable for acoustic isolation and of use when really low resonant frequencies are not required. In some cases, the life of the isolators may be questionable and some of the higher deflection isolators can be damaged by mis-installation or overload.

3. Preformed Glass Fibre Pads These are a relatively new development and consist of a compressed pad of glass fibre which is enclosed in a neoprene envelope. The trapped air within the glass fibre provides a useful degree of damping and the isolators have the advantage that their static deflection does not vary linearly with load. As a result, the resonant natural frequency remains constant over a wide range of loads. It is possible to obtain resonant frequencies down to the order of 8Hz. Isolators of this form are suitable for mounting machine tools and presses (where they have shown themselves capable of long life under impact conditions which have rapidly destroyed other forms of isolator). They can also conveniently be used in conjunction with plywood panels in order to support concrete bases.

4. Steel Springs The commonest form of steel spring used is a simple coil spring. Provided that the right combination of coil diameter, spring height and wire diameter is used, the springs are stable. They are capable of providing resonant frequencies down to the order of 2Hz. Because it is possible to design a spring so that, even when it is compressed so as to become coil bound, it is working within its fatigue limit. Springs of this type can be designed to have an infinite life. Coil springs are virtually undamped and, if damping is required, this has to be provided by auxiliary means. Steel springs have the disadvantage that at high frequencies vibration can travel along the wire of the coil, causing transmission into the structure. This is normally overcome by incorporating a neoprene pad in the spring assembly so that there is no metal-to-metal contact. Most commercially available springs contain such a pad as a standard feature.

5. Air Springs Air springs range from modified scooter tyres to purpose designed units. They consist of an air filled bag which acts as a spring between the two halves of the device. By varying the air pressure, the characteristics of the spring can be altered. With specialist designed air mounts, it is possible to obtain natural frequencies down to 1Hz. For installation where either a very low natural frequency is required or the positioning of the equipment is critical, it is normal to couple the springs to a level control device which varies the air pressure in the springs to maintain the equipment at the desired level, regardless of load.

Service Connections The principle of mounting equipment on vibration isolators is to break the mechanical connection between the equipment and the supporting floor. For this to be effective, it is essential that all other connections between the equipment and the structure are broken equally well. If this is not done, the installation of vibration isolators can make a vibration transmission problem worse rather than better.

If equipment is rigidly connected to a substantial floor and, at the same time it is connected by means of rigid service connections to the surrounding walls, the movement of the equipment will be relatively small. If the same equipment is now fitted on vibration isolators and the service connections are not modified, the equipment will no longer be held in place by the floor but by the service connections. The result of this will almost certainly be increased vibration levels in the walls. It is therefore absolutely essential that all of the service connections should incorporate sufficient flexibility so that their restraining effect on the equipment is negligible. Electrical connections are normally fairly simple and can be coped with by the use of suitable lengths of flexible cable enclosed in flexible sheathing.

Services that cause most problems are piped systems carrying either liquids or gases, particularly when under pressure. At low pressures, rubber or metal bellows can provide a high degree of flexibility provided that they are installed so that their natural directions of flexibility give freedom in the desired direction. In general, bellows are flexible in compression, tension and bending, partially flexible in shear and, to all intents and purposes, rigid in torsion. A study of the likely directions of movement will normally enable flexible connectors to be placed at the appropriate places in the pipework to provide the maximum flexibility.

In pressurised systems, there is a tendency for the pipes to be pushed apart at any joint by the internal pressure. This means that, unless some form of constraint is incorporated in the flexible joint, it will be stretched until it becomes rigid. Rubber bellows are normally provided with tie rods to prevent this happening. This means that the bellows are now only flexible in bending and only marginally in tension or compression. Metal bellows are normally enclosed with a woven wire braid to serve the same purpose. As the pressure increases, the braid becomes more and more rigid and the connector less and less flexible. To overcome this, it is necessary to use longer and longer flexible connections to preserve the flexibility. In extreme cases, lengths of 50 diameters or more may be necessary. Whilst this may be practicable for small pipework, it is not so for large diameter pipes.

In practice it has been found that it is more satisfactory to rely on the natural flexibility of the pipework itself by separating the pipework from the surrounding structure by the use of resilient hangers and clamps. Since the pipework is relatively rigid, this flexibility can only be achieved by making use of the long lengths of pipe – preferably including changes of direction – that are available within the system. It is therefore necessary to provide flexible support for 50 pipe diameters in normal circumstances and up to 200 in critical surroundings. Within these distances, these pipes should be supported on hangers or clamps having deflections comparable with those of the isolators under the equipment. Beyond this distance, the pipe needs to be supported on hangers which provide acoustic isolation only.

Typical Machines

Air Compressors Air compressors include some of the most difficult problems that are encountered. They range in size from fractional horsepower units to units absorbing many hundreds of horsepower. In most cases, it is appropriate to use free standing spring isolators, usually in conjunction with an inertia base. Reciprocating compressors fall into two general categories; those which consist only of a compressor and a driver unit, and those in which the compressor is already mounted as part of a larger piece of equipment.

In the case of individual compressors, it is necessary to mount them on a concrete base both to provide rigidity and also to provide additional mass to reduce the movement of the equipment. In most cases it is necessary to use relatively high deflection springs to ensure that all of the natural frequencies are low compared with the running speed of the equipment. In general, the primary forces and the couples are balanced within the machine vertically, but there are frequently residual horizontal forces which mean that the vibration of a compressor can only rarely be considered as a simple up and down motion. Where the compressor forms a small part of a large unit, the rest of the assembly will normally serve the same function as the inertia base.

Rotary Compressors and Chillers Where these are installed in basement or ground floor locations, relatively stiff rubber or glass fibre isolators are normally adequate. However, on floors above ground level, it is frequently necessary to resort to steel springs to avoid building resonance.

Inclinable Presses These should be mounted on comparatively stiff isolators of either rubber or glass fibre and should include a means of bolting the press down without short circuiting the isolators. Pads selected with a resonant frequency of approximately 20Hz should be adequate for operation rates up to 30 per minute.

Vertical Action Punch Presses As above but repetition rates greater than 60 strokes per minute are rare and a natural frequency in the region of 12Hz will normally be suitable.

Press Brakes For short bed machines up to about 2.5m, the machines may be vertically mounted on rubber or glass fibre isolators having a resonant frequency of 8 to 12Hz. Longer machines will require an inertia block to provide support for the frame. This can then be mounted on the appropriate isolators.

Guillotines – Small Machines These should be mounted on damped rubber or glass fibre isolators having a resonant frequency of around 12Hz.

Large machines will require the provision of a concrete base to maintain the rigidity. Attention must be paid to the weight distribution as the motor, gearbox and clutch are normally at one end of the machine, making the weight distribution far from symmetrical.

Lathes and Milling Machines These can be mounted on rubber or glass fibre with a resonant frequency of around 8 to 12Hz. Lathes with long bases will require mounting on a supplementary concrete base to ensure that alignment is maintained.

Jig Boring Machines and Precision Grinders These will normally require mounting on a large concrete inertia base to minimise movement and, in high precision applications or extremely unfavourable environments, it may be necessary to use high deflection coil springs.

Plate 1   A selection of typical vibration isolators used for industrial applications

Plate 2. Inertia Base

15
Noise Control by Room Treatment

WHERE control of industrial noise at or close to the source is not practical or sufficient, the application of room treatment can provide a highly significant reduction of the general noise level. It is important to be able to follow not only the acoustic guidelines based on the discussion in Chapter 4, but also to satisfy the other numerous constraints affecting the design, application and maintenance of such treatment. The aim of this chapter is to provide practical guidance to enable the reader to assess the value of this approach for specific cases and to ensure that the implications are fully understood.

Objectives The objectives in attempting to reduce the general noise level by room treatment may be:

a) To reduce noise affecting staff below statutory, advised or desired limits.

b) To improve communication, i.e. to allow direct speech communication between staff (e.g. for instructions or warning of imminent danger), and to improve attention to P/A, telephone, fire warning bells or other electro-acoustic systems.

c) To reduce the sound pressure level incident on the building envelope, thereby reducing the required sound insulation performance of the enclosure when considering noise breakout. Conversely, in cases where noise breaks in, treatment limits the amplification of the noise by the space itself.

In some cases the industrial process itself may be affected by noise (e.g. livestock industry).

Application It must be clear at the outset that the control procedures referred to in this chapter apply only to the reduction of the reverberant sound field (or general noise level) and not to the direct sound field (or local noise level) close to a noise source (see Chapter 4). It is clear that if the direct sound from the noise source produces a high sound pressure level, the application of room lining is likely to have little or no effect on the noise level close to the source, but room lining does limit the spread of sound energy from that and other sources. With the knowledge of the location and sound output of individual sources, an assessment can be made of the likely success of applying room treatment by adding the direct and reverberant components as described in Chapter 4 and determining the points at which the control of reverberant sound is worthwhile (see Fig 1).

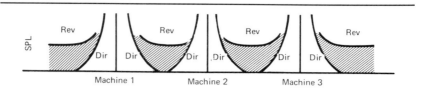

Figure 1. Relationship between overall, direct and reflected sound fields

In practice, it is found that the application of room treatment is particularly advantageous where specific areas of a factory layout are subject to very high noise levels and there is a requirement to reduce the spread of energy across the factory to areas requiring lower noise levels. The treatment tends to be effective where the noise sources are spread out and the output from individual sources is not particularly substantial. In this case, the summation of the reverberant component from a large number of sources is likely to have a marked effect on the overall sound level and room treatment becomes effective. On the other hand, where a number of sound sources has a high sound power output and they are located close together in a relatively small space, the application of room treatment may well have very little effect, simply due to the strength of the direct sound field – it will be difficult to escape the direct sound field in a small space with powerful sound sources.

The Potential Acoustic Value of Room Treatment The calculation procedures will vary depending on whether the building and the process already exist or whether concern is with a new project.

In the case of an existing situation, the execution of a site survey is clearly of great importance. This must establish the existing distribution of sound pressure levels (in octave bands over the audio frequency range), include a check on the limits of influence of direct sound from the various noise sources, and a note of existing absorptive treatment. Where noise sources are being introduced or where a new project is involved, estimation procedures must be used.

Site Surveys The techniques and instrumentation for the execution of site surveys are discussed more fully in Chapters 7 and 8. However, in order to make an assessment of the potential value of room treatment, it is necessary to ensure that the appropriate readings are taken to this end. The number of readings required is dependent on the layout of the industrial process and the form of the enclosure. Ideally, the survey should provide sufficient data to enable noise contours to be plotted over the plan area of the space. If the process involves more than one receiving height, it may be necessary to obtain contours for higher or lower levels. The height at which the sound pressure levels are measured should be related to the position of the ear of the operators – usually approximately 1.5m from the floor. With a production layout

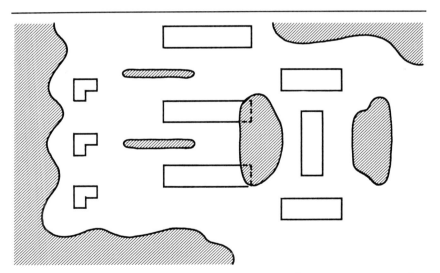

Figure 2. Noise contours – shaded areas indicate e.g. zones where reflected sound is highly significant

which is relatively repetitive, it may be possible to limit the number of readings and extrapolate results. Particular attention must be paid to any machinery which is highly directional in noise output. Whereas smaller machinery can often be treated as a point source, and assumptions can be made regarding the propagation of direct sound from these sources, a great deal of industrial machinery is relatively large and does present substantial directivity in noise output. It is necessary to take sufficient readings to allow sections such as shown in Fig 1 to be drawn. Fig 2 shows a plan of an industrial area with the zones which are subject to improvement with the use of room treatment shown shaded. It is of course important to bear in mind that many areas may be subject to improvement which is extremely minor, e.g. less than 1dB. Therefore it may be felt more appropriate to plot the areas which are likely to be subject to an improvement greater than 3dB. This will depend upon the degree of improvement required and the purpose of the treatment.

To carry out the above survey could, in many cases, be a lengthy process, particularly where the industrial process is complex and varied. But where the surveys are carried out by experienced personnel, the necessary findings can be acquired in a relatively short time.

Whilst measurements of sound levels are being made, the opportunity should be taken to record the current conditions of room treatment. A note should be made of the building structure, internal linings, openings and contents. In addition, a direct measurement of the absorption of the space can be obtained by measuring reverberation time. Tape recordings can be made of the decay of the sound field following, e.g. the firing of a starting pistol, or switching off a powerful broad band sound source. The tape recording can then be analysed in the laboratory and the time taken for the decay in each octave or third octave band can be read directly from the readout of a pen level recorder. The relationships between the reverberation time, room volume and absorption (as set out in Chapter 4) can then be used to estimate the amount of absorption present. The volume of the room is usually taken quite simply from drawings. In cases where the sound field could not be considered diffuse, it may be found that the reverberant sound component is not even across the area outside the zone affected by the direct sound field, but decays with distance from the source to an extent less than the inverse square law. This is likely to happen where the sound field is made up primarily from the multiple reflections between floor and ceiling, and is particularly evident in wide low industrial areas. Under these circumstances, measurements should be made of the decay of sound with distance from a number of individual sources, as a basis for relating this to Figs 10 and 11 in Chapter 4. A typical situation of this nature is shown in Fig 3.

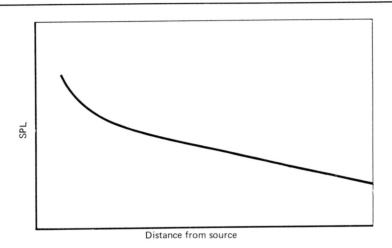

Distance from source

Figure 3. Typical variation of sound pressure level with distance from source

Estimation at the Design Stage Where the building in question does not as yet exist, it is necessary to make an assessment of the absorption of the building before determining the absorptive treatment required. This, by its very nature, involves less direct methods and a greater reliance on theory. From drawings, the surface area of the different components of the enclosure can be derived and layout drawings should enable an assessment to be made of the contents. Reliance must be placed on published literature or acoustic consulting files for the absorption coefficients for common building materials. The total amount of absorption is the sum of $S \times \alpha$, where S is the surface area of the material and α is the random incidence absorption coefficient to BS3638. It is important to include the absorption of air itself, which becomes significant above 1000Hz. (Note: Since the air is measured by volume rather than area, the coefficient has a different form.) Similarly, with room contents, it is often convenient to deal with numbers rather than surface area (e.g. number of occupants). The most frequently used absorption coefficients for this purpose are shown in Appendix 1.

The Acoustic Design In the case where the building already exists, we have acquired information about the existing absorption and we have as a bonus a certain amount of information regarding the sound

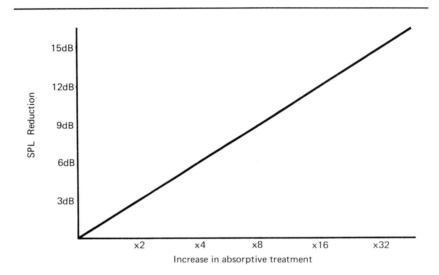

Figure 4. Effect of increase in absorptive treatment on reduction of reverberant sound pressure level

pressure level distribution. Where the building is new, we have an assessment of the degree of absorption and, if we have sufficient information regarding the sound power output of machinery, it is possible to derive an estimate of the sound pressure levels.

Whichever method is used, it is clear that a decision must be taken as to the degree of room treatment which is appropriate and its likely effects. It is important to remember that the subjective improvement resulting from only small reductions in the reverberant noise level is much greater than would be predicted merely from the change in noise level.

Fig 4 shows the likely reduction in reverberant sound pressure level in relation to the percentage increase in absorptive treatment. This simple relationship shows clearly that the application of absorptive treatment in industrial areas which are initially highly reflective is very effective. However, if the premises already exhibit a high degree of absorptive treatment, the provision of additional acoustic lining or contents will have very little effect unless large quantities are involved. It is therefore important to establish the cost/benefit relationship for the application of acoustic treatment, as will be discussed shortly.

In certain cases the sound field is not diffuse and an even reverberant sound field is not established. (reference Chapter 4)

Cost/Benefit Relationship At this point, it is necessary to consider very seriously the relationship between the improvement and the cost of achieving it. There are many non-acoustical aspects to be considered in the installation of room treatment. However, before a detailed assessment is made of any specific proposals, a broad guide on the costs is usually helpful. The following points should offer a useful check at this stage.

Comparison with Other Methods A useful rule of thumb when dealing with noise control is to start with the source. In most cases, control of noise at or local to the source involves less material and thereby tends to result in lower costs. There are, of course, many cases where machine quietening is very expensive or local absorption would result in increased production costs due to restriction on access to machinery. But it is worth remembering that the use of absorptive room linings is, in effect, an admission that one cannot control a noise before it is spread over a wide area. Because of this wide area, the treatment must be applied in large quantities to be effective. Fig 5 shows the typical relationship between costs of materials only for noise control using different methods as an illustration of this point.

Relationship between Costs and Extent of Treatment As with other building provisions, the unit cost of applying small quantities of treatment tends to be higher than the average cost if the treatment is carried

over a substantial area. Having incurred basic overheads on the installation (e.g. obtaining scaffolding), the increase in cost with quantity is
largely related to material costs and labour costs. There are, unfortunately, many factors determining the costs of acoustic treatment, such
as ease of access for application of treatment, the times at which the
premises are available for application of the treatment, the implications on services or lighting, and many similar influences. Nevertheless, as a broad guide, the relative costs of varying quantities of treatment are set out in Fig 6.

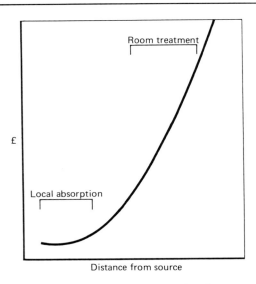

*Figure 5. Typical relationship between the distance of location of
treatment from the source and cost*

Detailed Design The choice of materials and methods for achieving
the acoustic performance is dependent on a large number of factors,
many of which do not relate to acoustic performance at all. Major
aspects which have to be considered include:
1. The acoustic performance of alternative materials
2. The available space for the location of absorptive treatment
3. The conditions of access for application of treatment
4. The potential health hazards presented by the treatment
5. The effects of moisture, condensation, and sunlight

6. Requirements for and methods of maintenance
7. The likelihood of and protection from impact or other damage
8. The effect on lighting levels, air movement or other services
9. The requirements for control of fire
10. The possible combination of treatment with thermal insulation
11. The compatibility of the treatment with the industrial process and any possible interaction (e.g. chemical attack)
12. Contract arrangements

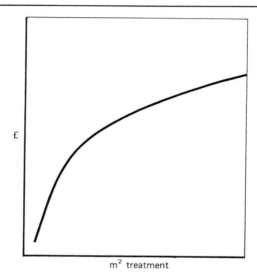

Figure 6. Typical relationship between area of room treatment and cost

The Acoustic Performance of Alternative Materials

Middle and High Frequency Absorbers The absorption characteristics of different groups of absorbers are outlined in Chapter 4. In practice, room treatment usually involves the use of material providing good middle and high frequency absorption. This is because this range of frequencies has the strongest effect on 'A' weighted sound pressure levels, and the dBA scale is most frequently used for assessment of industrial noise levels. Furthermore, the basic structure of the building envelope tends to offer some low frequency absorption, whereas, apart from absorption in the air itself, there is often little inherent middle and high frequency absorption.

The materials to be applied in such a case are the porous dissipative materials. As a guide, if it is possible to blow through the materials, but with some difficulty, the absorption characteristics are likely to be favourable. If the material is too open, there will not be adequate potential for viscous drag at the fibres or cells of the material. On the other hand, if the flow resistance is too high, the air will not gain access to the fibrous material. Examples of such material are quilts or semi-rigid slabs of glass fibre or mineral wool or open pore polymer foams. The selection of material is usually based on test data to BS3638: Measurement in an Impedance Tube; but the acoustic properties cannot, of course, be considered sufficient grounds alone for selection. The consideration set out in the paragraphs below will restrict the choice of material for non-acoustical reasons.

The acoustic performance of such materials improves with thickness; it's common to find significant reductions in absorptions after painting over the material with a non-porous paint.

Panel Absorbers If a reduction in low frequency noise is required, the application of panel absorbers is appropriate. This is often best achieved at the boundaries by ensuring that a panel construction is incorporated in the basic construction of the building. The outer sheeting, an air space (possibly filled with an absorbent quilt) and an inner board, together form effective panel absorption. The main concern is to see that this absorption is best at the frequency of interest; in particular, by careful selection of the inner board, in terms of surface weight, fixing and internal damping in relation to the air space over which it is set. It is worth bearing in mind that, in the absence of damping by absorptive material in the cavity, sound pressure levels at resonance can be very high and the danger of noise transmission to the exterior must be checked.

Cavity Absorbers The use of tuned cavity absorbers may be appropriate where very strong pure tones are evident. The efficiency of these absorbers is very high but only over a very limited frequency range. They also require fine adjustment and varying degrees of maintenance depending on the type. Should such measures be contemplated, specialist advice is essential.

Compound Absorbers Combinations of these absorber types can be achieved by, for example, the use of a perforated facing sheet over a porous dissipative absorber. The absorption characteristic will be determined by a large number of factors, one of the main ones being the percentage perforation of the front sheet. If the perforation percentage is low, the construction will act like a panel absorber giving low frequency absorption. As the percentage increases, the porous material becomes more exposed and the higher absorption performance

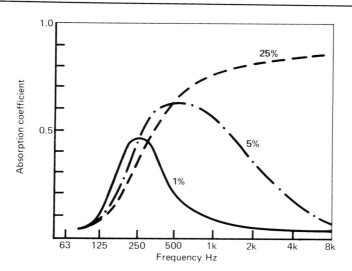

Figure 7. Effect of percentage perforation of facing on absorption

moves up the frequency scale. Furthermore, the subdivision of the area behind the sheeting will also create cavity absorbers. (See Fig 7.)

By careful design, it is therefore feasible to derive a construction suited to the case in question. It is advisable to seek specialist advice to help with this, since the potential cost of remedial work should the treatment not be effective is usually considerable.

Space Available for the Location of Treatment An examination of the existing premises or the proposals for new premises will enable an assessment to be made of the available space for applying acoustic treatment. In general terms, treatment is applied at boundaries or in the form of suspended units. The positioning of ventilation trunking or electrical conduit or other services may restrict the application of treatment to limited areas. It is not advisable to place absorptive treatment behind reflective surfaces such as sheet metal trunking, unless there is a substantial air space between the two. Treatment is frequently applied between structural members, or suspended from the structure as units set out in a suitable pattern. There may be areas which are not available for treatment simply because there is difficulty in gaining access or, in doing so, there would be a halt in the production in this area, which may not be allowable. Clearly the position of the treatment must relate sensibly to the position of the source or sources and the intended function of the material. Location as close to the source (or receiver) as possible is preferable. It is worth noting that location of suspended absorption units at high level may impede high level work in the area.

Access for Application of Treatment If the treatment is to be applied to a new building, there should be little difficulty in gaining access since the contractors' equipment is available and it is likely that the treatment will be built into the structure. But with existing buildings which are too noisy it is extremely important to take into account the cost of obtaining access to the roof area. In many cases the cost of erecting scaffolding and gaining access at high level can be a very significant component of the overall cost. It may be necessary to stop production or make special provisions to allow production to continue while access to high level is achieved. In certain circumstances it may be necessary to ask the contractor to work at night rates to avoid a clash with particular productive activities. The access is usually from below. Due to the form of construction frequently used for industrial buildings (e.g. corrugated asbestos cement), it is most dangerous to rely on access across the roof and entry via, for example, north light windows.

Health Hazards In certain industrial areas, particularly in areas where food is being prepared, it is important to check the proposals against potential health hazards. Materials can present a hazard directly by means of particle fall-out or surface migration. Materials may have the capacity to harbour organic growth, particularly under moist conditions. Attention must also be paid to the chemical stability of the material, the effects under conditions of high humidity, the effects of airflow on the surface of the material, and the requirements for regular cleaning. In many industrial areas this aspect is not critical but when such restrictions must be applied they can be very limiting on the choice of materials. Finishes developed for hospital use involving anti-bacterial materials with easily cleaned surface treatment can be particularly useful in such areas.

Moisture/Condensation Many materials may not be used because they decay in a moist atmosphere. This is particularly true of some organic materials such as wood based absorptive material. Where metal parts are involved in the framing or suspension of the material, attention should be paid to potential rusting in moist atmosphere. Generally speaking, damage is more frequently evident due to the effects of condensation. Any components of the treatment system which are at a very low temperature when located in an area with normal or high humidity will be subject to condensation unless there is adequate ventilation to carry away the water. An attempt should be made to avoid cold bridge links from the exterior of the building to hangers or framework to limit this problem. The most difficult condensation problem to deal with is condensation within the construction of the building envelope (interstitial condensation). This occurs when the temperature gradient across the wall or roof is such that the conditions of humidity and temperature which will cause condensation occur part way through the construction. If, therefore, moisture is able to permeate to this position and there is little ventilation at this point, there is severe danger of moisture deposit and potential damage to the structure (see Fig 8). The application of a vapour barrier on the inside of the building does restrict the migration of vapour to positions within the structure. However, this does not automatically solve the problem since moisture may be able to enter the construction from other sources. In some cases the presence of the vapour barrier might make matters worse since the inside surface is not able to act as an escape for moisture building up within the construction.

Maintenance Consideration should be given to the means of maintenance to be used with the treatment. This will of course depend on the material chosen and the frequency of maintenance which is permissible. There is clearly an advantage in tying the maintenance cycle to the maintenance of the structure generally. Consideration must be given to access, to cost and to any potential reduction in

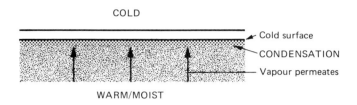

Figure 8.

Figure 9.

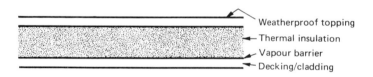

Figure 10.

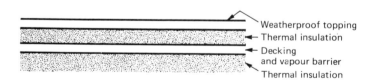

Figure 11.

Figure 8-11. Interaction between acoustic absorption and condensation at external constructions

performance of the material due to maintenance procedures. In areas where the industrial process involves extensive deposits on the treatment, the form of the deposits will determine maintenance requirements. For example, deposits of fats and oils present different problems to mneral dust. Consideration should be given to washing, vacuum methods and painting. With open pore materials, there is always the danger that either contamination or the maintenance process will result in blocking of the pores and thereby reduce the performance. There are a number of proprietary treatments which incorporate a thin, washable facing which is sufficiently light not to affect the sound absorption seriously. This type of absorber normally results in a small initial reduction in very high frequency performance, but this is preferable to a larger unknown drop in performance in use.

Impact Damage The material may be subject to impact damage if positioned either at low level or if subject to damage from cranes and mechanical handling at high level. It is rarely economical to go to impact resistant material and therefore the application of perforated impact resistant facings has become commonplace. However, it is important to take account of the potential loss of performance of the material if the percentage perforation of the facing is inadequate. Fig 7 illustrates the effect on absorptive treatment of placing materials with different percentage perforation over the face. It is worth bearing in mind that, when referring to specific percentage perforation, this applies to the use of continuously perforated material and not to broad sheets of reflective surface interposed with large openings. Apart from the fact that the latter would probably be ineffectual in dealing with impact damage at the openings, the large surface area of the reflective material in one position is likely to be sufficient to cause significant reflection. Therefore the spacing between the perforations should not exceed 50mm.

Lighting and Air Movement When planning for room treatment, attention should be paid to the implications on other services. Pendant absorptive panels (often referred to as 'functional absorbers') can present difficulties in relation to lighting or ventilation systems. If the lighting is located at a higher level, the screening effect can be serious. Apart from that obvious case, it is also as well to consider the reflectance of the surface of the material being used when the lighting is at a lower level. If this is not done, there may well be an indirect reduction in lighting level on introduction of the treatment. It is also important that sources of natural light (e.g. in factories with north lights in the roof) are not shielded by treatment.

The location of treatment may also be affected by any heating and/or ventilation system with units or terminal points at the same level or above. A brief check on this will normally allow a simple adjustment to be made.

Control of Fire Fire regulations normally call for boundary treatments to offer at least Class 1 Surface Spread of Flame specified in relation to BS476. Subject to the interpretation by the local fire officer, this tends to apply also to suspended absorbers. It is possible to use thin plastic facings or treated plastic foam, provided that the above rating is achieved, but the likely production of toxic fumes from foam plastic materials normally renders these unacceptable. There is therefore a preference for the use of incombustible materials such as glass fibre or mineral wool, perhaps with a thin surface membrane.

Combination of Treatment with Thermal Insulation Many of the materials which offer good sound absorption are also effective materials for thermal insulation. It is therefore well worth considering the possibility of using the same material for both functions if the practical problems of condensation can be resolved. This is most likely to apply to new industrial premises or where upgrading of the thermal insulation of existing premises is envisaged. On rare occasions it could be that the removal of existing facing material exposes thermal insulation material which is capable of good sound absorption.

The standards for thermal insulation of new buildings is controlled by the Building Regulations 1985, Approved Document L, Conservation of Fuel and Power 1990. Similar provisions apply or may be expected to apply to other locations. The regulations call for a thermal transmittance coefficient which can be achieved by many sound absorbing materials, although a number of materials are eliminated by the requirement to achieve Class 1 Surface Spread of Flame when tested to BS476.

The major difficulty which arises in making this combination is the potential for condensation within the building envelope construction as noted earlier in Fig 8. In order to combat condensation within the construction, the two sections shown in Figs 9 and 10 are currently considered to be reasonable building practice. The problem from the acoustic viewpoint is that the presence of a non-absorptive surface on the inside of the construction restricts its value for acoustic purposes unless low frequency absorption is required. From basic principles, there is an inherent problem, i.e. if the air can permeate the material thereby allowing acoustic absorption at middle and high frequencies, water vapour will also be able to permeate the material to meet a cold point within the construction. The use of a vapour barrier also restricts acoustic absorption. If we perforate the barrier in Fig 9, moisture transmission is then possible.

If the thermal/acoustic material is split into two layers separated by a vapour barrier, the lower layer can be used for acoustic absorption (see Fig 11) and the risk of condensation is much reduced. Alternatively, if the inside humidity is not too high, an increase in ventilation along the line of the underside of the decking, as in Fig 9, may allow perforation or removal of the vapour barrier. Or a very thin membrane can be employed but with some loss of performance. None of the above is necessarily a very good solution for any one particular application. Nevertheless, whatever system is used, it must restrict the potential for vapour transfer across a large temperature differential without restricting acoustic absorption. In practical terms, the benefits of dual use of one material are likely to be reduced by the extra costs of incorporating the detailing to deal with this problem.

Compatability with the Industrial Process It is important to check the properties of the absorptive treatment and, where applicable, its suspension system against the type of industrial process involved in the area. A number of processes will involve chemical reaction or excessive deposits damaging to the stability and/or absorption of the treatment.

For example, powdered foodstuffs with sulphur dioxide preservative may attract water. As a result, acid is formed. The consequent chemical damage can be considerable. It is therefore important to make this check before proceeding with room treatment.

Contract Arrangements Having checked the above items, it will be necessary to obtain prices from specific suppliers and follow the normal contracting procedures. Whereas a budget price may have been obtained at an earlier stage, the only real guide to costs must be a quotation to a specification.

In practice, deliveries are generally quite reasonable – the timing of the work in relation to other building work or the industrial process is usually more critical. If a competent acoustic consultant is used, there should be no difficulty in obtaining desired results. If, for some reason, the arrangement is carried out directly with a contractor, a method of checking the results should be derived and this should be written into the agreement with the contractors. A realistic guarantee of materials and, where applicable, the suspension system for the specific application should be sought over a reasonable life span. In order to achieve a good result it will be necessary for the consultants and/or the contractors to have adequate knowledge of the building structure and the industrial process.

Functional Absorbers A treatment which is often appropriate for noise control particularly in existing premises involves the suspension of absorptive material in panels or units to expose the sound field to a large area of absorptive material. These units are sometimes referred to as functional absorbers.

The size of these absorbers, taking the case of a rectangular panel, varies from $0.5m^2$ (surface area of one side) to 4 or $5m^2$ or more. Typically units are just less than $1m^2$ and are spaced at a density of one per $1m^2$ of plan area (see Fig 12). Thicknesses vary usually from 25mm to 200mm and the relative change in absorption characteristics with thickness must be taken into account. The density of absorptive material used tends to fall in the range 20 to $80kg/m^3$ (1.5 to $8lb/ft^3$). There : however a wide potential for variety in the form and distribution of suspended units. Clearly, if moved too far apart, units will lose their effect due to reflections at exposed surfaces between them. If, on the other hand, the units are moved too close together, the benefit in terms of increased absorption will be little and the cost will be very much increased. Therefore a balance must be struck to achieve a suitable density. As a guide, unless very little absorption is required, separation of absorbers by more than twice their depth is not recommended.

Separation by less than their depth is likely to result in a poor cost/benefit relationship. Material thickness and density must also be selected on a cost/benefit assessment and usually falls in the ranges noted above.

This type of absorber does not provide a quantity of absorption units directly related to the surface area times the published absorption

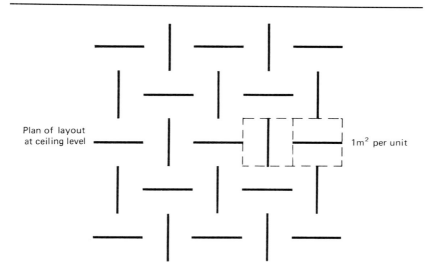

Plan of layout at ceiling level — 1m² per unit

Figure 12. Example of plan layout for suspended absorbers

coefficient of the material unless the absorption coefficient was measured using such suspended units. This is because doubling the area of absorber surface by using the opposite side of an absorptive material does not double the absorption because of the interaction between the two.

They must be lightweight, capable of easy maintenance, capable of resistance to chemical attack and so on. The usual dilemma centres around the extent to which the material can be 'bagged' for ease of handling and cleaning. The use of a non-perforated facing will reduce the absorption at the highest frequencies as indicated in Fig 7. If the skin is very light indeed, the danger of damage during handling is increased. Certain perforated materials such as mineral wool weave are capable of being wiped over with a marginal performance loss – this would not generally be adequate for food preparation areas. The potential for dust collection limits the application of this type of treatment in areas requiring high standards of hygiene.

Other Types of Treatment Apart from functional absorbers, room treatments are likely to take the form of suspended ceilings or boundary treatment.

Suspended Ceilings The traditional suspension grids and board or tile ceiling systems tend to be relatively expensive in terms of sound pressure level reduction per £ compared with boundary treatment or functional absorbers unless located close to the source. Nevertheless, the use of, for example, mineral fibre board or perforated metal with absorbent backing can be appropriate particularly in light industry and where small areas are involved. There can be advantages of appearance, maintenance and integration of services, but there are a limited number of industrial situations where this is appropriate.

Boundary Treatment Even if integration with thermal insulation is not practical, there are a large number of simple means of fixing material to the building enclosure which are very cost effective. This may take the form of a continuous treatment, or a series of absorptive 'patches' or even an absorptive insert in the corrugations of roof decking or wall cladding. It is also possible to redistribute the sound by considering the position of reflective surfaces to direct sound away from critical areas. This is, in practice, rarely considered and the geometry of industrial buildings is generally determined by the needs of many other design constraints.

An Outline Comparison The criteria for success are various but there is usually a fundamental requirement for an effective reduction in sound pressure level at reasonable cost, with a rider that the non-acoustic factors are also generally satisfied.

Cost comparison can only be general because of the variety of factors involved. Experience suggests that over a large number of applications, boundary treatment offers the best solution if other functions such as structural support for roofing or thermal insulation are achieved at the same time. Functional absorbers offer a very flexible treatment but are likely to be slightly more expensive. Suspended ceilings are generally more expensive again. For specific cases, however, any may be appropriate.

Conclusion For any one specific case, the potential acoustic value of room treatment must be established initially and alternative treatments assessed. The graphical data in this chapter should allow the effects of room treatment to be assessed but it is important not to overlook the non-acoustical aspects of the treatment.

Plate 1. *High levels of noise will be encountered in factory conditions such as these.* *Noise reduction at source is usually impracticable and absorbent treatment of the environment may provide significant improvements.*

16
Compressors
and Pumps

SINCE air and refrigerants can be classed as gases, they can be divided into two distinct groups. The acoustic performance of the different designs within these groups is more dependent upon their running conditions and basic design characteristics than their location in one or the other of the design groups. These two groups of machines are defined by whether or not the gas is positively displaced. The positive displacement compressor types are, as their name implies, machines which take a slug of gas and, by reciprocating or rotary action, force it into a smaller space.

Reciprocating Machines   The reciprocating machine is represented by the conventional engine type of machine with pistons and valves, and also by diaphragm types where the compressing element, either piston or cam, is separated from the compressed gas by a flexible membrane. The latter design is used where contamination of the compressed gas is undesirable. There are also certain types of piston machines which, when fitted with carbon or PTFE rings and special seals, can also be used for the compression of highly inflammable or toxic gases, or to provide 'clean' compressed air. The diaphragm compressor is used for small flows and at relatively low pressures because of the limiting strength of the membranes, whereas the piston type machine can be found working at pressures up to 40 000 bar. The rotational speed of these machines can vary from a few hundred to several thousand revolutions per minute. From this, it will be seen that the acoustic signature of a positive displacement compressor can vary from a slow-running piston compressor to that of a multi-cylinder high speed compressor, as shown in Fig 1. Between these two extremes is a multiplicity of shapes, sizes and considerations, all of which have in common certain principal sources of noise. These are inlet noise, noise radiating from the valve chest and crankcase, outlet noise, motor noise and noise from the motor cooling fan.

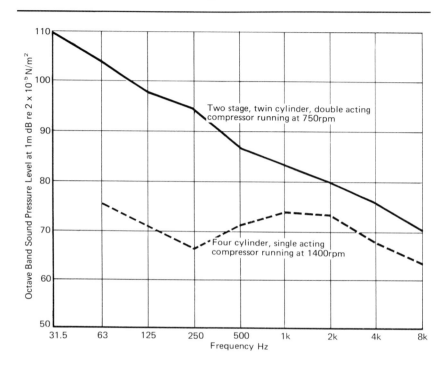

Figure 1. Typical spectrum for low speed and high speed reciprocating compressors

Intake Noise The majority of industrial installations concern relatively slow speed compressors which produce an intake noise spectrum with low frequency pure tones at compressor running frequencies or multiples, depending upon the number of cylinders. In some installations, the strong pure tones from the compressor intake can be at such a frequency to be below the normal audible range of the human ear, although harmonics of the tone could well come into this region. However, these pure tones can still cause discomfort and annoyance to individuals by the physical sensing of the pressure fluctuations or by their effect in causing vibration of windows, etc.

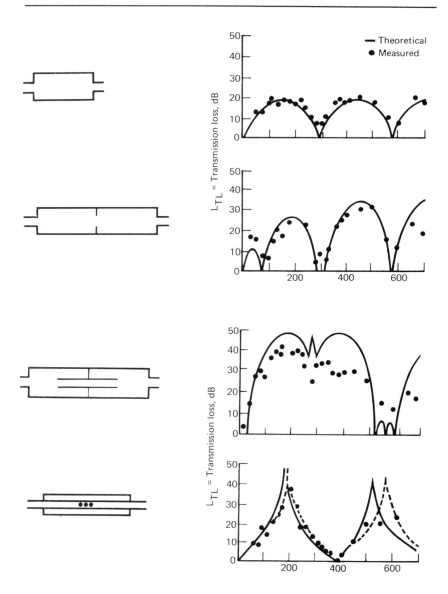

Figure 2. Selection of reactive attenuators after Davis. Moore and Stevens

A purely dissipative silencer would be useless at these frequencies unless a silencer of vast dimensions could be constructed. In general, there is little middle and high frequency noise from this type of machine and consequently a low frequency reactive unit can be used. These can appear in many forms, as shown in Fig 2. The simplest and most practical type for silencing the intake noise on most industrial compressors is the single side branch resonator depicted in Fig 3. The gas in the connecting section acts as a small mass and the gas contained within the volume of the device behaves like a spring. If the main

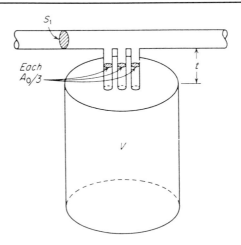

Figure 3.　Side branch Helmholtz resonator

container is pressurised and the pressure then released, the mass of gas in the connecting tunnel will oscillate at its natural or resonant frequency.

Since the 'plug' of air in the connecting section is moving in a relatively small passage, the pressurised gas in the main chamber will have to expend energy in overcoming frictional resistance. The resonant frequency of such a device can be predicted from the equation in Chapter 13. The performance of such a device is greater at the resonant frequency but falls off rapidly at frequencies either side, as shown in Fig 4. It is for this reason that this type of device is useful in this type of application where very strong pure tone sounds are emitted from the compressor intake. The lower line in Fig 4 shows the effect of filling the resonant cavity with acoustic absorbing material.

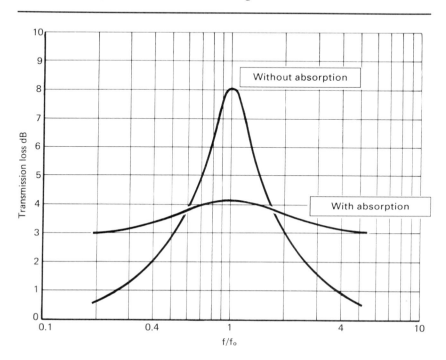

Figure 4. Transmission loss for typical side branch Helmholtz resonator with and without absorbent infill

There are many forms of resonant silencer, some of which are shown in Fig 2; these produce a great variety of attenuation characteristics which, unfortunately, cannot be dealt with in the space of this chapter. There are available, however, computer programmes specifically developed to formulate resonant silencer design, given the attenuation requirements at specific frequencies and the mass gas flow.

Casing Radiation Noise radiating from cylinder walls, valve chests and crankcase structures is often mistakenly considered to be of lesser significance than that produced by the compressor intake or outlet.

This is because the strong pure tone content of the latter sources is subjectively more noticeable than the broader spectrum noise from the machine's surfaces which still contain pure tones, but of less significance than that of the intake and outlet noise. In most installations the intake is provided with a silencer (although often this is not adequate for the task) and the outlet is piped away to cause noise problems elsewhere. The noise from the surfaces of the compressor will therefore become the dominant feature of the noise spectrum found in a compressor room. This spectrum consists mainly of middle or high frequency noise, again dependent on the type and speed of the machine. These frequencies and their levels are caused by the valve noise, the sudden changes of pressure within the cylinder(s) and are dependent upon the characteristics of this structure in radiating sound or vibration energy.

A typical frequency response for a cast machine structure is found to contain a broad peak at around 1000Hz with added peaks due to valve noise. The level of noise generated is governed by the piston speed and not by the power absorbed by the machine. A larger size machine will produce more sound energy, providing the piston speeds are the same, than a smaller machine because of the larger surface available for radiation of the sound energy. However, the work output generally rises at a much greater rate (15 times per 10-fold increase in machine size) than the noise levels (4-5 times per 10-fold increase in machine size). This leads to the common observation that for the same horsepower, the larger, slower machine is considerably quieter.

To reduce the noise radiating from the structure requires either the addition of mass to the structure, or a separate enclosure preferably isolated from the source. From this it can be seen that the cooling water jackets have considerable advantages in preventing cylinder generated noise and valve noise from breaking out of the structure by virtue of the considerable increase in mass. Another effective method is to attach close fitting damped panels over the cylinder block or other areas subject to high vibration levels. Generally, however, effective reduction of noise from the casing can only be obtained by attention to the machine structure at the design stage.

Outlet Noise The gas outlet noise normally causes problems with noise radiating from the air receivers, away from the compressor installation. This is a similar problem to the air intake noise and normally occurs at similar frequencies, sometimes amplified by the presence of a non-return valve in the air line between compressor and receiver. The noise breakout from the pipeline itself does not normally constitute a problem because of the thickness and small size of the pipe. However, the air receiver, although being of thicker material, has a greater surface area from which the noise resulting from the delivery pressure pulsations can radiate. The receivers should preferably be situated in a compressor house or a separate brick enclosure. Alternatively, a small receiver acting as a pulsation damper can be employed between the compressor check valves and the main air receiver. This will reduce the pressure fluctuations into the main receiver and reduce the resultant noise level.

Electric Motor Noise For low speed machines, electric motor noise can be more significant than noise from the compressor. This is covered in detail in Chapter 19.

Rotary, Positive Displacement Machines Rotary action positive displacement compressors come in three basic types: the 'Roots', sliding vane and screw. The Roots compressors are generally the noisiest and the screw variety the quietest. Working pressures normally do not go higher than six bar but multi-stage machines are available. The spectrum generated by all three types is dominated by the passage frequency of rotor elements and harmonics of this frequency. This is due to the sudden pressure changes which occur when the rotating elements expose the compressed gases at the delivery or suction port.

Although the Roots type machine does not have any internal compression, there is still a sudden pressure change as the rotor lobes pass the ports, due to the mismatch between the pressure of the trapped air and the delivery or suction port. As with the reciprocating machines, design of the ports and cavities of the inlet and outlet manifolds can affect the resultant spectrum shape. Again, as with the reciprocating machines, the principal sources of noise can be listed as – intake noise, outlet noise, noise radiating from the casing, and motor noise.

The inlet noise can normally be reduced by absorptive type attenuators because, unlike reciprocating machines, the frequency is much higher and in a range where a worthwhile reduction can be achieved by this form of silencing. There are cases, however, where slow running Roots type compressors generate pure tones at low frequencies; the fitting of reactive silencers in these cases will probably be more effective. On the outlet side, a pulsation damper in the delivery line can produce an effective reduction in the noise levels.

However, with the sliding vane and screw types, the predominant frequency is much higher and again an absorptive type attenuator can provide a useful reduction in the noise levels. An acoustic enclosure around the compressor and/or motor is the most common treatment for noise breaking out from the casing. It is possible, however, that the casing noise can be the result of 'ringing' of the casing at its natural frequency when excited by the compressor's rotary action. This reaction of casing structure to compressor forces can result in noise at a frequency at first sight not directly related to the periodic action of the compressor. The treatment of noise from a compressor is ideally made at the source, but, since this can often promote a lengthy and costly investigation programme, it is often more economical for the user to install a proprietary acoustic enclosure. Oil flooded rotaries, either the sliding vane or screw types, are generally quieter than their equivalent oil lubricated machines; which are themselves quieter than the oil free types of rotaries where the fabric or steel blades are replaced by carbon composite.

Non-Positive Displacement Machines or Aerodynamic Non-positive displacement compressors are manufactured in two extreme forms, the centrifugal and the axial with a hybrid mixed flow form. They are high flow rate and relatively low pressure devices where both the pressure rise and the capacity, increase with shaft speed. In both types the noise spectrum may be either broad band or predominantly pure tone, depending on the design of the machine. The major energy is generally confined to the higher frequencies. Sound levels generated by these machines are much higher than for the rotary positive displacement type machines because of the much higher total energy input into the system. The greater capacity and higher noise levels of these machines cause an additional problem over the other rotary machines, since noise breakout from the large size inlet and outlet pipework may be significant. In most instances this will need to be lagged with 50mm of glass fibre or mineral wool and covered with steel, lead or a plaster/cement covering having a weight of 10-12kg/m^2

(2-3lb/ft²). The high frequency content of the noise spectrum enables these machines to be effectively quietened by an acoustically designed enclosure. Inlet and outlet silencers of the absorptive type are most suitable for these machines for the same reasons.

An additional source of noise that is often present with machines of this type is the gearbox noise. Gearboxes of helical or epicyclic gear trains are often used for centrifugal or axial compressors when driven by electric motors to obtain the desired operational rotor speed. These can be a major source of noise if gear alignment or manufacture is not of a high standard. Vibration from the gearbox can also be transmitted to the surrounding structure.

Vibration With the slow speed reciprocating compressors, the out-of-balance forces may be considerable, even though running speeds are low. If the machines are installed other than at ground level, some form of vibration isolation will be required. The vibration is very rarely simply an up and down motion; rocking movements in at least one direction normally occur. Many of the machines are also relatively top heavy, so it is normal to install them on concrete bases to provide a stable support. These are then supported on springs or compliant materials as appropriate.

Vibration of the various rotary positive displacement machines can cause noise problems by setting the supporting structure in vibration. For example, if a Roots blower is mounted on a lightweight structure, fitting an enclosure round it will normally have little effect on the noise level unless the blower is mounted on vibration isolators which are at least capable of preventing the transmission of audible frequencies.

Aerodynamic compressors on the other hand generally represent a much simpler problem because a very much higher degree of balance is necessary for their satisfactory operation.

Fluid pumps, as with compressors, can be of a number of types and modes of operation, and to some extent they have similar problems in terms of noise control. The fluids pumped are generally incompressible and there is therefore no internal change of area or compression. Types most commonly found are similar to those mentioned previously for compressors: sliding vane, centrifugal, rotary piston and gear type. The rotary piston or axial piston pump may appear to be a contradiction of terms but is formed by grouping pistons in a circular array actuated by a cam type device or a flat plate (swash plate) set at an angle to the main drive shaft which, when rotated, drives the pistons up and down. This rotating plate device is sometimes used in a type of pump known as the orbital pump. A further recent development is that of adapting the Wankel principle to fluid pumps and compressors. The gear type pump is virtually an extension of the Roots type compressor, but with a large number of lobes formed by the teeth of the gears.

Sound is caused by pressure fluctuations or mechanical impacts. In a hydraulic system, the pressure fluctuations can be caused in a number of ways; by instability of flow, turbulence, by collision of areas of differing pressures (as at the valves or ports of pumps) and by 'cavitation' and 'water hammering'. By the nature of their operation, the sliding vane and piston type pumps produce pressure fluctuations at both inlet and outlet which generate noise. The degree of noise generated would depend on the pump's design and selection for the duty required. The latter consideration will also be a principal factor in the effect caused by instability of flow and turbulence, although again design of the pump itself does have some bearing on the matter. The noise spectrum of a pump would depend on its type, configuration, bearings and mounting, but generally hydraulically caused sound will predominate causing a series of pure tones at the pumping frequency and its harmonics.

The mechanical noise contribution of the pump itself is generally small and confined to its location only, unlike that of pipework noise. Bearing noise is likely to be the main cause of mechanically generated noise in a pump. There are available 'quiet' pumps where the conventional ball or roller bearings are replaced by sleeve bearings, thus removing the prime noise generating mechanisms. Pumps made of high damping alloys will help to prevent breakout of mechanically generated noise. The use of slower speed pumps will help to reduce hydraulically generated noise but may provide more problems in the control of the lower frequency mechanical noise. Lagging of the offending pump with a high damping material as mentioned previously, or total enclosure, are the only two practical and effective ways of controlling the mechanical noise from a fluid pump, with the exception of good design.

Plate 1. *A reactive inlet attenuator fitted to a large reciprocating
compressor in a paper mill. The low frequency noise from this type of
machine may still require careful attenuation to minimise external
noise problems*

Plate 2. A silenced screw type air compressor package. Developments in noise level reduction have enabled equipment of this kind to be sited practically anywhere that compressed air is needed. This is in direct comparison with noisier reciprocating type compressors which may need isolating in special plantrooms

17
Diesel Engine Noise

IN addition to being a common power unit for road vehicles and marine use, the diesel engine is widely used as a static or 'portable' power unit, driving plant such as standby generators, pumps and compressors. The problems of vehicle noise will be dealt with in Chapter 23. In 'static' applications, space and weight considerations which severely limit the reduction of, for example, truck noise are not a major problem and engine noise can be reduced using conventional noise control techniques.

Sources of Engine Noise The following sources contributing to overall engine noise levels can be identified:
1. Radiation from engine casing and connected structures (crankcase, sump, rocker covers, etc.)
2. Air intake (including noise from turbocharger)
3. Exhaust
4. Cooling fan and auxiliaries (injection pump, generator, etc.)

It is not intended to discuss methods of noise reduction at source, since this is extensively covered in technical literature. The relative significance of each noise source and the engine design and operating characteristics which affect noise emission are discussed in general terms. Different types of engines may have very different noise characteristics. The noise level data given is intended as a guide only, for initial design purposes or in the absence of manufacturers' data.

Casing-radiated Noise The predominant source of noise radiation from the engine casing is the rise in pressure in the cylinders during combustion, resulting in vibration of the external surfaces of the engine. The rapid cylinder pressure rise of the diesel engine results in high levels of the higher harmonics of engine firing frequency, producing a characteristic noise spectrum with a broad peak in the 500 to 3kHz range. Turbocharging produces smoother combustion and reduces casing-radiated noise under most conditions. The level of engine noise is most dependent on engine speed, generally increasing by 9 to 12dB for a doubling of rpm. The cylinder bore has also been found to be important. For a given capacity, engines with large stroke/bore ratios, or with more cylinders, are generally quieter. Unlike the petrol engine, the difference in engine noise between no-load and full-load operation is very small for a diesel engine.

Exhaust Noise Exhaust noise is produced by the periodic abrupt release of gas into the exhaust system as the exhaust valves open, and varies considerably between engine types depending on valve configuration and timing. Exhaust noise typically increases 15dB between no-load and full-load operation. The characteristic frequency spectrum peaks at engine firing frequency, given by:

$$\text{Firing frequency} = \frac{\text{rpm}}{60} \times \frac{\text{no. of cylinders}}{2} \quad \text{(4-stroke cycle)}$$

Turbocharging (compressing inlet air by an exhaust gas driven turbine) reduces exhaust noise significantly (6-10dB) in addition to reducing engine noise by smoothing combustion, as noted above.

Inlet Noise Inlet noise is generated by the interruption of airflow through the inlet passages by the opening and closing of the inlet valves. Inlet noise is load sensitive, increasing by 10 to 15dB from no-load to full-load operation. Where a turbocharger is fitted, noise from the compressor (a high speed centrifugal or mixed flow type) is radiated from the inlet duct. Turbocharger noise is characterised by a pure tone at blade passing frequency and harmonics, usually evident in the 2 to 4kHz range.

Engine Ancillaries Although noise from engine ancillaries, particularly cooling fan, injection pump and electric ancillaries, may contribute significantly to overall engine noise levels, when 'conventional' noise control measures are to be applied these sources may be considered to represent a contribution to casing-radiated noise.

Diesel Engine Noise Levels Typical noise levels of diesel engines are shown on Figs 1, 2 and 3, showing data for engine noise, exhaust noise, and inlet and turbocharger noise. This data is intended for use for initial design studies only and to illustrate calculation techniques for noise control or for use in cases where manufacturers' data is not available.

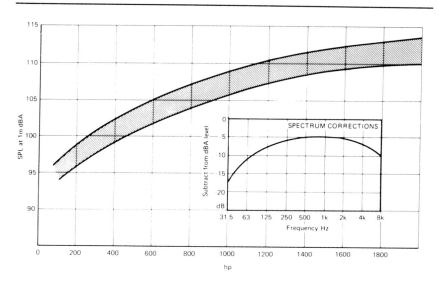

Figure 1. Estimation chart – engine noise levels

Noise Control The following techniques for reducing diesel engine noise will be considered:
1. Enclosure to control casing-radiated noise
2. Exhaust silencing
3. Inlet silencing
4. Vibration isolation

Enclosures Depending on the purpose of the engine, an enclosure may take the form of a building structure, a ship's engine room, or a purpose built enclosure. The basic principles are common; the power unit is completely enclosed by a 'sealed' structure. The enclosure must be ventilated for cooling air and generally for aspiration air; exhaust

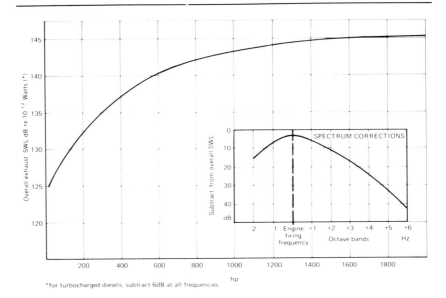

*for turbocharged diesels, subtract 6dB at all frequencies

Figure 2. *Engine exhaust noise levels (unsilenced)*

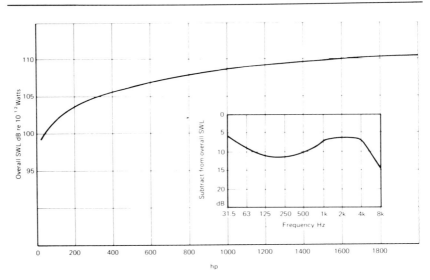

Figure 3. *Inlet/turbocharger noise levels (unsilenced)*

gases are discharged outside the enclosure. The principal design considerations can be illustrated by examination of a fairly common problem – the enclosure of a 350kVA motor-alternator set for emergency power generation, driven by an engine of approximately 450hp.

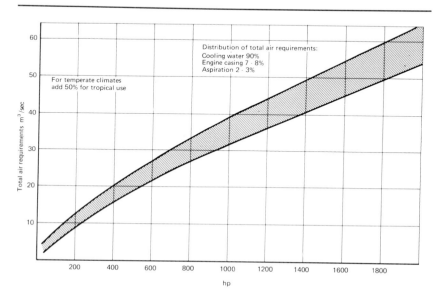

Figure 4. Estimation chart – air requirements for water cooled diesels

An installation of this type is usually cooled by an integral water radiator and engine driven fan. The total cooling air requirement for engines of various sizes operating in temperate conditions can be estimated from Fig 4 (again, manufacturers' data should be applied where available). It is observed that a 450hp engine may require a maximum total cooling airflow of 15-20m³/s (32-42000 ft³/min). Of the total cooling load, approximately 90% is via the radiator. Aspiration air (perhaps 2 to 3% of engine cooling air) can be neglected for initial calculations.

If a 'sealed' enclosure is required for noise reduction, the cooling air must enter and leave the enclosure via suitable attenuators to enable the noise reduction potential of the enclosure to be achieved. The usual configuration is shown in Fig, 7. The engine radiator is ducted (via a flexible connector) to the cooling air exhaust attenuator, whilst air enters via an unducted attenuator or acoustic louvre. The attenuators impose considerable pressure drop which has to be overcome by the engine driven fan, which will usually accommodate only 125N/m² (0.5in wg) additional resistance without serious reduction in flow. This generally imposes a limit of 2.5 to 3.5m/sec (500 to 700 ft/min) on the average air velocities approaching the attenuators. The resultant attenuator cross-sectional areas of 6.5m² for the selected example may prove difficult to accommodate, particularly in installations in buildings with limited area of external wall.

Two alternative cooling arrangements are possible:
1. A ducted cooling system with an additional fan matched to the system resistance. With such a system, duct velocities of up to 7.5m/sec 1450 ft/min are practicable using a single stage axial flow fan (which is of course powered from the emergency circuit). The fan must always be installed on the generator side of the attenuator.
2. The use of a remote radiator mounted outside the enclosure, or the use of a heat exchanger in the engine water system, with a remote cooling tower. These systems allow the air to the enclosure to be drastically reduced to about 10% of the volume shown in Fig 4. The remote radiator fan or cooling tower should be selected and located so that the noise from these items is not in itself a problem. The relatively small cooling air requirements for the engine room (for engine casing cooling, alternator cooling and aspiration air) are easily provided with small section ductwork and suitable axial flow fan.

Although the 'conventional' system of direct cooling is generally less costly, at least for engines up to 1000hp, space considerations often make remote cooling a necessary alternative.

The necessary noise reduction to be provided by the enclosure itself, and the specification of suitable materials, is determined as described previously in Chapter 5. The noise levels inside a minimum sized enclosure may be assumed to be the same as the noise levels 1m from the engine casing in Fig 1. Where the engine is housed in a larger plantroom, perhaps accommodating several similar units, a room sound pressure level should be derived from the engine sound power level and the room correction, as described in Chapter 4.

Exhaust Silencing The most objectionable components of engine exhaust noise are are the low frequency pulsations occurring at engine firing frequency and harmonics (and subharmonics depending on the engine configuration), usually in the frequency range 50 to 200Hz. As explained in Chapter 13, low frequency noise is most effectively reduced by an attenuating device working on the reactive principle, usually called a 'reactive' or 'snubber' silencer. Typical diesel engine silencers of this type consist of a series of chambers connected by perforated pipes, as shown in Fig 7, Chapter 13. This arrangement enables an attenuation spectrum with a fairly broad peak to be achieved, unlike the (theoretically) very selective attenuation provided by a simple resonator. This feature allows a single silencer configuration to be used for a variety of engines over a range of running speeds. Typical noise reductions achieved by proprietary 'standard' and 'residential' reactive silencers are shown in Fig 5.

Where a high standard of exhaust silencing is required, it is common practice to use a secondary silencer of the absorptive type, which is effectively complementary to the reactive (primary) silencer in providing high attenuation at mid to high frequencies (500 to 4kHz) but negligible low frequency attenuation (Fig 5). The secondary silencer also helps to avoid tailpipe resonances.

The primary silencer should be installed as close to the exhaust manifold as possible, with the secondary silencer spaced at least 10 pipe diameters downstream, with a tailpipe at least 10 pipe diameters long. Where an engine is enclosed, such as in a generator house, it is usual to mount the primary silencer inside the enclosure, connected to the manifold via flexible piping, and the secondary outside. Where the primary must be located outside the enclosure for reasons of space, it may be necessary to lag the silencer and ductwork up to the silencer externally (e.g. with 20g steel sheet over 50mm mineral wool packing) or to contain the system in a brickwork flue to reduce noise radiation from the silencer casing.

An alternative to the use of a secondary exhaust silencer is to use the cooling air discharge attenuators as the second stage.

Exhaust silencers will present some resistance to gas flow (back pressure) depending on the silencer internal configuration and the gas velocity at entry. Engines differ considerably in their tolerance to back

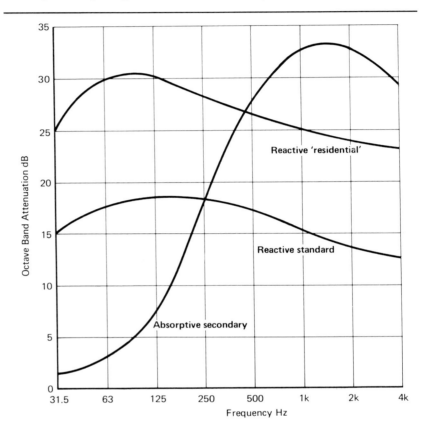

Figure 5. Typical attenuation of exhaust mufflers

pressure, although most types will accommodate at least 1250N/m² (5in wg). Engine and silencer manufacturers' data must be used to determine the maximum permissible back pressure and corresponding minimum silencer bore size.

Inlet Silencing For most static installations, engine aspiration air is drawn directly from the engine house. However, for larger engines

(1000hp plus) which are invariably turbocharged and are remotely cooled, it is usual practice to duct aspiration air from the exterior, generally via a filter. The requirement for an inlet air attenuator can be determined initially from Fig 3. A rectangular splitter attenuator immediately downstream of the filter section is most common used.

Vibration Isolation The principles of vibration isolation are covered in Chapter 6. The requirement for, and specification of, mounting methods depends on the range of running speeds and the size of the power unit. The most critical applications are usually when an engine is installed within a building to provide emergency power. For a 1500rpm, 50Hz set, the following general selection guide may be used:

| | Minimum static deflection of engine mounts | |
Location of engine	Up to 100hp	100hp plus
Basement	10mm (rubber)	10mm
Floor spans up to 10m	40mm (spring)	60mm
Floor spans over 10m	60mm (spring)	90-120mm

Design Study Application of the above techniques can be illustrated by a typical design example:
A 450hp eight cylinder diesel engine powering an alternator for standby power generation is to be located adjacent to a factory building, 60m from a residential area, as shown on Fig 6. Determine the requirements for enclosure and treatment of cooling air and engine exhaust systems to enable a maximum noise level of NR40 (approximately 45dBA) to be achieved at every house.

Initial investigation would probably indicate that an enclosure 8m long × 4m wide × 3m high would be the minimum required. Inlet and outlet louvres are better located at the ends of the building for convenience in connecting the engine radiator to the outlet ductwork and also to take advantage of directivity effects in reducing noise levels.

Complaints concerning noise are also less likely if the source of noise is not easily visible. The adverse psychological effect of louvres or similar openings directly facing residential areas should not be under-estimated.

The overall noise level at a distance will normally be a combination of noise from exhaust, cooling air inlet and outlet, and breakout from the enclosure itself. To achieve a level of NR40 overall, an initial design objective would be to reduce noise from each of the three sources to NR35, as follows.

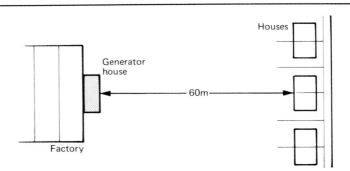

Figure 6. *Site plan showing position of generator house*

Exhaust Noise From Fig 2, assuming a firing frequency in the 125Hz octave band, the unsilenced exhaust SWL is:

octave band centre frequency	63	125	250	500	1k	2k	4k	Hz
Exhaust SWL	131	134	132	127	120	113	105	dB*
Distance correction (60m)	−47	−47	−47	−47	−47	−47	−47	
Directivity 90° (200mm dia pipe)	0	0	0	−1	−2	−2	−8	
SPL at 60m	84	87	85	79	71	64	50	
Comparing with NR35	63	52	45	39	35	32	30	
Excess over NR35 (= required attenuation)	21	35	40	40	36	32	10	

The SPL at a distance is calculated from SWL by applying correction for directivity (Fig. 8) and distance (Fig 9, Chapter 20)
*re 10^{-12} watt

From Fig 5, a 'residential' primary and an absorptive secondary muffler will be required.

Air Inlet/Outlet From Fig 4, the likely total air required for a conventional radiator cooled engine will be 20m³/sec. As an initial estimate based on a maximum face velocity of 2.5 to 3.5m/sec, a face area of 6.5m² for inlet and outlet louvres is assumed.

From Fig 1, average SPL in generator house is:

Frequency	63	125	250	500	1k	2k	4k	Hz
SPL	91	94	96	97	97	97	95	
SWL to inlet/outlet (SPL + $10\log A_L$–6=SPL +2dB	93	96	98	99	99	99	97	
Distance correction (85m @ 45°)	-50	-50	-50	-50	-50	-50	-50	
Surface Directivity (source at junction of 2 surfaces)	+6	+6	+6	+6	+6	+6	+6	
Source Directivity at 45° including 1 surface (Fig. 9)	+4	+4	+4	+4	+4	+4	+4	
SPL @ 85m, 45°	53	56	58	59	59	59	57	
NR 35	63	52	45	39	35	32	30	
Excess over NR 35 (= atten. required)	–	4	13	20	24	27	27	

The sound power emitted from inlet and outlet louvres is given by SWL = $SPL + 10\log A_L$-6, where AL (m²) is the area of the louvre. The SPL at a distance is determined by applying the appropriate directivity and distance corrections; the highest noise level in this case will occur at a position bearing 45° from each louvre, at a corresponding distance of approximately 85m. Moving away from this point in either direction results in lower noise levels due to an overall increase in the distance/directivity correction.

Reference to manufacturers' data shows that splitter attenuators with a length of 1200mm and a free area of 33% will provide the required attenuation, with a pressure drop of less than 70N/m² (0.25in wg) per attenuator.

Enclosure The minimum noise reduction to be provided by the enclosure is most easily calculated by 'working back' from the 60m noise limit, to provide a corresponding maximum sound power level emitted from the building.

Frequency	63	125	250	500	1k	2k	4k	Hz
NR35	63	52	45	39	35	32	30	
Distance correction (60m)	−47	−47	−47	−47	−47	−47	−47	
Directivity (junction of 2 surfaces)	+6	+6	+6	+6	+6	+6	+6	
Maximum SWL from enclosure	104	93	86	80	76	73	71	
External SPL (SWL−19+6)	91	80	73	67	63	60	58	
Internal SPL	91	94	96	97	97	97	95	
Minimum SRI of enclosure	0	14	23	30	34	37	39	

The corresponding maximum SPL outside the enclosure is related to SWL by $SWL = SPL + 10\log A_E - 6$, where A_E is the external area of the enclosure (m^2).

Subtracting the maximum external SPL from the internal SPL provides the required noise reduction of the enclosure structure.

A typical construction might comprise 150mm lightweight concrete blocks (rendered on one face) with a roof of precast concrete planks or wood wool cement roof units. A flat roof may in general have a sound reduction index 5dB lower than the walls, without reducing the overall noise reduction of the building to an observer at or near ground level. A personal access door with a rating of 30dB should be provided; access for plant installation and possible removal would normally be via the air inlet/outlet openings, following removal of the attenuators.

A sketch of the overall configuration is shown on Fig 7.

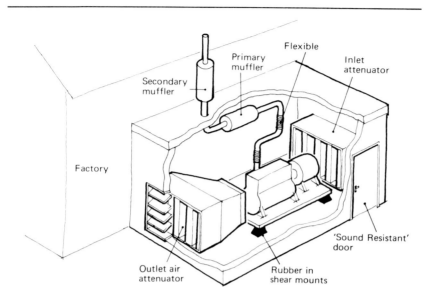

Figure 7. Diagrammatic view of generator house

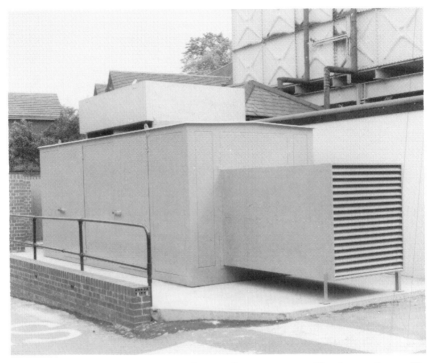

Plate 1. A specially built enclosure for an externally situated standby diesel generator. Inlet and outlet attenuators for cooling and combustion air are shown as well as sound resistant access doors

18
External
Factory Noise

THE control of noise to the community from factories has traditionally been instigated by complaints from neighbours. This is basically still true today. However, it has been modified to some extent by Acts of Parliament such as the Control of Pollution Act 1974, which was dealt with in Chapter 3. There is no specific legal limit to community noise. The allowable levels of noise in a particular area are determined by public tolerance, whether by the community as a whole or by individuals, and by the opinions of the local authorities as to how much noise is permissible in that locality. The usual method used for measuring, or as a last resort for calculating industrial noise affecting the community is set out in BS4142. This chapter is an attempt to relate the use of BS4142 to existing legislations and, in particular, to illustrate its use in problems which are more frequently encountered.

If we consider different types of noise emitted from factories, it may be seen that they are numerous. For example, fans may emit a broad band noise but more usually, and more commonly a problem, the noise may be a drone or a whine. Natural draught process furnaces are characterised by the roar at low to mid frequencies. In the case of noise emitted from pipes carrying steam, valves and vents tend to produce a middle to high frequency noise. The wide range of spectra from different sources is illustrated by Fig 1.

The noise may also be intermittent or impulsive, as for example in loading bays or drop forging works. All these factors have to be taken into account when assessing the likelihood of complaint, and not only the ultimate background noise level by reference to BS4142 will need to be calculated but also measured or notional background noise levels must be obtained.

When a new factory is to be built, or an extension or alteration to an existing factory, consideration should always be given to the effect the noise output from the factory will have on the environment. Therefore a noise survey should be carried out to establish the existing background noise levels. If it appears that noise emitted from the factory is

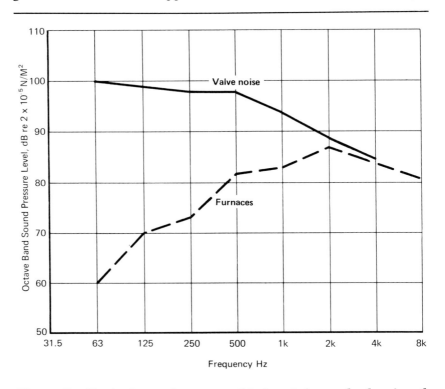

Figure 1. Typical sound spectra of industrial sounds showing the wide range of shapes that can be encountered

likely to be the subject of complaint, steps should be taken at the planning stage to rectify the situation rather than at a later stage which will inevitably prove more costly and may even involve a loss of production time.

As with any noise problem, there has to be a source, path and receiver. In considering noise to the exterior, we have discussed the many types of source, the path more usually is through the air (but it may also be transmitted through the ground as vibration) and the receiver is the community or individual. It has already been shown elsewhere that noise control at the source, or as close to it as possible, is often the most effective and economical form of treatment. Noise transfer to the exterior is no exception. Ideally, the quietest running items of equipment should be chosen. Many manufacturers are now able to quote measured sound power levels or sound pressure levels from their equipment. If this is not available, the measurement of a similar machine in an existing installation may be useful. When this is not possible, treatment may require to be applied, either by the use of damping compounds applied directly to the machinery or resilient materials to impact sources, or, in the case of noise from air or gases, a proprietary attenuator. If this is done and the levels are still too high, or if it is impractical to apply further treatment due to the operation of the machinery, then consideration should be given to enclosing the item of equipment in a sound insulating structure, or by screening the equipment as close as possible to the source.

In the case of a sound insulating structure, consideration may need to be given to the ventilation of any equipment enclosed. Orifices left in the structure will naturally reduce the effectiveness of the enclosure unless proprietary or purpose made attenuators are fitted to them.

In the case of equipment within a factory, the first consideration for marginal cases should be to provide a degree of sound absorption material within the factory. However, this can only be taken so far, remembering that a halving of the reverberation time by doubling the amount of absorption reduces the reverberant level by only 3dB.

Also, where the noise is predominantly low frequency, the use of sound absorptive materials is less likely to prove useful since the absorptive capacity of most materials maximises at middle or high frequencies. When the attenuation required is considerable, the only course of action is to improve the sound insulation of the structure.

For noise sources which are external to the building, such as ventilation fans or loading bays, some screening of the source often proves successful, particularly when middle and high frequency noise is a problem – low frequencies, being of longer wavelength, tend to bend around a screen. There is an added psychological advantage in the use of screens because the noise source is hidden from view. A large item of equipment in full view is expected to make a noise, so the observer becomes more critical. If the installation of a screen is likely to reflect sound to another area which was hitherto screened by the building, then a sound absorptive material should be applied to the face of the screen, having due consideration to its weathering properties. The structure of the screen need not necessarily be of heavy materials since noise will also travel around it, and its construction may well be dictated by the need for rigidity and stability. Other aspects to be considered are the effects of source directivity, screening by other buildings, and ground effects. For example, it may be possible to relocate the offending item of equipment on another elevation of the building where the distance to the nearest building is greater or it is screened from the receivers by the factory itself or by other buildings which are less critical, such as other factories. Again, some improvement will be obtained by having a landscaped area of grass and foliage between the source and receiver, rather than reflective hard tarmac. Although the effects may be more psychological than acoustic, they are nevertheless effective.

Receiver Acoustic treatment at the receiving end of the chain is unlikely to be an answer to a problem unless it happens to be one individual, and even then they are unlikely to take kindly to the installation of double glazing and artificial ventilation.

Measurement Procedures The basic procedure to be undertaken and the type of equipment to be used in assessing an existing noise problem are set out in BS4142. However, it is thought that some notes on the identification of sources after a problem has been established would be useful.

In order to identify a particular item or items of equipment responsible for the noise complaint, it may be necessary to use on site an octave band filter set (complying with BS2475) coupled to a sound level meter, a portable tape recorder, and possibly an accelerometer set.

The background sound should be measured at or near the point where complaints have arisen, at octave band intervals over the range 63 to 4kHz (seldom is the noise problem outside this range), initially with all plant and machinery switched off. After these readings have been taken, each item of equipment, if possible, should be switched on in turn and similar readings made, and again finally with all equipment in operation. A plot of these readings on graph paper should then establish which items of plant are a problem.

In some cases, when it is not possible to run items of plant individually, it will be necessary to take a tape recording of the noise for analysis later, using techniques described in earlier chapters. A survey of each item of plant should also be undertaken and, if possible, recordings made either of the airborne sound or by the use of an accelerometer fitted directly to the item of equipment. A note should be made of the type of equipment, its duty and its running speed. If a chart is later made of the recordings using a narrow band analyser and high speed pen level recorder, then it should be possible from the information recorded to establish the source of the problem. Once the offending item of equipment has been located, remedial treatment as described above can be initiated.

Case Studies
The following case studies illustrate some of the procedures and treatments described above.

Case Study No.1
Problem A new extension to a factory had been in operation for some six months and complaints had been received from local residents since its start up.

The new plant, about which complaints had been received, comprised a large plenum supply fan mounted on the roof at the northern end and a new supply fan with burner installed at the southern end of the extension, as shown in Fig 2. In addition, one of the existing fans had been changed to match the new one.

The main complainants were in two places, the occupants of houses A and B on the diagram. The louvred inlet to the fan/burner system faced straight down the entrance to the factory to house B.

Survey Surveys were carried out on two occasions, the first during the day at approximately 1600hrs and the second during the night at 0200hrs.

The instrumentation used on the survey consisted of a sound level meter coupled to an octave band filter set, a windscreen, an electronic calibrator and a portable tape recorder.

The analysis of these tape recordings was used to obtain chart recordings of the sound levels over a period of time to facilitate assessment and to eliminate problems due to variation in the background noise level.

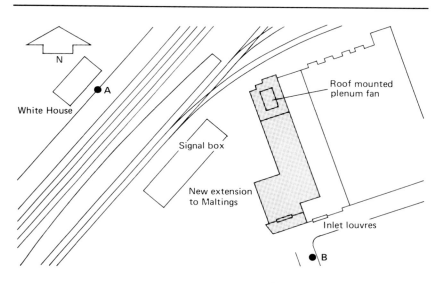

Figure 2. Sketch plan showing location of extension to factory

Measurements of the noise were made close to each item of plant for identification purposes during daylight. During the night-time survey, measurements were taken outside the houses with all items of plant running and also with various items of plant on or off.

Results Measurements outside house A indicated that the roof mounted plenum fan was the major noise nuisance since it raised the background noise level by 3dB. A secondary source due to the fan/burners raised this by a further 1dBA. As is usual, it was not possible to run all of the noise sources entirely separately.

Outside white house	'A' weighted sound levels in dBA
a) All plant operating	54
b) As a) but plenum fan off	52
c) As b) but kiln burners off	51
d) As c) but kiln fans off	50
e) As d) but plenum fan on again	53
f) As e) but kiln fans and burners on again	54

At house B the problem was found to be due entirely to the fan/burners. The plenum fan made no significant contribution.

Recommendations (see Fig 3); 1. Erect cladding panels of corrugated asbestos cement or metal around the plenum fan along the north and west parapets, together with a roof of similar material. The east facing side to be left open for air inlet.
2. Erect an 'L' shaped screen wall around the fan/burner intake.

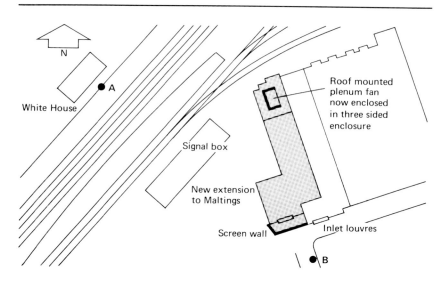

Figure 3. Sketch plan showing modifications to factory

The recommendations were carried out and a further survey was commissioned in order to measure the improvements. The operation of the equipment following treatment caused no increase in background level at either of the residential measuring positions.

Case Study No. 2

Problem Prior to the installation of a new rod mill, measurements were taken of a similar installation in another plant in order to establish the likelihood of any noise problems from the new mill. It was computed that the plant would exceed the background level by about 13dBA and that complaints were likely. Recommendations were made for the plant to be enclosed by a sound resistant enclosure built of 150mm concrete blocks roofed with pre-screeded wood wool slabs. All openings were to be treated to prevent noise breakout.

Results The plant was installed without its enclosure, thus giving the opportunity to take noise level measurements with the object of confirming previous recommendations. These measurements showed an excess over background of 15dBA.

Case Study No. 3

Problem Complaints had been received from the occupants of the factory directly opposite a newly installed diesel generator set. A fan, driven by the engine, blasted air over the engine radiator and then directly to the atmosphere through the external wall of the factory. The air inlet was by means of wood louvres approximately 2m to the right of the outlet on the same external wall. The size of the air inlet was approximately 2m × 2m. The generator room was 'L' shaped and separated from a test area by a 300mm cavity wall. Access to the room was via a double door set having a mean sound insulation of 45dB (100 to 3150Hz).

The set was normally run for approximately three days, twice a month during the hours 1000 to 1800.

Measurements of the noise levels were made both with and without the generator set in operation, in the generator room, in front of the premises of the complainant and also in the managing director's office of this company, which directly overlooked the installation.

Measurements were made manually in dBA and octave bands and in addition recordings of the noise were made on the tape recorder using the sound level meter as a calibrated microphone.

Results Applying BS4142 to the noise levels measured it may be seen that complaints were justified.

Time of day – 1130hrs.

Measured noise level	78dBA
Tonal correction	+5dBA
Corrected level	83dBA
Background level	60dBA

Corrected level – background level = 23dBA so vigorous complaints would be expected.

Measurements inside the managing director's office indicated that the generator running raised the background levels from NR30 to NR48. The sound insulation requirement of the enclosure was computed by subtracting the correction for distance and the sound insulation of an open window from the levels measured within the generator room and comparing these with the target of NR30 for the managing director's office.

The major weaknesses were found to be at the air inlet and discharge. In order to remedy this, it was necessary to install proprietary attenuators. However, it was found that this would increase the pressure drop to $250N/m^2$ (1in wg) and the engine radiator fan was only capable of operating against $50 N/m^2$ (0.2in wg). However, by changing the fan for one which is intended to operate in tropical climates against $300N/m^2$ (1.2in wg), this problem was overcome.

The attenuators were installed external to the building and housed in a 225mm wall, as shown in Fig 4. To prevent rain penetration, a sloping roof was constructed and an expanded metal screen placed across both inlet and outlet ducts to prevent birds or debris entering the enclosure.

To assist the distribution of cooling air over the generator, a 100mm blockwork wall was constructed within the generator room, as shown in Fig 4.

No further complaints were received.

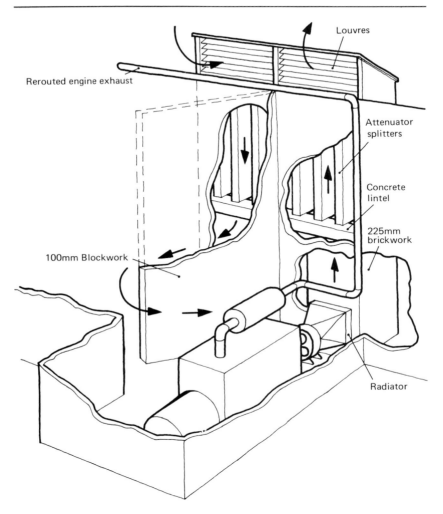

Figure 4. Modifications to diesel generator installation

Plate 1. Large plant can produce significant environmental noise problems.

19
Noise from Electrical Equipment

NOISE sources in electrical equipment conveniently sub-divide themselves into four main types:
1. Mechanical noise
2. Aerodynamic noise
3. Electromagnetic noise
4. Thermal/electrochemical noise, for example, noise produced by sparks, arcs and corona discharges

Mechanical Noise Mechanical noise in electrical machines will originate from three main causes, unbalance, bearing noise and brush friction on slip rings or commutators. In the case of defective motors, these noises will be greatly increased by the presence of loose components or the rubbing of rotating or stationary items.

Unbalance Unbalanced noise always occurs at the rotational frequency of the machine $(N_r/60)$ Hz, where N_r is the speed of rotation in rpm. Unbalance can arise in two ways, in the first case, the centre of gravity of the rotating mass is off centre from the axis of rotation. This leads to static unbalance which in extreme cases can be seen to exist if the rotor always stops in the same rotational position, i.e. with the heavy side at the bottom. Even if the centre of gravity is on the centre of rotation, dynamic rotation can occur if the axis of symmetry is not parallel with the axis of rotation. This unbalance only shows when the machine is run. Both forms of unbalance can be cured by correct mass balance of the motor.

Occasionally, due to lack of symmetry in the rotor, magnetic unbalance can occur where an unbalanced radial magnetic force due to uneven air gaps produces symptoms similar to normal mass unbalance. Magnetic unbalance cannot be cured by mass balancing of the rotor. It can, however, be identified by the fact that magnetic unbalance disappears immediately the current is turned off on an electric motor. The only cure is replacement of the rotor.

Quality grade	Speed	Maximum r.m.s. values of the vibration velocity, in mm/s, for the shaft height, H, in mm		
		$80 < H \leqslant 132$	$132 < H \leqslant 225$	$225 < H \leqslant 400$
	r/min			
N (normal)	$> 600 \leqslant 3600$	1.8	2.8	4.5
R (reduced)	$> 600 \leqslant 1800$ $> 1800 \leqslant 3600$	0.71 1.12	1.12 1.8	1.8 2.8
S (special)	$> 600 \leqslant 1800$ $> 1800 \leqslant 3600$	0.45 0.71	0.71 1.12	1.12 1.8

Figure 1. Limits of Vibration Severity.

Fig 1 sets out advisory guides of vibration severity for rotating electric machines in accordance with BS4999: Part 142.

Bearing Noise Bearing noise is not normally a problem except for very quiet applications, or unless bearings are defective, in which case they should be replaced. For super silent applications, plain journal bearings can be used instead of rolling element bearings, provided that the loading on the bearing can be carried by bearings of this type.

The major noise source with most rotating electrical machines, and especially with squirrel cage induction motors, is aerodynamic noise.

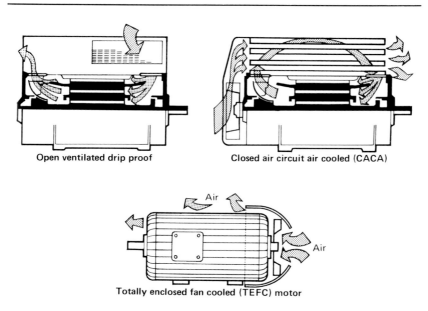

Open ventilated drip proof   Closed air circuit air cooled (CACA)

Totally enclosed fan cooled (TEFC) motor

Figure 2. Principle methods of air cooling electric motors

This is caused either by the cooling fan or by the interaction of the rotor and stator. Particularly with the smaller sizes of motor, there is a requirement that the motor as supplied should be capable of running in either direction. This means that the fan must operate equally well while running in either direction. This leads to a forced choice of a radial bladed fan. Unfortunately such a fan is one of the least effective ways of providing a cooling air flow because of the high tangential velocity of the emerging air, and, more important in this context, it is also very noisy. As a general rule, totally enclosed motors (TEFC or CACA) (Fig 2) tend to be more noisy than open ventilated motors because of the greater quantity of cooling air that is required to maintain a similar temperature.

The fan noise can be reduced by fitting a backward curved blade fan, which has the disadvantage of operating in only one direction, but may well improve the cooling of the motor despite its lower nominal performance. If operation in both directions is required, the manufacturer's normal approach is to reduce the size of the fan which may lead to an increase in motor frame size for the same output, or alternatively the use of higher temperature insulation for the windings. Standard motors can be quietened by the fitting of shrouds and mufflers to the fan or ventilation openings. In the case of TEFC motors, great care has to be taken with the design of the shroud round the body as its presence

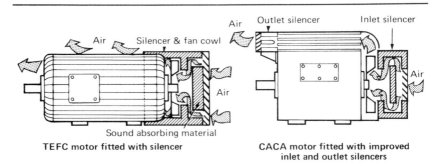

TEFC motor fitted with silencer

CACA motor fitted with improved inlet and outlet silencers

Figure 3. Sound attenuating modifications for TEFC and CACA motors

may either improve the cooling of the motor or interfere with it catastrophically (Fig 3).

In large induction motors where there are radial slots through the rotor and stator for cooling, these can produce intense siren noises. In this case it is necessary to incorporate some sound attenuation into the air inlet and discharge apertures.

Elecromagnetic Noise – Alternating Current Machines The commonest type of electric motor is the three-phase induction motor. A rotating magnetic field generated by the stator produces a torque on the rotor due to interaction with a field set up by current flow in the rotor windings. The rotor windings normally consist of copper or aluminium bars short-circuited at their ends by rings, and often referred to as a squirrel cage winding. The rotor runs at a lower angular velocity than the velocity of the magnetic field. The difference between the two angular velocities is referred to as 'slip' and depends on the load on the motor. Associated with the rotating magnetic field are radial mechanical forces which will rotate with the field. These forces depend not only on the position of the poles of the magnetic field, but also on the number of stator slots, the number of rotor slots and the slip between the rotor and the magnetic field. This radial force system is complex and can be resolved into individual waves whose frequency is determined by the factors listed above. Associated with each frequency component there will be a specific force pattern. If the fre-

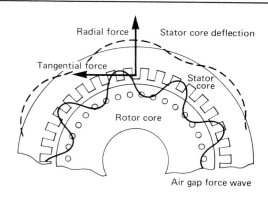

Figure 4. Production of magnetic noise

quency and force pattern coincide with a form of natural vibration of the stator, the stator will vibrate and radiate noise at this frequency (Fig 4). This problem is normally avoided by careful selection of rotor and stator slot numbers. It normally only occurs in large machines, but when it does occur the results can be spectacular, leading to a very intense high pitched scream which is quite unexpected from a piece of machinery of this size (Fig 5).

Magnetic noise in direct current motors is caused by variations in flux distribution as the armature slots traverse the magnetic fields under the poles. This can cause rocking of the pole pieces which, being coupled to the yoke, can set up resonances of the total structure. This particular noise source can be designed out of the machine by skewing the slots or by tapering the air gap at the entry and exits of the pole pieces, and by ensuring that the fundamental resonances of the main assembly do not coincide with any of the range of rotational frequencies at which the motor will be operated.

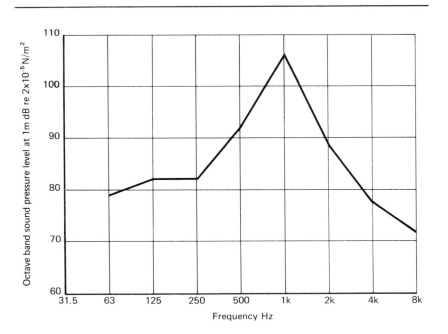

Figure 5. Noise due to stator shell vibration in 2200hp 3-phase induction motor running at 490rpm

Classification of Noise Emission by Rotating Electrical Machines Various national and international Standards have been proposed for measuring and classifying the acoustic noise emitted by rotating electrical machines. Foremost amongst these Standards are ISO Recommendation R1680, International Electrotechnical Commission Publication IEC 34-9 and BS4999: Part 109: 1987. Since there is now a degree of international agreement on the dimensions of small and medium power electric motors, it follows that there should be an attempt to establish limits for their noise emission, irrespective of the individual sources from which this noise arises.

All the Standards above, and other information sources from which they are derived, have established standard techniques for measuring the noise of electrical machines, whether on-load or no-load, and then converting this acoustic data to an equivalent sound power level. It has been established that for electrical machines a single value 'A' weighted sound power level provides a good basis for comparing the sound outputs of various electrical machines and consequently the 'A' weighted sound power level is frequently quoted in this context. Table 1 is reprinted from BS4999. Part 109 and sets out upper limits of sound power level for machines rated up to 16MW. These maximum noise rating values conform with good modern engineering practice but it is already acknowledged that good designs can achieve noise levels significantly less than the limits specified here. However, care must be taken when utilising the data set out in Table 1, or manufacturer's published sound power data, since the on-load noise of a motor direct coupled to the driven assembly can be considerably greater than the no-load value. Also, in order to compute anticipated sound levels in the vicinity of a motor commencing with a given sound power level, it will be necessary to know fairly exactly the type of acoustic environment into which the unit will be installed and whether or not there is likely to be any variation in distribution of noise around the motor.

Transformer Noise Transformer hum is a good example of electromagnetic noise. Although transformers have no moving parts, the alternating magnetic field causes changes in shape of the core of the transformer which radiates noise. The change of shape of the core is caused by magnetostriction – a name which is given to the effect whereby a piece of iron changes its shape when magnetised. The change of shape is the same regardless of the polarity of magnetisation. As a result, the core will change shape at twice the supply frequency since the change of shape is the same for each direction of magnetisation. The process is not linear and the resulting wave form is complex in shape and produces many harmonics. For a 50Hz supply, the magnetostriction frequency is 100Hz, but harmonics up to 1000Hz or more may be detected. Gross mechanical vibration of the magnetic core can also occur and add to the noise. With small air cooled transformers, vibration of loose laminations can also produce a buzz. In large transformers, friction forces between the interleaved laminations help to control this effect. This is further assisted by the damping which may be provided when the transformer is immersed in a tank of

Table 1.

Limiting mean sound power level L_W in dB(A) for airborne noise emitted by rotating electrical machines

Protective enclosure		Rated speed (rev/min)											
		960 and below		961-1320		1321-1900		1901-2360		2361-3150		3151-3750	
Rating kW (or kVA)		Sound power level dB(A)											
Above	Up to	IP 22	IP 44	IP 22	IP 44	IP 22	IP 44	IP 22	IP 44	IP 22	IP 44	IP 22	IP 44
	1.1	—	76	—	79	—	80	—	83	—	84	—	88
1.1	2.2	—	79	—	80	—	83	—	87	—	89	—	91
2.2	5.5	—	82	—	84	—	87	—	92	—	93	—	95
5.5	11	82	85	85	88	88	91	91	96	94	97	97	100
11	22	86	89	89	93	92	96	94	98	97	101	100	103
22	37	89	91	92	95	94	97	96	100	99	103	102	105
37	55	90	92	94	97	97	99	99	103	101	105	104	107
55	110	94	96	97	101	100	104	102	105	104	107	106	109
110	220	98	100	100	104	103	106	105	108	107	110	108	112
220	630	100	102	104	106	106	109	107	111	108	112	110	114
630	1100	102	104	106	107	107	111	108	111	108	112	110	114
1100	2500	105	107	109	110	109	113	109	113	109	113	110	114
2500	6300	106	108	110	112	111	115	111	115	111	115	111	115
6300	16000	108	110	111	113	113	116	113	116	113	116	113	116

NOTE.   IP22 corresponds generally to drip-proof, ventilated and similar enclosures.
IP44 corresponds generally to totally enclosed fan-cooled, closed air circuit air-cooled, and similar enclosures (see BS 4999 : Part 105).
No positive tolerance is allowed on the above sound power levels.

Reproduced from BS4999. Part 109.

oil for cooling purposes. However, even when a transformer is contained in such a tank, noise can be radiated from the tank walls due to the fact that oscillations of the core may be either directly coupled to the external surface via the support assembly, or transmitted via the liquid infill. The thickness and construction of the tank has little bearing on the radiated sound. Large tanks will radiate low frequencies very efficiently and the characteristic sound of transformers in electrical distribution systems is invariably 100Hz (120Hz in North America). Smaller transformers tend to radiate less noise at the fundamental frequency, but may tend to radiate more of the high frequency harmonics. In all cases, limited control of such noise can be achieved by applying vibration damping material to the oil tanks.

In general, the following guidelines should be considered when designing transformers for low noise output:
1. Provide special damping and binding of the core laminations by selected organo-silicon varnishes.
2. Use special lamination materials. Ferromagnetic compounds with high silicon content reduce the magnetostrictive effect.
3. Decouple the transformer core from the tank walls by vibration isolators. Ensure that cable connections and earth straps are as flexible as possible.
4. Reduce the core flux density. This unfortunately will give rise to larger and more expensive transformers for a given application.
5. Enclose the unit in a special enclosure or hood.
6. Alternatively, screen noise radiation to adjacent areas by walls. Such walls can incorporate cavity absorbers tuned to the low frequency sound output if it is necessary to limit reflections off the screens.
7. Where heat transfer is achieved by circulating cooling oil through external radiator banks, the piped oil circuit should incorporate flexible links to decouple vibration which would otherwise be transmitted along the rigid pipes.
8. If cooling fans are required to assist heat transfer from the radiator cores, such fans should incorporate sound attenuators on both the air inlet and discharge paths.

Solenoids and Relays A solenoid is an electrical device for producing linear motion over a relatively short distance, such as when a valve or latching mechanism is actuated for a larger mechanical system. Solenoids operate by establishing a source of attraction between two iron poles which are energised when a current is passed through a coil which surrounds them both. Normally a metal plunger is arranged to be drawn into the coil which is surrounded by a thick magnetic yoke. Both electromagnetic and electrodynamic noise can be generated by solenoids. Electrodynamic noise is created when motion of the plunger, together with the component which is moved, is arrested by a mechanical stop. The noise so emitted will depend not only on the momentum of the moving element but on the method of decelerating its motion. A metal-to-metal contact will obviously make much more noise than impact with a resilient pad. Electromagnetic noise will be generated if the solenoid is actuated by alternating currents. (For ultra-quiet applications it is desirable that a constant direct current should be used to actuate the device.) Alternating current can potentially give rise to a magnetostrictive hum at twice mains frequency which can coincide with the mass-spring resonance of the plunger on its compliant stops. In these circumstances, a rattle or buzz can be emitted by a loose fitting plunger. (It is often found in these circumstances that a light coating of grease on the moving parts is effective in reducing this noise source.)

Relays and similar contactors can give rise to the same noise problems as solenoids as they are clearly from the same family of electrical devices. Relays function by attracting a pivotted armature on to an iron pole piece which is energised when a current passes through the surrounding coil. The small motion of the armature is linked to pairs of electrical contacts which are either opened or closed by the limited travel of the armature, thus making or breaking the circuits controlled by the unit. As with solenoids, electromagnetic noise may be caused if the units are actuated by alternating current or direct current with a superimposed AC ripple. This noise may be eliminated by using constant voltage direct current in the control circuit. Alternatively, more sophisticated relay circuits can make use of secondary 'slave' relays which will hold the armature in the 'on' position even after the energisation of the main coil has ceased. Such relays require a second pulse of energy to release the armature.

If the electric load to be handled by the relay contacts is not excessive, the alternative of using reed relays may be considered. These devices consist of two metal reeds encapsulated in a glass tube which form both the contact arms and armature. They are brought together by the action of a magnetic field induced by a surrounding coil and, because the moving parts are so light and totally encapsulated, there is virtually no mechanical or arcing noise to be heard. As an alternative to reed relays, the use of solid state semi-conductor devices may be considered. Although such units are inherently quiet, they sometimes require auxiliary cooling, particularly where heavy loads are handled. Forced heat exchange can be achieved by the use of blown air or a circulated cooling fluid, but in either case there is the possibility of additional noise being generated by the auxiliary cooling plant.

Circuit Breaker Noise All electrical distribution systems must incorporate switches and circuit breakers. These are mechanical devices which bring together and separate conductors so that power supplies can be made or broken at will. Whenever two conductors move apart or come together, an electric spark may be generated. This spark is more correctly referred to as an arc – the flow of electrical current along ionized gases between the two switch poles. The length of the arc will be determined by the applied voltage. A 10mm arc in air requires a breakdown voltage of 30kV. Consequently, when switching the high voltages associated with the national grid network, arcs of up to 60mm in length could be encountered. Extremely high temperatures are generated by the ionized gases if the current densities are high and, in consequence, the switch poles could be rapidly burnt and eventually destroyed by the electrical discharge. For this reason, most modern heavy duty switchgear incorporates an air blast mechanism whose function is to extinguish the arc as rapidly as possible by blowing it out with a blast of compressed air. The sudden release of a large quantity of compressed air is similar to the explosion of a gun and a similar noise is generated. Such sound is clearly unacceptable in switching centres located in urban areas, and specialist forms of silencer/attenuator units are needed to limit this noise. Severe constraints are imposed on the designs for air blast circuit breaker attenuators. They must not give rise to excessive back pressure otherwise the arc will not be extinguished. Also they must handle large volumes of air while at the same time being limited in physical size by other electrical and mechanical design constraints.

Plate 1. Attenuated electric motors operating in a noise critical petrochemical installation. 300kW 3000rpm CACA type fitted with inlet and outlet attenuators

20
Air Moving Systems

MOST industrial plants contain fans to move air for heating/cooling purposes, or for the transport of materials, e.g. in dust extract systems.

The type of fan selected will depend upon the properties of the air to be moved, and the volume and pressure required. The following types are often encountered in industrial applications (see Fig 1).

Propeller Fans These are normally used for the extraction of large volumes of air at relatively low pressures (less than $125N/m^2$ (0.5in wg)). They consist of a fairly crude impeller mounted in a diaphragm plate and generally with no shrouding around the motor. Mounted in a wall, they would have a free air intake and discharge. Due to the low pressure development, they are usually considered unsuitable for use in ducted systems or where attenuation is required. Attempts at quietening this type of fan are not usually successful as the pressure loss imposed by the attenuators substantially affects the aerodynamic performance of the fan. Air cooled condensing units often use this type of fan, and if residential housing is nearby, consideration should be given to substituting axial flow fans which can then be attenuated if necessary. An inherent disadvantage of the propeller fan is its tendency to generate pure tone components at the blade passage frequency. i.e. $\dfrac{\text{rpm} \times \text{no. of blades}}{60}$. Should noise complaints occur regarding the pure tones, a fan replacement would be inevitable.

Axial Flow Fans These have higher efficiencies, aerofoil type blades and can generate relatively high pressures, particularly when used in series and with guide vanes. Invariably the impeller and its associated

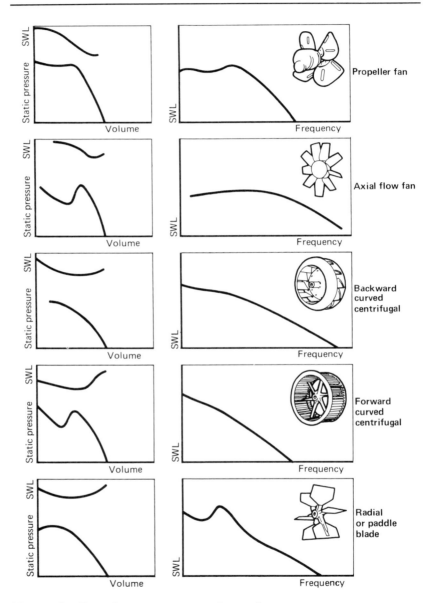

Figure 1. Fan characteristics and sound spectra

motor is contained within a cylindrical casing to which cylindrical attenuators can be bolted.

For corrosive or inflammable gases, the motor may be mounted externally and plastic impellers used.

Sound data for axial fans can be provided by most manufacturers with a reasonable degree of accuracy, although care should be taken to ensure that all relevant correction factors are added where necessary.

The noise generated by an axial fan tends to predominate in the middle frequencies rather than the lower ones, and can be attenuated by the use of standard bolt-on cylindrical attenuators. When a very high degree of noise control is required, it will be necessary to transform the duct from circular to match up with a rectangular splitter attenuator to achieve the necessary performance.

An idling standby impeller in series with the duty fan will create a 6dB increase in overall sound power. To achieve the catalogue sound figures, the airflow must pass over the impeller before the motor. Should the reverse occur, increases of up to 8dB can be expected. The catalogue data also assumes a fully ducted system with ducting upsteam and downstream of the motor. If the fan is used without ductwork or coned intakes, both the acoustic and aerodynamic properties will suffer.

Centrifugal Fans There are three common types of centrifugal fans which may be encountered. The basic configuration of each is similar but the impellers are of a different design.

Backward Curved Fans As the name implies, the blades are tilted backwards compared with the direction of rotation. This tends to make the fan stable over a wide range of its operating characteristic, although the maximum pressure is less than theoretically possible for a forward curved fan. As with all centrifugal fans, the air enters along the axis of the driving shaft and then turns through 90° to be discharged to the scroll of the fan.

Centrifugal fans will generate maximum sound energy at low frequency with a considerable fall-off towards the higher frequencies. It is for this reason that a centrifugal fan is often considered to be quieter than an equivalent axial type, i.e. for the same volume and pressure, the axial will generate a higher mid frequency level which will produce a subjectively higher noise level. However, the centrifugal type may be more difficult to attenuate to a specific design level due to the minimal performance of absorptive attenuators at low frequency.

Forward Curved Fans The impeller consists of many small blades which are curved in the forward direction, giving a high discharge velocity and potentially higher pressure development. However, fans of this type are more likely to stall violently. This, combined with their less stable operation, results in their main application being to move a large quantity of air at relatively low pressure (i.e. less than $500N/m^2$ (2in wg)).

Radial or Paddle Blade Fans These are very common for industrial applications as their large flat blades are self cleaning and can be used for dirt laden atmospheres without erosion or loss of efficiency. However, the basic efficiency of the fan is low compared with other centrifugal types due to their generally crude construction. The radial blade, like the propeller fan, tends to generate strong pure tone components at relatively low frequencies which can cause complaints at nearby critical locations. Attenuation can reduce the problem but it should be remembered that absorption attenuation maximises at middle and high frequency, which can result in the pure tone becoming more prominent.

Roof Extract Units These are produced in many forms, but due to their design do not lend themselves to being attenuated on the atmosphere side, which can limit their use in residential areas. Most manufacturers produce an attenuating curb which will help to control the fan noise reaching the conditioned space. Another point to remember with this type and propeller fans is that they create a weakness in the structure of a building which will lead to noise breakout from any internal processes in the building.

Fan Noise Levels When selecting fans for a project, all comparisons should be made on a basis of the sound power levels re 10^{-12}watt as defined in BS848:Part 2. Sound pressure levels at various distances can be misleading for comparison purposes due to the variation in measurement techniques between different manufacturers.

The sound power of a fan will vary depending on its duty, size, speed and general configuration, but the overall level will be dependent on the horsepower needed to drive the fan. This in turn is proportional to

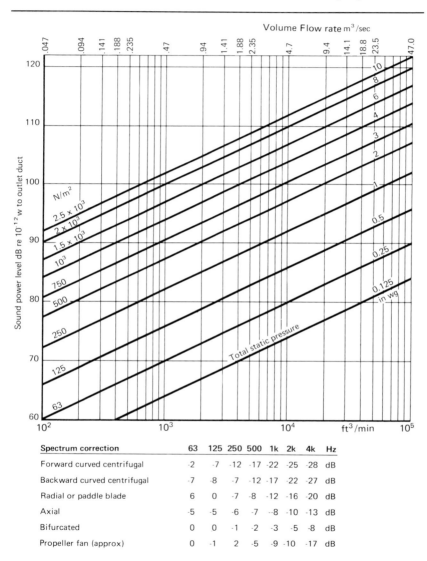

Spectrum correction	63	125	250	500	1k	2k	4k	Hz
Forward curved centrifugal	-2	-7	-12	-17	-22	-25	-28	dB
Backward curved centrifugal	-7	-8	-7	-12	-17	-22	-27	dB
Radial or paddle blade	6	0	-7	-8	-12	-16	-20	dB
Axial	-5	-5	-6	-7	-8	-10	-13	dB
Bifurcated	0	0	-1	-2	-3	-5	-8	dB
Propeller fan (approx)	0	-1	2	-5	-9	-10	-17	dB

Figure 2. Estimation of fan sound power level

the volume and static pressure requirement. An approximate idea of the overall sound power level can be gained from:

$$SWL = 10 \log Q + 20 \log P + 37dB \qquad (1)$$
Q   = flow rate in m^3/sec
P   = static pressure in N/m^2

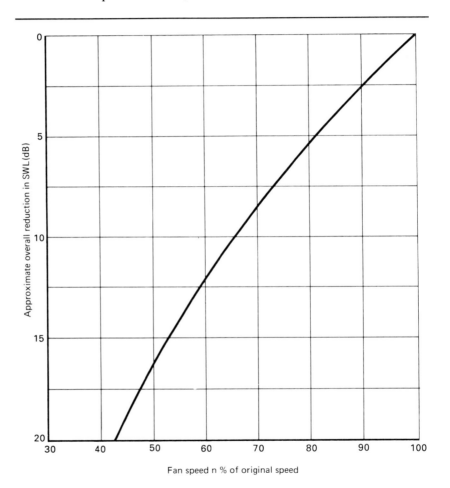

Figure 3. Fan sound power level as function of fan speed based on SWL α $N^{5 \cdot 5}$

This is diagrammatically represented in Fig 2. Note the correction factors for the different fan types, i.e. the radial blade will be noisier for the same volume and pressure.

For a given fan, the sound power level will vary between the fifth and sixth power of the tip speed, therefore a reduction in speed will produce a significant drop in noise level, i.e. approximately 16dB for a 50% lowering of speed (see Fig 3).

Ventilation Systems There are two basic types of system, known as high and low velocity. This can be confusing as it does not necessarily apply to the velocities in the ducts but more to the type of distribution equipment that is being used.

Low Velocity This is the conventional type of system whereby air is fed into a sheet metal or builders work duct and then finds its way to the room via grilles and diffusers. However, the duct velocity is not necessarily low and, for poorly designed installations, local velocities can be nearly double the design value, resulting in noise generation problems.

For industrial applications, the design noise level may lie in the range of NR40 to NR60 depending on the type of work involved and the ambient background level due to any processes. To ensure that the selected design criterion is not exceeded, it is necessary to analyse the distribution of noise from the fan and compare the resultant room levels with the design figure.

For all practical considerations, supply and extract fans can be considered together, as the air velocity is minimal compared with the velocity of sound in air.

Noise from the fan will be reflected back by bends, expansions, contractions and grille outlets. Sound energy is also dissipated into the duct walls if they are rectangular, and there will be marginal reductions from any filters or heater/cooler batteries in the ducts.

The standard calculation sheet (see Fig 4) can be used to calculate the amount of attenuation required. The starting point is the sound power level of the fan from which the following reductions are made.

SRL

CONTRACT TITLE	New Factory	C/C		SHEET NO	Fig 4
SYSTEM DESIGNATION Metal Working Area Supply		REF. NO. 1			HIGH/LOW VEL
SOUND SOURCE Centrifugal Fan		UNIT REF NO		PATH TO Heat Treatment	

ENG	MAKE & TYPE DIDW Backward Curved	DUTY	5 m³/s at	750 N/m² in wg running at	1000 rpm

	OCTAVE BAND CENTRE FREQUENCY Hz

DATE	SPL			63	125	250	500	1k	2k	4k
OVERALL SWL Estimated 101		SPECTRUM CORRECTION		-7	-8	-7	-12	-17	-22	-27
CORRECTIONS TO SWL DATA										
STRAIGHT DUCT		UNIT SWL		94	93	94	89	84	79	74
LENGTH m	SIZE mm	TREATMENT								
4	1500 × 600	—		2·56	1·28	0·64	0·40	0·28	0·28	0·28
				3·20	2·56	1·28	0·64	0·64	0·64	0·64
				5·76	3·84	1·92	1·04	0·92	0·92	0·9
				6	4	2	1	1	1	1
BENDS & TAKE OFFS										
NO.	TYPE	SIZE mm	TREATMENT							
2	R	750	—				2	4	6	6	6
1	R	400	—					1	2	3	3
OTHER ATTENUATION										
END REFLECTION	REF	0·3 × 0·3 = ·09 m²		12	7	3	1			
		SWL LEAVING SYSTEM		76	82	87	82	75	69	64
SOUND POWER TO ROOM 1 m³/s	20 %			-7						
ROOM SIZE 10 × 7.5 × 4 = 300 m³				-11 } -16						
MID FREQUENCY REVERBERATION TIME 1·8 (secs)				+2						
		REVERBERANT SPL		60	66	71	66	59	53	48
SOUND POWER TO OUTLET 0·5 m³/s 10 %				-10						
DISTANCE TO LISTENER 1·5 m				-14						
DIRECTIVITY (FLUSH/CORNER/) 0·09 m²				+7	+7	+8	+8	+8	+9	+9
		DIRECT SPL		59	65	71	66	59	54	49
		RESULTANT SPL		63	69	74	69	62	57	52
cf DESIGN CRITERION	NR 50			75	65	59	53	50	47	45
ADDITIONAL ATTENUATION REQUIRED				0	4	15	16	12	10	7
SWL ENTERING ATTENUATOR										
REF DRG NO	NOTES									

Calculation sheet No1 Ductborne noise

© Sound Research Laboratories Limited

Figure 4. *Calculation sheet for attenuation requirements*

Duct Attenuation Rectangular ductwork is efficient in attentuating low frequency sound due to the energy dissipation into the duct walls. The reduction to be expected in the different octave bands can be assessed fromFig 5. Note that the attenuation of spiral wound circular ductwork is very poor due to its inherent stiffness and can virtually be ignored except for very long lengths.

Attenuation per metre of unlined ducts

Rectangular ducts

Duct size mm	63	125	250	550	1k	2k	4k	Hz
75-175	0.16	0.32	0.48	0.32	0.32	0.32	0.32	dB
200-375	0.48	0.64	0.48	0.32	0.23	0.23	0.23	dB
400-750	0.80	0.64	0.32	0.16	0.16	0.16	0.16	dB
800-1500	0.64	0.32	0.16	0.10	0.07	0.07	0.07	dB

Circular ducts

Duct size mm	63	125	250	550	1k	2k	4k	Hz
75-175	0.07	0.10	0.16	0.16	0.32	0.32	0.32	dB
200-375	0.07	0.10	0.10	0.16	0.23	0.23	0.23	dB
400-750	0.07	0.07	0.07	0.10	0.16	0.16	0.16	dB
800-1500	0.03	0.03	0.03	0.07	0.07	0.07	0.07	dB

Attenuation per foot of unlined ducts

Rectangular ducts

Duct size in	63	125	250	500	1k	2k	4k	Hz
3-7	0.05	0.1	0.15	0.1	0.1	0.1	0.1	dB
8-15	0.15	0.2	0.15	0.1	0.07	0.07	0.07	dB
16-30	0.25	0.2	0.1	0.05	0.05	0.05	0.05	dB
32-60	0.2	0.1	0.05	0.03	0.02	0.02	0.02	dB

Circular ducts

Duct size in	63	125	250	500	1k	2k	4k	Hz
3-7	0.02	0.03	0.05	0.05	0.01	0.1	0.1	dB
8-15	0.02	0.03	0.03	0.05	0.07	0.07	0.07	dB
16-30	0.02	0.02	0.02	0.03	0.05	0.05	0.05	dB
32-60	0.01	0.01	0.01	0.02	0.02	0.02	0.02	dB

When calculating attenuation in rectangular ductwork, it is valid to take both duct dimensions into account. i.e. attenuation per metre of 750mm x 250mm duct at 63Hz is 1.28 dB (0.80 + 0.48) dB.

Figure 5. Attenuation of unlined ducts

Radius bends will give reductions at high frequency due to reflections but the use of a mitre bend (Fig 6) will produce fairly substantial reductions at low and middle frequency depending on the duct size. This type of bend should always be used with short chord turning vanes to minimise the pressure drop for the fitting. If large turning vanes are

Dimension D of Duct		Octave band centre frequency, Hz						
mm.	in.	63	125	250	500	1000	2000	4000
75 – 100	3 – 4	–	–	–	–	1	7	7
110 – 140	4.5 – 5.5	–	–	–	–	5	8	4
150 – 200	6 – 8	–	–	–	1	7	7	4
230 – 280	9 – 11	–	–	–	5	8	4	3
300 – 360	12 – 14	–	–	1	7	7	4	3
380 – 430	15 – 17	–	–	2	8	5	3	3
460 – 510	18 – 20	–	–	5	8	4	3	3
530 – 580	21 – 23	–	–	6	8	4	3	3
610 – 660	24 – 26	–	1	7	7	4	3	3
680 – 740	27 – 29	–	1	8	6	3	3	3
760 – 820	30 – 32	–	2	8	5	3	3	3
840 – 890	33 – 35	–	3	8	5	3	3	3
910 – 970	36 – 38	–	5	8	4	3	3	3
990 – 1040	39 – 41	1	6	8	4	3	3	3
1060 – 1120	42 – 44	1	6	8	3	3	3	3
1140 – 1200	45 – 47	1	7	7	4	3	3	3
1220 – 1280	48 – 50	1	7	7	4	3	3	3
1300 – 1350	51 – 53	2	8	7	3	3	3	3
1370 – 1430	54 – 56	2	8	6	3	3	3	3
1450 – 1510	57 – 59	2	8	6	3	3	3	3
1520 – 1580	60 – 62	3	8	5	3	3	3	3

Figure 6a. Attenuation of mitre bends

		Octave band centre frequency, Hz						
mm.	in.	63	125	250	500	1k	2k	4k
62.5 – 125	2.5 – 5	–	–	–	–	–	1	2
150 – 250	6 – 10	–	–	–	–	1	2	3
275 – 500	11 – 20	–	–	–	1	2	3	3
525 – 1000	21 – 40	–	–	1	2	3	3	3
1025 – 2000	41 – 80	–	1	2	3	3	3	3

Figure 6b. Attenuation of radius bends (or mitre bends with large turning vanes)

used, the attenuation is reduced and tends towards that for a radius bend.

End Reflection At the end of the duct run, unless the ducts are very large, a considerable amount of the sound energy is reflected back towards the fan as a result of the sudden change from the enclosed duct to the open space. The maximum reflection occurs at low frequency as the wavelength is greatest compared with the size of the opening (see Fig 7).

According to the calculation sheet, we have now reached the point where the amount of sound energy leaving the system can be calculated. This is not strictly true as no account has been taken of the division of sound at junctions and branches. Sound energy will divide in proportion to the relative areas of the branches and, assuming the velocity difference is not excessive, a comparison can be made of the volume flow differences. For convenience, this is taken account of in the ensuing reverberant and direct level calculations, where the air volumes to room and listener respectively are compared with the total fan volume.

Returning to the line on the calculation sheet 'SWL leaving system', this is completed by arithmetically adding all the attenuation figures together in their respective octave bands and then subtracting them from the fan sound power level.

The final corrections are then taken for the reverberant and direct level in order to convert the sound power figure to a sound pressure in the room. This is analogous to heat transfer where the thermal energy in kW is known and the room heat loss factors are applied to give the final temperature. Sound power and thermal energy cannot be directly measured in a room. This calculation can follow the procedure given in Chapter 4 but more often the procedure is based on Figs 8 and 9 where factors are tabulated to enable the reverberant and direct noise levels to be calculated. The reverberant level is calculated using the factors in Fig 8 and the direct level for the nearest listener is found from Fig 9. However, this listener is hearing not only the direct level from the nearest grille but also the reverberant level in the room, therefore the resultant which he actually hears is the logarithmic addition of the two. This is obtained from the rule of thumb given in Chapter 1.

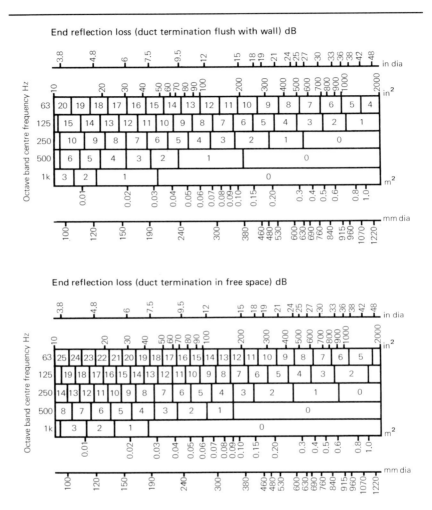

Figure 7. End reflection loss

This resultant sound pressure level can then be directly compared with the design level and the difference is equal to the additional attenuation required. If the resultant level is required in dBA, the following figures must be subtracted from the octave band readings to weight them according to the 'A' scale. The reduced figures are then added together using the rule of thumb to give the single figure dBA level.

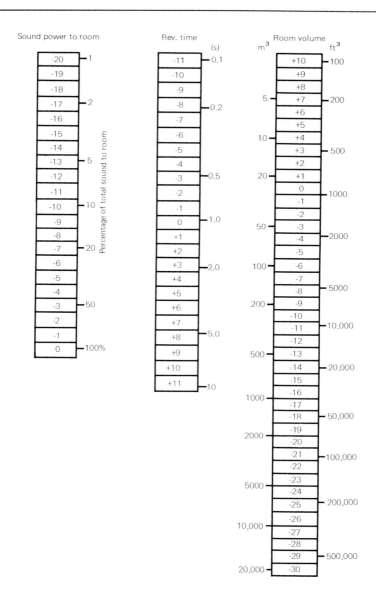

Figure 8. Reverberant sound pressure level computation

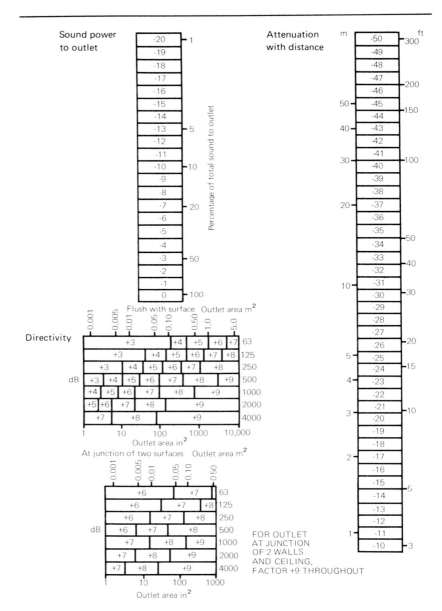

Figure 9. Direct sound pressure level computation

'A' scale reductions to be subtracted from resultant SPL

63	125	250	500	1k	2k	4k	8K	Hz
−26	−16	−9	−3	0	+1	+1	−1	dB

Note that it is not possible to specify attenuation requirements by comparing the resultant level in dBA with a design level in dBA. All attenuation should be quoted in octave band reductions since the effect of an attenuator on the dBA level will depend on whether the dBA level is the result of high or low frequency noise. Having determined the required reduction in fan noise, a suitable attenuator must be selected to achieve this value.

All attenuators are capable of behaving as noise generating sources if air passes through them at high velocity. The situation can occur where the attenuator is regenerating noise at a level which is higher than the required attenuator leaving level, in which case the overall attenuation is reduced. For example:

Sound power level	= 70dB
Required attenuation	= 20dB
SWL leaving attenuator	= 50dB

If the air velocity through the attenuator is excessive, it could generate a level of 60dB, in which case the overall system attenuation has been reduced from 20dB to 10dB.

Balancing dampers are fitted to ducts to control the air distribution between the various take-offs. The noise generated by the damper will increase by about 9dB for each doubling of the pressure drop, which may necessitate the use of further attenuators downstream for low noise level areas.

The assessment of air regenerated noise in ventilation systems is still fairly crude due to the very large number of variables which are involved. For instance, noise regeneration at tees, bends, etc., can be predicted from formulae but does not take account of any upstream or downstream turbulence which can modify the predicted value by several decibels. However, for industrial applications, regeneration is not often a problem as the duct velocities will be controlled by the need to maintain a low pressure loss through the system.

High Velocity Systems Again, this name applies more to the type of equipment used than the actual velocities, although they will invariably be higher than those in the previous low velocity systems. If air is passed at high speed through circular ducts of low frictional resistance, the duct area will be much smaller than the equivalent low velocity rectangular duct for the same volume flow rate. However, the air must be discharged to the conditioned space at a lower velocity and pressure, which entails the use of a terminal unit to reduce the velocity to a level suitable for discharge into the room.

Terminal units consist of a damper or series of adjustable vanes which reduce the pressure and allow the air to reach the room via a low velocity discharge duct. The damper will generate noise dependent on the airflow and pressure drop and will invariably necessitate the use of a secondary attenuator. Noise can also break out through the valve case, but this is unlikely to be a serious problem unless the design level is below NR45. Some terminal units incorporate constant flow-rate controllers. These have the advantage that they will control the discharge volume independent of any fluctuating upstream pressure. Typical maximum inlet pressures are $1.5kN/m^2$ (6in wg).

The high velocity side of the system should preferably be constructed of spirally wound circular ductwork, as the circular shape and the spirals give a high degree of natural stiffness which combats any tendency towards duct drumming. It is for this reason that rectangular ductwork should be avoided. For velocities in excess of 15m/sec, the take-offs from the circular duct should be coned to reduce pressure loss and noise due to turbulence.

This type of system is more often used for conditioning office buildings, although it is used in industrial applications. For more information on high velocity systems.

Dust Control Systems For industrial situations where large quantities of dust or shavings are produced, it is necessary to remove them near the source in order to prevent a health hazard. This usually involves a hood or canopy over the machine, designed to extract the dust. The velocity of the air in the system must be sufficient to carry the dust or shavings along, and the heavier the particles, the higher will be the required air velocity. The velocities will vary between about 10m/sec

(1800ft/min) for light grain dusts and 20 to 25m/sec (3500 to 4500ft/min) for wood shavings and metal dust. These velocities give rise to high air friction losses in the distribution ductwork which in turn lead to high pressure requirements and noisy fans. The radial or paddle bladed fan is often used for dust laden air as the blades are flat and self cleaning. The number of blades is usually few and this causes a very marked low frequency pure tone at the blade passage frequency.

Apart from the simpler forms of filter and settling chambers, large quantities of dust are separated in a cyclone (see Fig 10). This consists of a cylindrical hopper into which the dust laden air is discharged tangentially. The dirt particles fall to the bottom of the hopper, from where they can be collected. Meanwhile the air inside the hopper discharges vertically through the inner cylinder.

Two main problems occur with this type of system. The first and usually most serious is noise radiation from the fan. This will be apparent as breakout from the fan case, ductwork or cyclone, and also directly from the intake and discharge of the ductwork. The second problem is noise breakout from the ductwork and cyclone body due to the impact of the particles on the metal casing. With smaller particles this is not usually serious, but where heavier particles are being carried the breakout can cause a problem, particularly if the flow of materials is not constant.

Ideally, cyclones should not be installed near residential areas. The sight of a cyclone is often sufficient to cause complaints and, if it is also noisy, the complaints can be particularly vigorous. The following points should be considered when controlling cyclone noise.
1. The fan is the main noise source and should be sited inside a sealed plantroom and not on an open roof.
2. Ductborne fan noise to the intake hood and cyclone can be control-led by suitable attenuators. For a typical fan with six blades running at 1440rpm, a pure tone will be generated at its blade passage frequency, i.e $\dfrac{1440 \times 6}{60} = 144\text{Hz}$. Standard cylindrical attenuators have minimal reductions at this frequency and, if the pure tone is very pronounced, it will be necessary to use large rectangular splitter attenuators. These must have perforated facings to prevent fibre erosion and membrane linings if the perforations are liable to clog. The attenuators should be

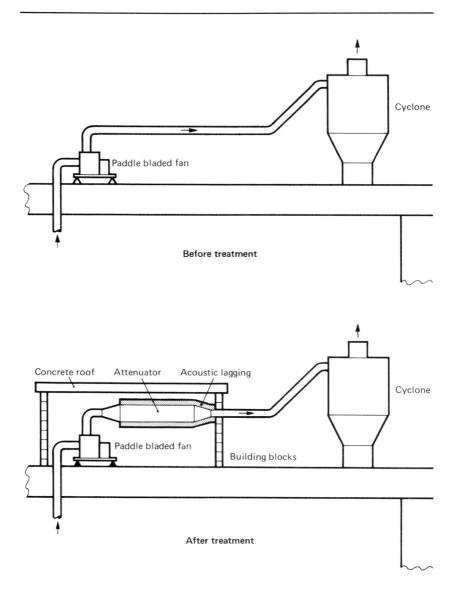

Figure 10. Acoustic treatment for cyclone extract system

fitted as close to the fan as possible so that the ducts emerging from the plantroom are 'quietened'. Authorities in the United States are advocating the use of tuned stub resonators (see Chapter 13) on dust control systems to deal with the pure tone and to avoid the problem of clogging.

3. Where heavy particles are separated, noise breakout from the cyclone can occur. Screening can reduce the noise provided the barrier is substantially higher than the cyclone. Alternatively, lagging of the cyclone body with dense material will provide a reduction but the benefits do not often justify the expense and difficulty of carrying out the lagging effectively.

Duct Breakout Noise breakout can occur when high levels of noise are contained within light structures, i.e. sheet metal ducts and cyclone bodies. Wherever possible, noise should be controlled at source, which would necessitate the installation of attenuators to reduce the noise inside the duct. If this is not possible, duct lagging can be applied, but the overall reduction will not be as great as fitting an attenuator, particularly where large areas of exposed ductwork are involved.

The sound power breakout from a duct can be estimated from the formula:

$$\text{SWL breakout} = \text{SWL in duct} - R + 10 \log_{10} \frac{S}{A} \qquad (2)$$

where S = duct surface area m² (ft²)
$\quad A$ = duct cross-section area m² (ft²)
$\quad R$ = sound reduction index

For large areas of ductwork, $10\log_{10} \frac{S}{A}$ can be greater than R at low frequency, in which case a figure of 3dB is taken, i.e. half the sound power will break out through the duct wall. The addition of mass lagging may still be insufficient to show an appreciable increase in the effective value of R. Note that breakout from a section of ductwork cannot always be controlled by selective lagging. If the first section of duct is lagged, the breakout may then appear via the second unlagged section. Where possible, lowering of the noise within the duct will provide a far greater reduction in breakout compared with conventional duct lagging.

Before embarking on a programme of lagging, it is essential to look at the problem in overall terms. If the fans and ductwork are mounted externally, then lagging the ducts will have negligible effect as the fan is the strongest noise radiator. In this case, the fan should be installed in a blockwork enclosure and the intake and discharge ducts lagged to achieve maximum reduction.

Examples
Example 1 A factory process involved the mixing of chemicals which needed a high air change rate in order to maintain reasonable working conditions. A conventional low velocity ductwork system was installed with an axial flow fan to extract the air to atmosphere. Soon after completion, complaints were received of excessive noise from the outlets nearest to the fan.

A survey of the noise levels at first suggested that it was a simple case of fan noise as no attenuation had been fitted to the working side of the fan. Closer inspection of the fan revealed that it had been very badly installed, with the ductwork of the system not aligning with that of the fan. Long floppy connections had been used to overcome the misalignment and, with the fan working, they were being sucked into the ductwork to form an obstruction local to the fan. The ductwork was modified to remove the misalignment and shorten the flexible connections. At the same time it was noted that the airflow passed over the motor before the impeller. This form of running is known to cause excessive noise (see section on axial flow fans earlier in this chapter). The motor arrangement was reversed so that the air passed through the impeller first.

These modifications reduced the noise level at the working position by approximately 10dBA, which was considered to be sufficient. It should be remembered that all manufacturers' data is based on optimum aerodynamic conditions and any deviation from this caused by poor transforms process, etc., can only increase the noise output.

Example 2 A cyclone extract system consisted of a radial bladed centrifugal fan within a roof enclosure, with the discharge ductwork connecting to the cyclone on the roof. Complaints were received from nearby residents of excessive noise from the installation, and in particular a low frequency pure tone.

A survey was carried out and tape recordings were taken to determine the frequency of the pure tone. A narrow band analysis of the recording indicated a pronounced peak at 128Hz, which corresponded to the fundamental frequency of the fan, i.e. $\dfrac{1280 \text{ rpm} \times 6 \text{ blades}}{60} = 128\text{Hz}$.

The most effective way of treating the problem was to attenuate the noise at the fan discharge, as any reduction achieved here would effect a similar reduction at the complainant's property. The fan itself was

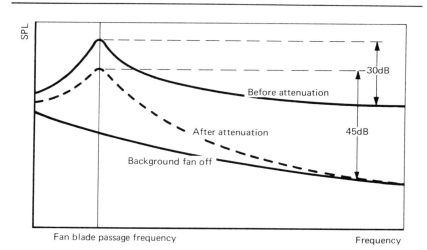

Figure 11. Effect of differential between pure tone and background

located inside a brick built plantroom, therefore breakout from the fan case could be ignored. A 400mm circular duct connected the fan to the cyclone and the first suggestion was to fit a circular attenuator directly into the duct. The problem with this solution is that a circular attenuator has limited performance, being most effective at middle and high frequency. Therefore the high frequency fan noise would be substantially reduced but the 128Hz pure tone would be only slightly reduced. This could have the effect of making the noise more objectionable as the differential between pure tone and background would be increased (see Fig 11). The solution to the problem was the installation of a 2.1m long rectangular attenuator which had the capability of reducing the pure tone at 128Hz to below the ambient noise level.

Example 3 A 500mm × 400mm, 20 gauge duct passed above the false ceiling of a cellular office in a factory. Breakout from this duct was causing excessive noise in the office space and a survey was carried out to determine the most effective way of controlling it.

Ideally, an attenuator could have been fitted to the fan but, due to the number of branch take-offs close to the fan, and a limit on any further system resistance, this method of control was ruled out. This left two alternatives; either lagging the duct or increasing the mass of the false ceiling. The former course was taken as being the most practical.

The sound reduction index of 20 gauge ductwork is as follows:

Frequency	63	125	250	500	1k	2k	4k	Hz
R for 20 gauge	3	8	14	19	24	30	35	dB

Length of duct = 3m
using equation 2
$$\therefore S = (1.0 + 0.8) \times 3 = 5.4m^2 \text{ duct surface area}$$
$$A = 0.5 \times 0.4 = 0.2m^2 \text{ duct cross-section area}$$

$$\text{Effective sound reduction of duct} = \left(R - 10 \log_{10} \frac{S}{A}\right)$$

$$= R - 10 \log_{10}27 = R - 14$$

The term R − 14 cannot give a greater breakout level than there is inside the duct. Therefore at low frequency the effective reduction is taken as 3dB. The effective reduction of the unlagged duct is then:

Frequency	63	125	250	500	1k	2k	4k	Hz
Effective reduction in sound power level	3	3	3	5	10	16	21	dB

The addition of 10kg/m² lead with 50mm glass fibre on the duct would give the following approximate increase in the sound reduction index:

Frequency	63	125	250	500	1k	2k	4k	Hz
Reduction	3	5	9	13	13	8	8	dB

These figures must be added to the original value of R and then corrected to give the true reduction of breakout. The effective reduction for the lagged duct is therefore:

Frequency	63	125	250	500	1k	2k	4k	Hz
Effective SRI	3	3	9	18	23	24	29	dB
$\therefore$ Reduction in breakout	0	0	6	13	13	8	8	dB

The noise source associated with the breakout problem was an axial flow fan with maximum breakout at middle frequency. Lagging the duct gave reductions as predicted and the office noise level was considered acceptable. Note that this treatment would not have been successful for a centrifugal fan where the maximum energy generated is at low frequency. With all acoustic problems, the treatment must relate to the spectrum shape of the noise and for this reason octave band figures must always be taken as well as the single figure dBA.

Plate 1. ***Axial flow fans located in a plantroom fitted with cylindrical attenuators. The complete fan/attenuator package is mounted on
vibration isolators with flexible sound attenuating duct connectors***

21
Gas Turbines

THANKS to aeronautics and metallurgical developments, gas turbines have improved by leaps and bounds. They are already found in numerous applications, some of the more important of which we can mention as propulsion (rail, sea and road transport, etc.), pumping and compressor stations, and generation of electricity (mobile and standby units).

It is not possible in this chapter to consider all the different forms of gas turbine, although certain similarities of function are found in the various applications. We shall therefore devote ourselves exclusively to the power generation, pumping and compressor installations.

The gas turbine can be described in a rather oversimplified way as a heat engine consisting of a compressor using air more or less polluted by the products of combustion as its ancillary fluid. The air must be compressed to a fairly high pressure and must then be heated, usually by direct combustion. Expansion of the gas of combustion is then used to drive a power turbine. (Fig 1)

Let us note in this connection that the term 'gas turbine' is wrongly used to define a turbo-engine assembly including a compressor which is no less essential than the turbine.

Such a turbine, driven by the expanded gases, acts as a sort of motive unit capable of driving the compressor, alternator, etc.

The gas turbine has found considerable acceptance to the detriment of the diesel engine in the equipment of gas and oil pipelines.

The expansion of the market for the gas turbine continues, particularly for electricity for auxiliary and emergency supply applications. New markets in the oil producing and developing countries are being discovered all the time.

Figure 1. Diagrammatic view of a gas turbine

The primary object of the user or of the acoustics expert is to determine all the factors contributing to the creation of noise in order to decide which treatment is able to provide the best possible results at minimum cost.

Identification of Sources   The gas turbines with which compressor and pumping stations or electricity generating units are equipped are usually mounted on a supporting metal frame on which are installed:
The gas generator, comprising the air compressor and the combustion chamber
The power turbine
The lubrication circuit air coolers

For the electricity generating unit:
The gearbox (if applicable)
The alternator and its ventilation

For the compressor station:
The gearbox (if any)
The gas compressor coupled to the turbine

Definition of a Noise Criterion Before any gas turbine is installed in position, a study of the existing environment will make it possible to define a noise criterion.

In the case of an installation in a rural or residential area, it is not unusual to find criteria as low as NR30 at 100m from the turbines, which makes it necessary to comply with a criterion of around NR70 at 1m from the machines, which is why it is important to break down the whole unit into elementary sources with a view to applying the most appropriate remedy to each of them.

Analysis of Sources and Definition of Necessary Treatment – Gas Generator Intake The noise at the gas generator intake rises from the blade rows of the air compressor. It is typified by a wide band spectrum to which is added a discrete frequency noise located in the high pitch sector (generally in the octave bands with centre frequencies of 4 and 8kHz).

Table 1 gives, by way of information, some figures for measurements taken at the intakes of gas turbines.

Table 1 *Estimated Sound for Power Level Values for Unmuffled Air Intake Noise of Gas Turbine Engine*

Continuous Rating of Engine kW	SWL (in dB re 10^{-12}w) in Octave Band Central Frequency in Hz							
	63	125	250	500	1k	2k	4k	8k
200-329	102	103	103	106	112	117	117	114
330-529	105	106	106	109	115	120	120	117
530-849	108	109	109	112	118	123	123	120
850-1299	111	112	112	115	121	126	126	123
1300-1999	114	115	115	118	124	129	129	126
2000-3299	117	118	118	121	127	132	132	129
3300-5000	120	121	121	124	130	135	135	132

These noises take two main paths: either they are radiated from the inlet of the air filter installed in the intake, owing to the high degree of directivity of the high frequencies from the extension of the high intake, or they are radiated from the connecting duct between the air filter and gas generator, or from the filter casing.

How can these noises due to the stages of compression be reduced? The simplest method is clearly to install a dissipative attenuator in the connecting duct as close as possible to the gas generator, or failing this in the air intake. A unit with relatively narrow air passages should be used to attenuate the discrete frequencies located in the high frequency range.

Inserting such a system in the intake of a gas turbine makes it necessary to take certain precautions in the manufacture of the attenuators. In fact, in order to avoid any possibility of the material being drawn into the turbine, the attenuators must be of robust construction and completely welded. The rate of flow must be such that it is unable to produce any deterioration of the facing protecting the mineral fibre so that the latter cannot find its way into the gas generator.

Casing Radiation The main sources of noise are:
1. The accessory drive housing
2. The air compressor body
3. The combustion chamber
4. The power turbine body
5. The compressor body (pumping or compressor station)
6. The casing of either the reduction gearbox or the current generator with its ventilation
7. The supporting frame for the entire unit and, in particular, the pedestal for the gearbox (if there is one) which radiates in the form of acoustic energy the vibration energy transmitted to it by the reducer.

Table 2 shows the typical noise spectrum radiated by the bodies of the machines.

Taking into account the difficulty of applying direct measures to the source to reduce the noise, the method to be considered is an acoustic enclosure.

Table 2 *Estimated Sound Power Level for Casing Noise of Unenclosed Gas Turbine Engine*

Continuous Rating of Engine kW	SWL (in dB re 10^{-12}w) in Octave Band Central Frequency in Hz							
	63	125	250	500	1k	2k	4k	8k
200-329	111	113	114	114	114	114	114	114
330-529	112	114	115	115	115	115	115	115
530-849	113	115	116	116	116	116	116	116
850-1299	114	116	117	117	117	177	117	117
1300-1999	115	117	118	118	118	118	118	118
2000-3299	116	118	119	119	119	119	119	119
3300-5000	117	119	120	120	120	120	120	120

This enclosure can take various forms:
1. Single enclosure using concrete or steel as the basic material
2. Double metal enclosure

Let us point out in passing that, in the case of a double metal enclosure, there must not be any mechanical connection between the two enclosures as otherwise the result obtained may not be satisfactory.

A large number of parameters must be taken into consideration in the design of the acoustic enclosures:
1. The insulation of the walls
2. Internal absorption
3. The means of access
4. Passages for pipes, ducts and electricity supplies
5. Closures, port holes or glazed inspection holes
6. The tightness of the joints
7. The internal ventilation
8. The isolation of vibration

For a more detailed account, please refer to Chapter 12 on acoustic enclosures.

One of the most troublesome factors for these enclosures is the heat radiated by the body of the machine. It will therefore always be necessary to ensure that the forced ventilation is sufficient to keep the enclosures well supplied with air. This heat, which may exceed the normal operating temperature when starting up, likewise makes it necessary to take precautions with regard to the joints, not only those which ensure perfect tightness of the panels but also those which ensure that the exhaust duct is not rigidly connected to the enclosure.

Another important factor relates to the pressure losses in attenuators mounted on the turbine intake, on forced ventilation units and on the air type gas or oil coolers. In all cases these should be minimal so as not to affect the performance of the turbine and to ensure the highest possible rate of cooling or ventilation airflow.

The intake of air for cooling should preferably be from outside the enclosure by means of separate ducts to obtain the advantage of colder air. The air should likewise be exhausted directly to the oustide in order to avoid increasing the temperature inside the enclosure.

Let us point out in passing that, in the case of low power turbines, forced ventilation can be provided with the aid of the cooling circuit fan.

Most gas turbines with which we are concerned in this chapter are started with the aid of an electric motor or an internal combustion engine (petrol or diesel). The latter are always contained in the enclosure so that there is no need to bother with their carcase noise. On the other hand, it is always necessary to provide a reactive type attenuator on the exhaust circuit to trap low frequencies.

Noise Break-in from Pipework In compressor stations the pipework upstream and downstream of the compressors can radiate discrete noise from the compressor and also noise produced by the gas flow. The most effective method of reducing the noise from these pipes is to bury them so that no surface is exposed. If this cannot be done, attenuators must be fitted in the pipelines. These ideally should be installed in straight sections of pipe to provide the best flow conditions and as close to the compressor as possible, since the problem is greatest immediately upstream and downstream of the compressor. In addition to fitting the attenuators, it is necessary to supplement the treatment by the acoustic thermal insulation on the pipes, provided by a sandwich of mineral fibre, lead foil, glass fibre and a sheet steel weather cover.

The vital rule to be observed in this combination is to avoid mechanical contact between the piping, the lead foil and the sheet iron cover. This treatment might prove insufficient to satisfy a very low noise criterion at 100m, in which case it may be necessary to use an acoustic enclosure to provide protection of the pipe and any line attenuators.

A final very important detail – vibration of the enclosure by contact with the pipe when passing through it must be avoided.

Exhaust The acoustic power spectrum found in gas turbine exhausts is very rich in low frequencies. Table 3 shows typical acoustic power spectra measured at the exhaust outlet of untreated turbines.

Table 3 *Estimated Sound Power Level for Unmuffled Exhaust Noise of Gas Turbine Engine*

Continuous Rating of Engine kW	SWL (in dB re 10^{-12}w) in Octave Bank Central Frequency in Hz							
	63	125	250	500	1k	2k	4k	8k
200-329	120	122	122	121	119	117	113	107
330-529	122	124	124	123	121	119	115	109
530-849	124	126	126	125	123	121	117	111
850-1299	126	128	128	127	125	123	119	113
1300-1999	128	130	130	129	127	125	121	115
2000-3299	130	132	132	131	129	127	123	117
3300-5000	132	134	134	133	131	129	125	119

This problem is aggravated in the change in wavelength of the sound waves due to the increase in the speed of sound brought about by the higher temperatures. The normal treatment is to use dissipative attenuators. When estimating their performance, it is necessary to take into account that the change in wavelength shifts the performance curve towards the higher frequencies, i.e. the attenuator is less effective at low frequencies.

Discharge of the hot gases at the outlet from the turbine takes place with a change of direction, preceded by an initiation of rotation in the fluid. The consequence of this double phenomenon is the occurrence of very strong turbulence which gives rise to wide variations in pressure producing pulsations perceptible at a great distance.

There are several existing techniques to reduce such turbulence. The simplest consists of achieving an aerodynamic route in which flow straighteners and a plenum chamber are used to smooth the gas flow and lower its speed.

It is likewise desirable to provide a vibration break at the turbine outlet in order to prevent the propagation of vibrations from the turbine towards the exhaust circuit. Once all these conditions have been realised, it is possible to decide the most appropriate treatment to reduce the sound energy emitted at the exhaust outlet.

The two types most frequently used are:
1. Zigzag silencers, consisting of plenum chambers installed in series and thus promoting the elimination of low frequencies. The disadvantage of this system is that the pressure drop in these switchbacks is very considerable and may reduce the performance of the gas turbine.
2. Low frequency silencers, consisting of boxes in which splitters of considerable thickness are installed to trap low frequencies, and small splitters very close together to trap high frequencies.

Whichever method is used, strict engineering precautions have to be taken with regard to the engineering.

In fact, the high temperature of the gases (which might sometimes reach 500°C to 600°C during starting up) creates problems of mechanical behaviour, corrosion and expansion.

The material chosen for the splitters must be capable of resisting high temperatures. It must be of sufficient density and of limited dimensions so that it does not compact over a period under the effect of the vibrations.

As the steel sheets forming the casing and the support for the splitters are directly exposed to hot gases, they must be subjected to special treatment and be either stainless or very thick with a suitable coating.

During manufacture it is necessary to bear in mind the problems of expansion which are aggravated by the infill material. Since the latter acts as a good heat insulator, it increases the difference in temperature between the parts directly exposed to the hot gases and those protected by the absorbent material, increasing the problems of differential expansion.

Another important factor in exhaust treatment is possible breakout problems from the exhaust stack. In this case it is necessary to provide acoustic insulation for the exhaust attenuator body, at least in the lower part where the energy is greatest.

Certain designers attempt to improve the performance of exhaust attenuators at low frequencies by combing Helmholtz type resonators with the splitters. These attempts are all too frequently thwarted by a phenomenon called regeneration, which is often neglected by designers. There is, in fact, a limiting rate of flow of gas through an attenuator above which the latter becomes a source of noise due to the aerodynamic noise generated by the airflow.

It is important to remember that certain gas turbines are equipped with waste heat boilers on their exhaust circuits designed to produce steam to operate a steam turbine, a district heating system or energy recuperators to increase the output of the turbines. However, although these boilers and regenerators do provide some degree of natural attenuation, they have shown themselves to be inadequate to achieve low noise criteria. They have a further disadvantage in the acoustic sense of increasing the radiating surfaces participating in noise break-out.

Auxiliary Equipment Of the auxiliary equipment, we can mention the following:
1. Lubrication pumps
2. Electric motors
3. Pneumatic controls
4. The gearbox
5. Relief valves

None of these devices is very noisy compared with other elements of the turbine. They are mostly housed in the enclosure of the turbine so that there is no need to worry about them except in exceptional cases which might require local treatment.

Vibration When compressors or pumps are directly coupled to the power turbine, the amount of vibration set up by gas turbines is very small, particularly if the designers have not allowed displacements significantly greater than 10μ (peak to peak) on leaving the test bench.

The frames on which the equipment rests have a comparatively low natural frequency compared with that of the equipment. It is therefore very unusual to encounter complex problems of vibration, particularly since present methods of calculation make it possible to estimate with great accuracy the critical speed of the shafts. The actual design of the frames and their welded construction also enables modifications to change the natural frequency; it is in fact simple to insert a strut to displace the natural frequency if it is found necessary.

There are, however, cases in which the vibration can affect the acoustic environment of gas turbines. This occurs when there is a step down or step up gearbox between the power turbine and the driven machine, and manifests itself as intensive dynamic excitation of the gearbox pedestal which communicates its energy to the frame assembly and thereby to the enclosure if it rests directly on the latter.

Improvements in gearbox design will reduce these problems. Nevertheless, if vibrations due to the gearbox are present, it will be necessary to take precautions in respect of the acoustic enclosure.

Figure 2. The structure is mounted on an isolating sandwich material

The following illustrations show two possible ways of isolating the structures on which the panels are mounted:

In the first (Fig 2), the structure rests on a sandwich material isolating it from the ground.

In the second (Fig 3), the structure, which should be mounted on a frame rigidly anchored to the ground, is flexibly connected to this frame by means of flexible mounting studs which can distort in tension and in shear.

Figure 3. Here the structure is mounted on a frame rigidly anchored to the ground. It is connected to this frame by flexible mounting studs

A Priori Treatment The following is an example of what has previously been stated and shows how it can be applied in the acoustic treatment of a 25MW gas turbine. All the following elemental sources were revealed following a series of measures (sound power level in dBA) carried out on an identical turbine installed on another site.

	dBA
Body of the machine	107
Gearbox pedestal	114
Opening of burnt gas exhaust stack	95
Housing of the burnt gas exhaust attenuator	102
Ventilation of the cooling circuit – suction	96
delivery	101
Ventilation of the alternator – suction	92
delivery	87
Gas generator intake – intake opeing	93
duct before attenuators	100
duct after attenuators	85
duct perpendicular to attenuators	92

Moreover, measurment of vibration carried out on the concrete block on which the turbine was resting showed high levels in the octave bands centred on 125 and 500Hz. With the aid of all this information, it was necessary to reduce the sound level at 120m to an acceptable level for the vicinity (this being around the NR40 curve).

Using the following formula, it was possible to estimate the soɪ pressure level at 120m:

$$\Sigma \, Np = \Sigma \, Nw - 20 \log d - 8 - R$$

in which Np = sound pressure level at 120m
$\quad\quad$ Nw = sound power level for each elemental source
$\quad\quad\quad$ d = distance separating the source from the measuring point
$\quad\quad\quad$ R = correction coefficient allowing for the directivity of each source, atmospheric absorption, the nature of the ground and the effects of any baffles positioned between the source and the listening point.

Taking into account the high sound levels, the method of separate treatments was rejected in favour of an acoustic enclosure surrounding the main sources. The high levels of vibration made it necessary to isolate the primary structure from the ground by means of a flexible system in order to avoid the panels comprising the enclosure re-radiating this vibrational energy in the form of acoustic energy. The supporting frame for the exhaust attenuator likewise rested directly on the ground and it was necessary to provide a secondary structure which was flexibly connected in order to avoid setting up vibrations in the panels forming the housing. All the ventilation openings were dealt with by means of absorption type attenuators producing only a slight drop in pressure (streamlined baffles) in order to maintain the nominal rates of flow. They were flexibly connected to their supporting frame and the enclosure by means of rubber studs and elastic sleeves.

Heat removal was effected by means of axial flow fans flexibly connected to the hood by rubber studs. Fresh air intakes were provided at the four corners by elbow type attenuators. It was necessary to make them in the form of elbows in order to preserve the appearance of the structure as a whole and to maintain acoustic isolation equal to that provided by the enclosure (other than in relation to the surface area). This also improved their performance at low frequencies.

Figure 4 shows a partial view of this enclosure enabling the sound level at 120m to be reduced to the values shown in the following graph (Fig 5).

Figure 4. Steel enclosure around a 25MW gas turbine generator, designed to meet acoustic specification of NR40 at 120m

Background Noise Rating Curves

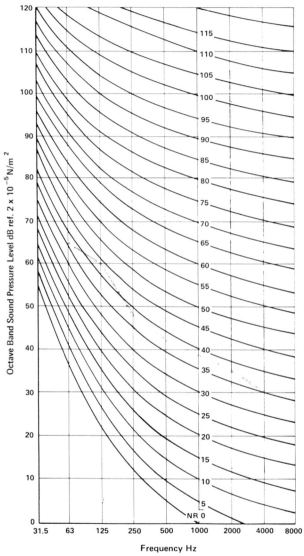

Figure 5. *Sound pressure level measured at 120m*

Plate 1.   A gas compressor station for the British Gas grid system. The gas generators and turbine drivers are extensively silenced to match the quiet rural surroundings. Equipment fitted includes intake attenuators, acoustic enclosures and exhaust attenuators

22
Internal Factory Noise

THE general position in a factory from the noise point of view is that a number of machines (using machine in its broadest sense) are disposed in an area of a building which is usually relatively live or reverberant. There are a number of factors which determine the noise levels in and around such an area. These are the relative positions of the machines, their sizes, how noisy they are individually, the size of the area, and the type of surroundings. These all interact to produce a final result and this chapter will explore the factors and the implications of any changes made for noise control purposes.

The Acoustic Situation On a simplified basis, the situation in a typical factory can be summed up in a diagram (Fig 1) which shows the noise level as a function of distance from a number of different sound sources in a perfectly reverberant space. The different 'plateau' levels are for different values of reverberation time in the room. As the reverberation time is reduced, so the reverberant field noise level between the peaks of direct field from the sources falls off. The lowest curve shows the effect of a low reverberation time – fairly dead surroundings.

The level of the reverberant field where there are multiple sources in an area will be made up by contributions of sound power from each source, so that the resultant is the total sound power level of all the sources. These are added up in the usual way (see Chapter 1). In some cases, the total may accrue from a large number of identical or similar sources, or there may be a small number of dominant sources influencing the total. Careful measurement and logical inspection of the results will reveal which situation it is. This decision on the relative contribution of a number of noise sources is most important as it is the key to the solution of the problem.

The level of noise to which a worker in a typical industrial situation is subjected may arise for three reasonably distinct reasons:

1. The direct field noise from his machinery only, or one very near him.

2. The reverberant field from one or more machines further away from him.

3. In a less than perfect reverberant situation, the combination of the direct field of the nearest machine and the falling off reverberant field of the bulk of the machines.

These are illustrated in Fig 2.

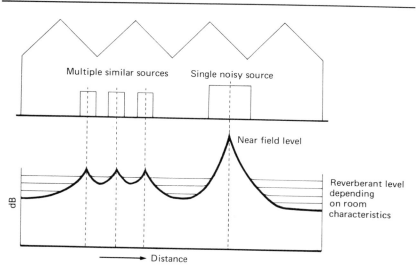

Figure 1. Noise level against distance from source in reverberant surroundings

In practice, the results even in a very reverberant space will be somewhere between the two extremes because the surroundings will not be so perfectly reflective as to give a completely diffuse sound field. In particular, if the central area of a large factory building is filled with a large number of similarly noisy machines, then the 'noise plot' of the area will show a general plateau across the middle with many peaks for the noise sources, but there will be a fall off outside the area towards the walls. This is illustrated in Fig 3.

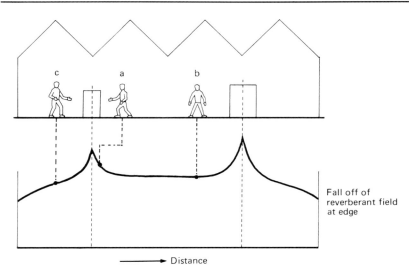

Figure 2. Operator noise levels in reverberant surroundings

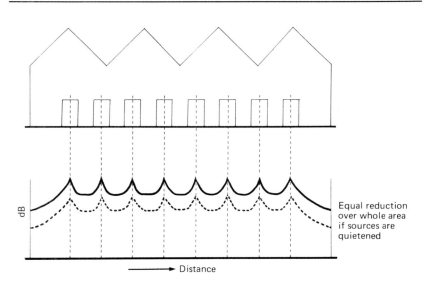

Figure 3. Noise levels from multiple identical machines in reverberant surroundings, showing the effect of noise reduction at source

The effects of the range of different types of noise control will be related in each case to this concept of direct field and reverberant field, and the results illustrated with similar diagrams.

The range of relevant methods of reducing noise is as follows:
a) Reduction at source or by changing the process (see Chapter 11)
b) Reduction by enclosures or screens (see Chapter 12)
c) Reduce reverberation time by adding absorbent (see Chapter 15)

Reductions of Noise Level at Source Any reduction of noise at source by modifying the noise generation mechanisms will have a beneficial effect by reducing the peaks of direct field. If the reduction is made on each of a large number of similar machines, then this reduction in source level will result in a corresponding reduction in the reverberant field. This is illustrated by the lower curve in Fig 3.

If the noise level is dominated by one or more noisy sources, together with other less dominant sources, then reductions of the lower level sources will not have any significant effect on the reverberant level. This is obvious when the charts for decibel addition and subtraction in Chapter 1 are studied. For a similar reason, with a large number of like sources there will be only a small total reduction in the reverberant level if only some of the machines have their noise reduced. Typically, if half of a number of similar machines have individual noise reductions of 10dB applied, or are switched off completely, then the reduction in the reverberant level will be only 3dB. The results of any exercise of this type, where individual noise sources are reduced in level, can be calculated or predicted by reference to the procedures and charts in Chapter 1.

Again, it must be emphasised that a firm understanding of this general principle is essential to any noise control measures in any field. In an industrial situation, there are two 'separate' aspects to consider – the direct and reverberant fields – and this is rather more complex than the simple external noise situation with a number of sound sources in the open air, where only the direct field needs to be considered.

The effects on the immediate operator of reducing the noise of a single machine may or may not be significant or worthwhile, depending on whether he is affected by the direct field of that machine or by the general reverberant level from this and other machines. Usually, no great calculations need to be done and, in most cases, a very simple measurement survey of the area will reveal the situation, particularly if machines can be turned on and off logically and the results observed.

The usual outcome of the survey of a typical noisy area of a factory is that a small number of dominant sources are identified which it may or may not be possible to reduce. If this is possible, and carried out, a larger number of less significant sources are revealed which may then need to be dealt with. The final result is often that there is then a very large number of similar level noise sources, each contributing equally to the noise level. To gain any further significant reduction, all of the sources must be reduced together. With experience, at least the first few steps in this process can be recognised at the start, although in a complex situation it will be necessary to approach the final solution in a series of stages, simply because it is often impossible or impracticable to identify the importance of each contributor to the total. Again, in a practical situation, the experienced noise control engineer will soon recognise that there exists a final overall level below which it is uneconomic or impracticable to go.

Summary Reduction of machine noise levels at source can be a very rewarding exercise in total noise reduction, provided that the limitations of the process are understood. It is very easy for the inexperienced practitioner to recommend spending large sums of money on treatment to a single machine or part of it, when, although noisy, it is not a dominant source and therefore no significant total reduction will result.

Reduction by Enclosures or Screens

Enclosures Putting a correctly designed sound resistant enclosure round a noisy machine will give substantially the same result as reducing the machine noise at source and this method may be more convenient in the case of an existing machine. The advantages and disadvantages of this method have been discussed in Chapter 12. In practice, however, the leakage of noise from the access and cooling apertures means that the noise reduction is less than perfect and the result will be a small reduction of direct and reverberant sound. The exact reduction will depend on the circumstances according to the rules described previously in this chapter. The process of enclosing machines can be reversed and the personnel enclosed in a sound resistant control room, etc. The rules are basically the same as above.

Screens The use of screens or incomplete enclosures is a more complicated subject because the total results depend not only on the original dominance of the individual sources but also on the acoustic environment.

In the open air or very dead (anechoic) conditions, the placing of an acoustic screen or barrier between a noise source and an observer will reduce the received noise level by an amount that can be calculated with reasonable precision. The reduction obtained will depend on the effective height of the barrier above the line joining source to observer, and on the position of the barrier will respect to both. The reduction varies with frequency, being much less at low, than at high frequencies. It is not necessary to construct the barrier of any material more substantial than will give a sound reduction of 5 to 10dB greater than the calculated screening reduction at any frequency, provided that there are no holes in it. It is rare for any acoustic screen to produce more than 10dBA noise reduction in a practical situation.

Unfortunately this screening is nothing like as effective in the reverberant or semi-reverberant conditions found in most internal industrial situations. In a typical reverberant factory, the screening of the direct noise (which is the calculable effect referred to above) usually makes little difference to the noise level affecting personnel. The reverberant or reflected noise 'spreads over' the obstruction with little impediment.

If, for example, at a particular position, the direct and reverberant noise levels are equal and a screen is erected calculated to reduce the direct noise by 10dBA, it is likely that the received noise level at the observer will only be reduced by approximately 3dBA. In a practical case, the final result will probably be less because of reflections round the barrier from adjacent machinery, etc., which were not allowed for in the calculation.

Obviously a range of values will be obtained for the various levels of dominance of direct and reverberant noise in other positions and situations.

Clearly there are cases where an acoustic screen will have a useful effect but this is less often than is generally thought and is dealt with later in this chapter.

Summary Correct enclosure of machines to reduce noise will have substantially the same effect as noise reduction at source.

The use of acoustic screens to reduce noise in a typical reverberant situation if often a waste of money if the installation is applied without very careful assessment.

Modification of the Acoustic Environment by Adding Absorbent So far, this chapter has been generally concerned with reducing the direct noise level affecting an observer. This section deals with reducing the reverberant noise level in a number of ways which all involve adding acoustically absorbent materials to reduce the reverberation time of the area.

It is usually difficult to calculate an accurate reverberation time for a typical factory building using the normal rules applicable to other buildings such as concert halls and offices, etc., but it will probably be in the range 2 to 4 seconds. In reasonably diffuse conditions, a reduction of 3dB in reverberant noise level is produced by a halving of reverberation time, so that a useful result will be obtained if enough absorbent material is added to reduce the reverberation time to a third or a quarter of its original value. Again it must be emphasised that this reduction will only be significant in the correct context where both direct and reverberant contributions are assessed.

The most obvious and useful place to apply a large area of absorbent surface treatment is the roof because it is the largest continuous area apart from the floor (where carpet would not be appropriate in a factory).

In practice, the use of a large area of absorbent material in the roof fairly close to the noise sources has rather more of a beneficial effect than at first sight would seem possible. The main reason in factories is that the low roof height in relation to the floor area means that the normal inverse square law of a 6dB reduction in noise level with a doubling of distance is modified in 'two dimensional spaces' such as those with large absorbent surfaces. The effect is increased if the absorbent material is low over the machines but this usually means a false ceiling which will cut out any natural daylight from the roof lights.

One useful and important modification of this treatment is to substitute 'modular acoustic absorbers' or 'functional absorbers'. These usually consist of flat panels or slabs of acoustic absorbent material hung vertically in a grid or egg crate pattern just above the machines. This treatment is generally the most economical and best way of disposing a given amount of absorbent material in an industrial situation (see Chapter 15).

If the absorbers are coloured white and hung in a sensible pattern, then very little interference with natural light will occur. If a white plastic finish is used, carefully selected so as to degrade the absorbent effect as little as possible, then the absorbers are easily kept clean in most situations. Being very light, they can be suspended simply on thin wires attached to the structural frame without having to be extra careful about their exact position, because this is not critical.

Modular absorbers are of most use in a typical reverberant factory area with a large number of similar machines producing middle and high frequency noise at a level of 85 to 95dBA, where it is not possible for operational reasons to reduce machine noise at source significantly or to enclose machines. This situation is surprisingly common and covers food packaging, printing, small presses, bottling halls, etc. The noise level is often very irritating and objectionable but only marginally, if at all, hazardous.

A reduction overall of 5 to 10dB would be achieved, except at positions very close to individual machines where the immediate direct noise field would be dominant. This small but significant objective noise reduction would be accompanied by a considerably greater subjective improvement than the sound level meter readings would suggest. This phenomenon is well known but not yet fully understood. One suggestion is that people do not like a situation where the noise arrives from all directions (a diffuse field) and prefer to know where the noise originates (direct field).

Because the modular absorber has its greatest absorbent effect at middle and high frequencies, the treatment is not generally appropriate for low frequency noise. It would almost certainly be a waste of money and effort to install them in an area dominated by low frequency noise from large furnaces or fans.

Whilst it has been emphasised that the most effective use of absorbent is on the roof or ceiling of a large area and not the walls, it is often appropriate to treat walls to control local reflections. An example would be a partial enclosure or screen in front of a single noisy machine if there was a wall behind. Application of absorbent treatment to the wall in the immediate area of the machine would reduce degradation of the performance by reflection from the wall. In the same way, the inner side of the screen facing the machine should also be treated for the same reason to reduce reflection to the operator.

Returning to the use of partial enclosures or screens, it was said in a previous section of this chapter that they were generally ineffective in reverberant areas. If the reverberant area is treated first with absorbent roof linings or modular absorbers, then a screen or partial enclosure may become a useful method of further reducing a noise problem. Again, the solution to noise problems in factory areas hinges on the correct assessment of the dominance of individual noise sources and the difference between the direct and reverberant noise at any point.

Summary Reduction of the reverberation time of a factory area by application of absorbent in the form of surface treatment or modular absorbers will have a useful effect if the individual conditions are carefully studied and assessed.

Case Histories As a worked example of the type of calculation covering most of the situations, let us consider a case where 12 machines are going to be installed in one large work area 15m × 12m × 6m (Fig. 4). Let us assume that it has been possible to get access to a prototype machine working in a smaller room 4m × 5m × 3m. In addition, we have been able to estimate the reverberation time for the proposed installation and to measure noise levels around the prototype machine and the reverberation time in the room where it was installed. The data can be summarised as below for one mid frequency octave band. The

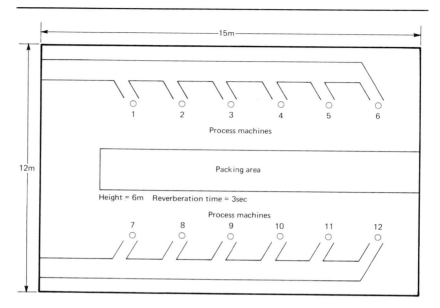

Figure 4. *Plan of workshop showing position of machines and packing area*

other octave bands can be treated similarly and the results summed to give an overall level if required.

	Prototype Machine	Workshop
Number of machines	1	12
Volume of room	60m³	1080m³
Reverberation time	0.5sec	3sec
Mean SPL at points remote from machine	80dB	
SPL at operator's head position	85dB	

1. What will the noise level be at the operator's head position?
2. What will the noise level be at the packing area?
3. Will screens round the packing area reduce the noise level in that area?

4. Will absorbent treatment reducing the reverberation time in the
    workshop make a worthwhile improvement?

. In this example, we have problems of multiple sources and the two
transmission means, i.e. by direct and reverberant paths.

In the measurements on the prototype machine, the noise at the
operator's head position (OHP) was 85dB, compared with the reverberant level of 80dB. From the rule of thumb for level subtraction, it
follows that the direct contribution is about 83dB.

In the large workshop, the reverberant level can be calculated as
shown below. The reverberant level is clearly so high that at the
operator's head position the direct field from the other machines will
not be important.

It is convenient in this calculation to work backwards from the prototype measurements to obtain the sound power level (SWL) of a
single machine by applying the corrections for room size and reverberation time of the small room (see Chapters 4 and 20).

Therefore:

Reverberant SPL of single machine	80dB
Reverberation time 0.5sec	+3dB
Room volume 60m³	+4dB
SWL for single machine therefore	87dB

In the workshop with 12 machines, the total reverberation SPL can be
calculated using the new room corrections in the normal sense.

SWL for single machine	87dB
Correction for 12 machines	+11dB
Room volume 1080m³	−17dB
Reverberation time 3sec	+5dB
Reverberant SPL therefore	86dB

This calculation could have been carried out without going back to
sound power level, by taking the differences between the two room
constants together with the correction for the 12 machines.

Thus the answers to the questions are:

1. At the operator's head position	dB
Reverberant field	86
plus direct field	83
Therefore total field	87

2. In the packing area	
Reverberant field	86
Direct field	negligible

3. In the packing area the sound level is entirely governed by the reverberant level so non-absorbent screens will have no useful effect whatsoever. If absorbent screens are used these will be effective but mainly because of their absorbing effect rather than because they act as screens.

4. If, by the installation of absorbent treatment, we can reduce the reverberation time to 1sec, will the effect be worthwhile? The reverberant field will drop by 5dB (see Chapter 15) so that the totals above are changed as follows:

1. At the operator's head position	dB
Reverberant field	81
plus direct field	83
Therefore total field	85

2. In packing area	
Reverberant field	81

i.e. the increase in absorption has a significant effect on people in the area well away from the machines but gives very little benefit for the individual operator. Whether or not the treatment is economically worthwhile will depend on many other factors.

To illustrate the above situations and methods of treatment, a number of relevant case histories will be quoted, each dealing with one or more of the important factors involved.

The Importance of Silencing the Correct Noise Source A steel stockholder had a problem with noise from a steel coil cut-up line. Coiled steel sheet was unrolled, flattened and cut off to length by a large guillotine in a highly reverberant building. Proposals were in hand for a multi-thousand pound enclosure covering the guillotine completely and having attenuated inlet and outlet tunnels for the material to reduce noise leaking from these points.

A preliminary survey revealed that the majority of the noise was being produced not by the guillotine but by a 'hump' table before the guillotine, employed to take up the slack in the continuously moving steel strip when the guillotine clamps are applied during the cutting stroke. The strip rose in a hump and then crashed on to the rollers of the hump table when the clamps released. These crashes were producing peak levels of up to 107dBA at 2m away from the hump. In contrast, the guillotine produced only 90 to 92dBA and most of this was from the exhaust ports on the pneumatic actuators which could easily be quietened with cheap plastic silencers.

An enclosure around the guillotine would have had absolutely no effect on the total noise problem. The solution adopted to solve the problem was very simple. The table was changed to one having a solid hump surface covered with low friction plastic sheet. The geometry of the hump surface was carefully tailored so that air trapped under the sheet during the last part of the fall cushioned the impact which was then quiet.

The Importance of the Reverberant Field A large food manufacturer was about to build a new packaging factory. Large numbers of identical machines were to be installed under a very low ceiling faced with asbestos cement sheet. The walls and floor were also covered with very highly reflective ceramic tiles. The packaging machines were pneumatically operated with unsilenced air exhausts. A survey in the existing factory of the identical machines confirmed that the acoustic result would be very objectionable high level of middle and high frequency noise throughout the area caused by the reverberant nature of the area.

Recommendations were made that the new area would be an 'acoustic disaster' unless the machines were at least partially silenced and the low ceiling was covered with some form of acoustically absorbent material. Due to economic considerations and the difficulty of finding a suitably hygienic acoustic material, this was not done and the result was as predicted.

Soon afterwards, a further new factory was designed and considerable effort was made to apply hygienically acceptable acoustic absorbent to the low ceilings. Specialised sound absorbent tiles, originally designed for use in operating theatres where similar hygiene problems exist, were used to cover all ceiling and some wall surfaces. In addition, as many as possible of the air exhaust ports were silenced with inexpensive plastic silencers. The final result was very satisfactory indeed compared with the previous factory.

Plate 1. Modular absorbers suspended from the roof in an automatic lathe area to reduce the reverberant noise level. In this form modular absorbers can be an inexpensive method of reducing irritating middle and high frequency noise levels

23
Trucks and Tractors

THIS chapter is based on experience with road vehicles. However, the principles are equally true for all commercial plant, e.g. cranes, earth-movers, quarry machines. The design of the machine will obviously affect the relative importance of the various noise sources but experience shows various recurring problems which will be detailed later in the chapter. The following basic subjects will be covered:

Noise Standards
This is a brief discussion of the present standards for noise in and outside vehicles. Methods of making noise measurements are discussed.

Noise Sources
A description is given of the various noise sources and mechanisms and their importance.

Transmission Paths
The various transmission paths by which noise enters the cab are detailed and their importance assessed.

Methods of Control
Recommendations and details of methods for noise control are given for use in design and remedial work.

Noise Standards
External Noise Most countries have standards for external noise emission from vehicles. In Britain this is given in the 'Construction and Use' regulations and permits a noise level of 81dBA at 7.5m from

an unladen vehicle under specified test conditions. Other international codes vary within a range of approximately ± 2dBA of this figure. EEC regulations vary with the installed engine power and on highway or off highway use. These levels are continually being reviewed downwards. They represent a practical limit with present technology. It can be expected that these noise levels will be gradually reduced as technology improves and quieter engines are produced, and it is with this in mind that the government has in the past sponsored various programmes of development of quiet engines.

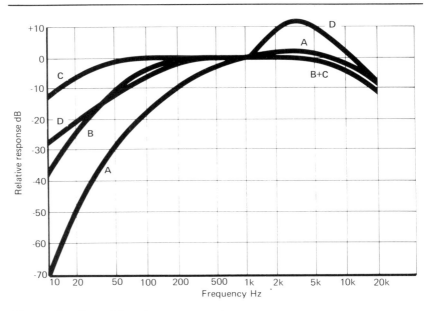

Figure 1. Sound level meter, weighting curves

Internal Noise In Britain, the only standard applying generally to vehicle internal noise is the Noise at Work Regulations. This is intended primarily for factory noise and gives a limit of 90dBA L_{eq} with an action level at 85dBA L_{eq} and is designed to avoid hearing damage. This takes no account of any effects on driver performance, i.e. loss of concentration, and hence it is open to debate whether this is a suitable target criterion. Research on the effects on driver performance has been negligible and hence it is difficult to make recommendations for suitable criteria. However, psychological tests in the past have not shown any measurable effects of noise on reaction time, etc., below 80dBA. 80dBA is also a level which may be achieved in cabs practically and therefore it is recommended that this is a good level to work to in design. This level cannot readily be achieved in remedial work on many existing cab designs and therefore it will be some time before such a level can be enforced. It has become a generally accepted practice to measure noise levels by placing the microphone at approximately 200mm from the centre of the driver's head level with the ear. The microphone is normally positioned to face forwards. Noise levels are made in dBA L_{eq} as this is a measurement which can be related to hearing damage work. However, subjective effects noted by Sound Research Laboratories (SRL) and other workers indicate that this does not give sufficient weighting to higher frequencies. The 'D' weighting, which was developed primarily for jet aircraft noise assessment, has been suggested as a useful alternative as this weights the 500Hz, 1kHz, 2kHz frequency region (Fig 1), which corresponds to the effects of diesel knock. However, this is not confirmed and it is as well to gather as much information as possible by making octave band sound level measurements.

Noise Sources

Engine The obvious major noise source, both external and internal, in any commercial vehicle is the engine. Reduction of noise emission from the engine therefore has a double benefit of reducing both external and internal noise simultaneously. This is the area in which a considerable amount of research has been, and is being, carried out. However, quiet diesel engines have not yet been constructed on a commercial basis so other methods must be applied at present.

Research has shown that a rough formula for the noise emission by the engine is:

$$I_0 \propto N^n B^5$$

where I_0 = overall engine noise in dBA
N = engine speed
B = bore
n = constant for type of engine

This shows that the noise is largely dependent on the speed and the bore, i.e. given two similar engines, a slower revving, smaller bore, engine is likely to be quieter. This may be found useful in selection of the most suitable engine when purchasing a vehicle. There is little that can be done to an existing vehicle to improve the engine noise.

Peripheries A considerable proportion of the general engine noise emission can be caused by the essential peripheries on the engine. In particular, the compressor and the fuel pump/injector system can cause high noise levels near to body panels. The operating principles of the majority of these parts are usually very similar. If a choice is available in make of these parts, the manufacturer should be consulted and asked to provide noise emission levels.

Wind Although the majority of commercial vehicles are very badly shaped aerodynamically and do create turbulence which produces noise, this is rarely a major contributor to external or internal noise. This is because other noise sources create higher noise levels. However, if in-cab noise levels are reduced to the region of 75dBA, wind noise will begin to be important.

The use of deflector panels mounted on the cab roof is designed to reduce drag and will not have a significant effect on cab noise levels except in very severe wind conditions where buffeting may be reduced, thus reducing any drumming noise on the cab roof.

Vibration Vibration from the road and from the engine is transmitted around the chassis structure and then radiated by the cab panels as noise. Except in extreme cases where something loose vibrates when the vehicle is on a rough road, this does not cause external noise problems. However, the engine vibration can cause a significant level of noise in the cab. Road vibration appears to make only a minor contribution to the in-cab noise levels. Measurements by SRL on the road show that, in the 31.5 and 63Hz octave bands, appreciable peaks can be measured, but at frequencies above these and on an 'A' weighted scale, there is little effect. On the 'A' weighted scale the difference between a vehicle running 'on the governors' in a low gear and the highest gear is of the order of 1dBA. Calculations predict that in the majority of standard vehicles the road induced noise levels are of the order of 75dBA. These are, however, steadily coming down.

As stated before, the engine vibration can contribute significantly to the internal noise levels. This obviously depends very much on the engine mounts but it is almost impossible to select mounts to give good isolation through the entire frequency band. Selection of engine mounts is at present very much a trial and error exercise.

Tyres Tyre noise is a high frequency noise generated at the contact area between the tyre and the road. This noise is directional and is directed away from the cab from which it is shielded by the tyre itself. It is therefore not a significant noise source within the cab. Until recently, tyre noise has not been considered important externally. One tyre manufacturer has, however, measured external noise and recorded levels of 80dBA at under 30mph in heavy rain. This indicates that, although this is still a minor contributor to external levels at present, it will become a major factor if engine noise research work is successful and the legal standard in the external noise test is lowered.

Cooling The importance of fan noise varies greatly between vehicles. It has been found on some earth movers that up to 50% of external noise is due to the fan. SRL have measured a 2dBA reduction in noise inside a 32ton tractor unit when a thermostatically controlled fan is switched off, implying a 30% reduction in energy. Fan noise has a subjectively annoying pure tone and can therefore cause noise problems without giving a measurable increase in overall noise levels. The fan is usually well enclosed on road vehicles and is rarely a major source of external noise.

Inlet and Exhaust Noise Inlet noise can be a major contributor to internal noise but rarely has an effect on external noise. This is because, where an unsilenced inlet is used, the air cleaners are usually on top of the engine, near the floor, but well screened from outside. Where remote type cleaners are used, the cleaner itself usually provides sufficient attenuation. Exhaust noise, provided the silencer is maintained in good condition, can be reduced to the point where it is approximately equal to the general engine noise level. However, in practice the silencer will often deteriorate and the exhaust will become the major noise source.

Internally, exhaust noise is insignificant if the exhaust is carried back along the vehicle chassis. Petroleum regulations call for the exhaust to be in front of the fire screen so that, for vehicles covered by these regulations, this often leads to the exhaust outlet being just under the driver's door. With the window closed and a properly fitting door, this makes no difference to the measured noise level. With the window open, on the majority of roads, this is a minor contribution to the noise levels. In heavily built up areas with narrow streets, the reflected external noise becomes a major contribution to the internal noise levels at the driver's ear, and if the exhaust outlet is on the driver's side this will be a significant proportion of the external noise on that side.

It has been noted by SRL that in cases where the exhaust is under the driver's door there are more complaints from the drivers than measurements would lead one to expect. This is worth considering in design and, if this arrangement cannot be avoided, the system should preferably be 'oversilenced'.

It has also been noted that drivers comment that the exhaust outlet is preferable behind the front wheel rather than in front. This is not borne out by measurements or theory. The distance from the exhaust to the driver's ear is identical in either case, and the speed of the lorry is low compared with the speed of sound, so there is no significant effect of 'leaving the noise behind'. This effect can be explained to some extent in that the forward exhaust tends to be close to the door seal, which may be acoustically weak, whereas the exhaust behind the wheel may be screened from the driver by the mudguard.

Transmission Noise Gearbox noise is included under engine noise as this is one unit and treatment usually affects both, although the gearbox noise is usually insignificant compared with the engine noise. Differential noise is not important as regards internal cab noise due to the separation of the differential from the cab. It is a minor external noise source at present, but may become significant as diesel engine noise is reduced or on off highway vehicles.

The importance of these noise sources can be summed up as in Table 1:

Transmission Paths
Seals In every vehicle there are a large number of seals, seams and gaps around services entering or leaving the cab. These may or may not be opened during regular maintenance. In SRL's experience, these

Table 1

Noise Source	Internal	External
Engine	Major noise source	Major noise source
Peripheries	Significant noise source when located near floor or bonnet panels	Negligible
Wind	Negligible	Negligible
Vibration	Major noise source due to engine vibration	Negligible
Tyres	Negligible	Significant noise source, will become major problem as engine noise decreases
Cooling fan	Varies between 0 and 50% of overall noise level	Significant noise source on road vehicles, major noise source when not enclosed, i.e. earth movers
Inlet	Significant low frequency noise source	Negligible, except where turbocharger used, when it may become significant
Exhaust	Minor noise source except when silencer old or placed next to worn door seal	Major noise source
Transmission	Negligible	Minor noise source, may become important as engine noise decreases

have been the major path by which noise enters the cab interior. As yet, they are unimportant in external noise considerations as there are no vehicles with engines so fully enclosed that small gaps will cause any loss in acoustic performance.

The decibel scale is logarithmic so that if a panel is inserted with half open and half closed area, between a noise source and the receiver, the drop in noise level at the receiver will be 3dB. If the panel is quarter open, three quarters closed, the reduction is only 6dB. Where slits of one tenth of the panel area are open, the reduction is 10dB and for one hundredth open area the reduction is 20dB, minus any extra noise through the panel itself. It can easily be seen that, if a vehicle is constructed with a number of bonnet panels, a large proportion of the noise energy emitted by the engine is incident on these panels and the joints between them. Therefore, even if the gaps at the joints are only one hundredth of the area of the bonnet, the reduction between the engine and the cab is limited to approximately 20dB. For a vehicle with noise levels in the engine compartment in the region of 115 to 120dBA, this limits the noise level in the cab to 85/90dBA.

Typical improvements that may be achieved by attention to seals and seams are up to 5dBA at the driver's ear in new vehicles, or 10dBA in extreme cases in old vehicles.

This reduction of 10dBA on old vehicles is important as this will very easily undo any good work carried out in other directions. It is almost inevitable that certain panels will become deformed after being removed many times for maintenance, especially if they are difficult to reposition. Where possible, seals should be sufficiently compliant to allow for some error in replacement of the panel and the panels themselves should be designed such that they can easily be refitted correctly. In extreme cases, if the panels are very difficult to reposition and are not obviously essential, there is a strong possibility that they will not be replaced at all. This obviously will have major consequences on the acoustic performance of the cab structure.

The position of the seal is a major factor in how important a link in the structure that seal will be. It often happens that the bonnet seal is placed very close to a major noise source on the engine, such as the top cover, manifold or air intake. This subjects the seal to very high noise levels and, if it is not a good seal, it will become a major weak link in the structure.

Cab Structure As was explained in Chapter 5, the insulation provided by a panel of material usually follows the pattern shown in Fig 2. At low frequencies the sound reduction index varies as the stiffness of the panel is varied. As the stiffness is increased, the low frequency sound reduction increases. At higher frequencies the sound reduction index is controlled by the mass of the panel; as the mass is increased so the sound reduction index increases. Above this region is the coincidence region, where the wavelength of the incident sound coincides with waves in the panel itself and a decrease in the sound reduction index is noted, known as the coincidence dip.

In the majority of vehicles, it is rare to find a panel which is not pressed and is therefore not stiff, except for the roof. Low frequency drumming, or resonance, is usually not experienced and there is usually little to be gained by stiffening the panels. When a panel is stiffened, this has the effect of moving the resonant frequencies up the frequency scale

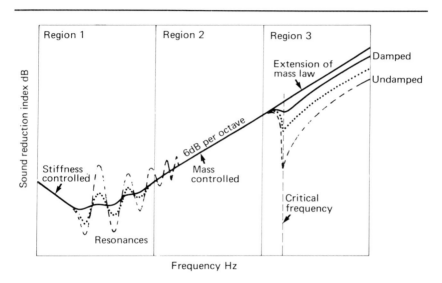

Figure 2. Transmission characteristics of a panel

and may indeed cause new problems by moving these into a sensitive frequency region. In such a situation, damping materials applied to the panels may be found very effective. These damping materials will also have an added effect of increasing the mass of the panel, thereby improving the performance in the second region – the mass control region. The coincidence dip may be shifted up or down the frequency range by increasing or decreasing the stiffness, altering the boundary conditions or changing the thickness of the material. However, this will remain a problem at the majority of frequencies and can most easily be overcome by making a double skin construction with panels of different thickness or material, or by fitting barrier materials with foam or felt sandwiched between them which provides a partial double skin effect.

The design of the majority of vehicle cabs is such that waves can propagate around the entire cab, hence causing resonances in the cab structure. This is usually best tackled at the design stage as it may often be required that mounting points should be modified.

Windows At present the windows are estimated to give only a small contribution to the total internal cab noise levels. Calculations show that, if the bonnet and floor panels were treated sufficiently to reduce the noise effectively through these areas, the top of the cab structure and windows would limit the noise levels inside the cab. This assumes no treatment to the engine and appears to have been borne out as a limit to noise reduction in some of the better trucks.

Heater The heater air ducts have often proved to be a limit in remedial treatment to internal cab noise at approximately 85dBA. These are traditionally situated with the air intakes near the fan, under the dashboard. Levels of approximately 100dBA have been measured at the inlet to heater ducts, and 115 to 120dBA are typical noise levels at the fan just underneath the ducts. There is usually very little room provided for attenuation in these ducts as the requirement is for a large volume of air from a low pressure fan. These can therefore be a very significant noise source in the cab. Experiments by SRL on mock-up cabs have shown that large reductions in noise transmission through heaters could be achieved by repositioning heater intake ducts. With the advent of air conditioning systems for cabs, it is expected that packaged units situated on the cab roof should become a feature of cabs. It should be ensured in the design of these that attenuation for fan noise is included.

Pedals It is very difficult to provide gaiters that will always give a good acoustic seal behind the pedals and the floor where large travels on the pedal are required, as in the traditional foot pedal arrangement. Where possible, air controlled pedals should be used such that only air lines need penetrate the cab structure.

These can easily be sealed. Where the traditional type pedal with long travel is required, an attenuator principle should be used to provide an attenuated passage for the pedal to travel through. This is a long passage fitted closely around the pedal stalk filled with acoustic absorbent materials.

Methods of Control
Engine As stated before, reduction of noise from the engine has the double benefit of reducing both external and internal noise of the vehicle. This approach has therefore been encouraged by the government and considerable amounts of research have been carried out on this. The main noise emitting areas on engines have been identified and a formula, as given before, developed to predict engine noise. The

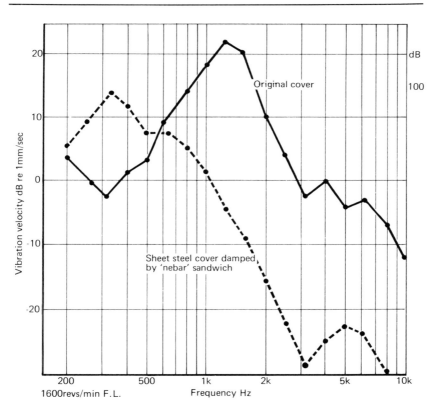

Figure 3. *Averaged results of vibration of rocker cover*

main noise emitting areas on the engine are the top cover, the front plate and the sump. Some engines have already been produced with these parts pressed from naturally damped materials such as sound deadened steel. This is a sandwich of two steel sides with a bitumastic compound between them (Fig 3). Damping compounds, as mentioned previously in the section on the cab structure, can also be used. These

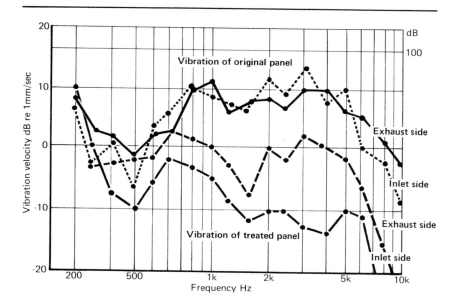

Figure 4. *Crankcase and water jacket panels – close shields on both sides of small diesel engine (3000rpm, full load)*

treatments will give effective reductions, sometimes up to approximately 7dBA. However, at present there are few damping compounds which will stand up to the conditions experienced on diesel engines and, unless specially pressed parts are made for the particular engine, this is a very expensive exercise.

Close shielding techniques are another current approach. A shaped panel of glass fibre or similar material is fitted approximately 10mm away from the engine, held to the engine by isolating mounts, sometimes with acoustic absorbent material sandwiched between the engine and the panel. This can be arranged with several panels to cover the entire engine area and makes a very effective barrier (Fig 4). Its main fault lies in the fact that the panels must be removed for maintenance and are difficult to replace, and therefore tend not to be replaced after a few maintenance runs.

Total redesign of the engine is the approach being followed at present. An engine has been constructed which consists of a basic frame with

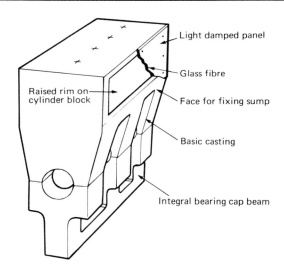

Figure 5. Experimental quiet engine

bolt-on jackets which form the oil and water casings (Fig 5). These jackets can be constructed of a deadened compound and can be to some extent isolated from the main frame. Reductions of the order of 10dBA have been achieved by such designs. There are still problems of cost, production techniques, wear, etc., to be overcome.

Other methods, for example the redesign of injectors and combustion chambers to give a smoother burn, are being tested.

There are, therefore, quieter engines on the way. However, it will be several years before such engines are commercially available. The designer should therefore, at present, be designing with existing engines in mind.

Encapsulation Moving away from the engine, the logical next step to reduce noise, particularly external noise, is to encapsulate the engine. This implies building a complete enclosure round the engine, and providing absorption within the enclosure to reduce noise levels within the enclosure itself. Ideally the enclosure should be a totally separate body from the remainder of the cab structure and experiments in America along these lines have produced reductions of the order of 15dBA externally. However, such enclosures require a large amount of space to be used and, with most vehicles being designed to take a number of different types of engine, can very rapidly become uneconomically large. Some vehicles have been produced with part encapsulation. This usually consists of panels above the chassis members and up to the floor, and small panels below the chassis members. This is designed to reduce external noise in the main. However, it tends also to reduce internal noise by reducing the noise level at the floor panels and hence the noise breaking through the floor area. Reductions of the order of 4dBA in external noise may be achieved by such panels.

Unfortunately, encapsulation methods suffer from the same problems as close shielding in that the panels are difficult to replace, and in the workshop, where time is at a premium, they tend to be discarded. This is to some extent a problem of education in that the mechanics very rarely appreciate the results of omitting these panels.

The use of acoustic absorptive materials, as used in enclosures, may also be applied under the engine covers. Reductions of up to 5dBA have been achieved by simply providing absorption in the upper half of the engine compartment and hence reducing noise build up within this compartment. Acoustic absorptive materials can also become oil absorptive and hence they can be major fire risks within the engine compartment. This can be overcome by using foams with skinned surfaces. The skins used must be very thin to prevent loss of acoustic performance and obviously must be strong enough to withstand wear during servicing.

Fan and Cooling Systems As was stated earlier, experiments on earth movers and such vehicles have shown that fan noise can be up to 50% of the total radiated noise from the engine. The fan therefore merits attention at present and, as engines are quietened, will become a major noise source and therefore must be considered.

The noise generated by a fan varies roughly as the fifth power of the blade tip speed. This means that for a small increase in fan speed, a large increase in noise level may be noted. The position of fans in most vehicles, i.e. very close to the radiator and also to the front of the engine, is far from ideal and reduces the efficiency of the fan itself by up to 50%. There is therefore a large improvement in noise levels to be gained by increasing the efficiency of the fan as the first stage.

Any obstruction placed near a fan blade will cause a distinct pure tone noise at the blade passage frequency – that is the frequency at which blades pass a given point. At about 2200rpm for a six bladed fan, this gives a tone in the region of 250Hz. There is also a considerable broad band noise generated by airflow and these two components tend to balance equally in producing the overall noise level. The fan should therefore be located as far away as possible from any fixed objects and the spacing between the radiator and fan should be as large as possible. Reductions of the order of 2 to 3dBA have been achieved by increasing the distance between fan and radiator from 100mm to 200mm. A similar reduction of 2 to 3dBA has also been achieved by increasing the distance between the fan and the engine by the same amount. All objects such as radiator hoses should be routed as far away as possible from the fan.

The use of a shroud to direct airflow through the fan is essential. If this is not used, turbulent flow will result around the blade tips and recirculation of air around the fan can reduce the efficiency of the fan markedly. The design of the shroud itself can alter the efficiency and noise generation of the fan considerably. Optimum airflow and noise performance appears to be achieved with approximately a 60% coverage of the fan (see Fig 6). The clearance from the tips to the shroud is also important. As this clearance is decreased, the noise level is reduced and the airflow is increased. Hence optimum efficiency and lowest noise levels may be achieved by having as small a clearance as

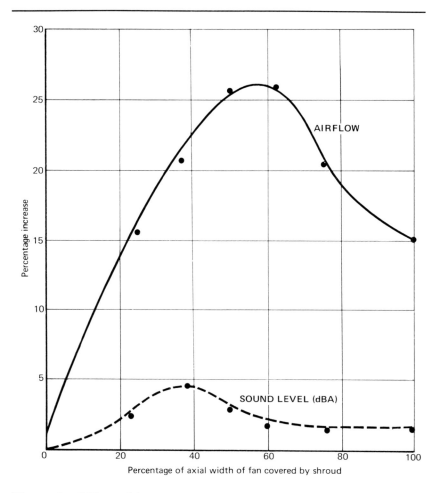

Figure 6. *Effect of fan average on airflow and noise (fan speed held constant) after International Harvester Co of Great Britain Ltd*

possible. In typical mounting conditions where the shroud is fixed to the radiator and fan obviously to the engine, this small clearance is difficult to achieve due to movement of the two related to each other. However, improved clearance could be achieved by mounting the shroud as part of the engine assembly so that the shroud moves with the engine. It is important that if this type of assembly is adopted the shroud should seal closely to the radiator as the pressure drop across a radiator tends to be high, therefore small leaks can reduce the efficiency of the system drastically. The shroud should be designed to give as good an air distribution across the radiator surface as possible. Cylindrical type and venturi type shrouds (see Fig 7) tend to give better air distribution than the orifice type box shroud. Increasing the distance between the fan and the radiator when used in conjunction with a shroud obviously helps to improve the air distribution across the radiator. Hence reducing the airflow required allows a reduction in the size or speed of the fan.

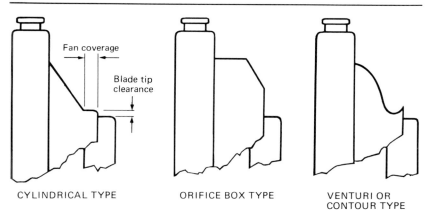

CYLINDRICAL TYPE   ORIFICE BOX TYPE   VENTURI OR
                                                          CONTOUR TYPE

Figure 7. Typical fan shrouds

Conventional fans are not well designed aerodynamically. The blades are of uniform thickness and are considerably less aerodynamically efficient than contoured cross-sections. The spider or central portion of the fan is not aerodynamically designed so that air over this portion produces turbulence and noise. Rivets used to attach the blades to the spider also disturb the airflow over the blades and increase drag. However, the potential improvement in performance gained by improved aerodynamic design is severely compromised by the environment in which the fan must operate and hence the increased cost of producing such aerodynamic fans is not fully justified at present.

A further method of noise control which may be considered is increasing the temperature of the coolant in the radiator. The heat rejection,

Q, for a given radiator design is approximately proportional to the square root of the airflow, $\sqrt{q}$, and to the temperature difference, ΔT, between the incoming coolant and the incoming air. The airflow is proportional to the fan rpm and the fan sound level is proportional to the fifth power of the tip speed. Combining these results, we find that:

$$\text{SPL(dBA)} \; \alpha \; 100 \; \log_{10} \frac{Q}{\Delta T}$$

thus a small increase in coolant temperature can bring about a large reduction in fan sound level. However, increasing the temperature of the coolant either requires the use of specialised coolants, e.g. ethylene glycol, or pressurizing the system further, and unless carried out during the design of the vehicle this is not economically viable.

Conventionally the fan is fixed to the engine either directly on the crank shaft or via belt drive, which means that the fan runs at a fixed ratio to the engine speed. For a large proportion of the time the fan is running unnecessarily and coolant temperatures lower than design are often encountered. The engine therefore runs inefficiently, power is wasted in driving the fan, and unnecessary noise is generated. One fairly simple method of reducing the airflow through the radiator when lower volumes are required is to fit variable shutters which close when airflow is not required. These tend to make the fan run in a stall condition when they are closed and hence can increase the noise level from the fan. Increases of up to 5dBA may be caused by running the fan in this condition. The shutters themselves reduce noise radiated from the front of the vehicle but internal noise levels may be severely affected by such shutters. Variable speed fan drives are by far preferable. These take several forms. One type senses the temperature of the air behind the radiator and switches the drive and the fan off altogether when the temperature is low enough, hence reducing fan noise and wasted power consumption. Other types vary the fan speed by altering the amount of slip in the drive, therefore the fan will be running most of the time with varying degrees of slip. This can result in large reductions in noise level. For instance, a reduction of the fan rpm to 44% of maximum design rpm can give a noise level reduction of 20dBA.

Increasing the surface area of the radiator can also give reductions by reducing the pressure loss across the radiator for a given airflow. Hence the noise emission can also be reduced.

Another method of reducing fan noise being considered at present is the use of remote cooling systems. These have several advantages – one that the cooling system may be moved away from the engine compartment, hence enclosure of the engine can be made simpler. Secondly, conventional air conditioning type fans may be used. These are generally far more efficient than vehicle fans and therefore should consume less power. Thirdly, conventional air conditioning type attenuators may be used before the radiator and after the fan to reduce external noise emission from the fan, hence reducing the noise problem. Also the cab ventilation system may be combined with the cooling system as one package, hence reducing the need for a separate radiator and separate fan for the cab system. The major disadvantages in remote systems are that the only position generally feasible to situate such a system is on the cab roof. This necessitates using electric fans and hence a generator must be attached to the engine to provide sufficient current for this, which brings with it additional servicing problems. Also, if the assembly is mounted on the cab roof, the filler point for the cooling system must be at this height and problems occur for daily checking of the water level. Hence it is unlikely that this type of system will be adopted until noise levels from the engine itself have been reduced to such an extent that the fan noise becomes very important.

Engine Mounts Selection of engine mounts is at present very much a trial and error exercise. Engine mounts themselves are simply vibration isolators as described in Chapters 6 and 14. They are selected to give a natural frequency of the order of 5Hz. This implies that the static deflection is of the order of 12mm (½in). 5Hz corresponds to 300rpm and it is unlikely that any engine will be running at this speed. However, it will pass through this point when starting and stopping. The engine mount deflection must therefore be limited to prevent excessive rocking at this speed. The natural frequency could only be reduced if a buffer was provided to prevent excessive movement of the engine. However, this would also prevent the engine moving under high acceleration or braking loads and would effectively 'short circuit' the engine mounts by providing a rigid connection between the engine and the chassis when the isolation was most badly needed. So the compromise choice of a mount with a natural frequency below tickover speed, but high enough to give a low deflection and acceptably small movement of the engine is usually taken.

A vehicle is in fact a very complicated system. The engine-engine mount-chassis-suspension-wheels-tyres-road gives a mass-spring-mass-spring-mass-spring-fixed configuration. This makes it almost impossible to predict how the resonant frequencies in the various modes of movement will interact with each other. It is almost inevitable that there will be certain resonances. For example, Fig 8, shows graphs of the difference in vibration (in dB) across the front and rear engine mount on a 15cwt forward control van, and the ideal

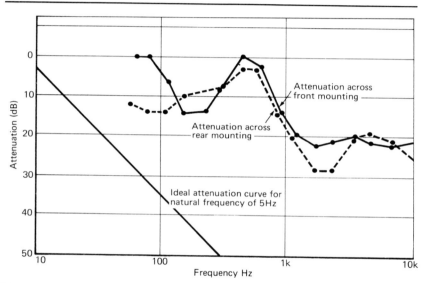

Figure 8. Vibration attenuation across engine mountings in a 15cwt forward control van

attenuation for these mounts which have a 5Hz natural frequency. It shows that at 500Hz there was no actual attenuation across the front mount and only 3 to 4dB across the rear mount. In this case a peak in the 500Hz octave band was measure inside the vehicle. Trial and error experiments obviously will enable mounts to be selected which, if a weak point is unavoidable, can give this weak point at a point of frequency where the vibration in the engine is at a minimum.

Inlet and Exhaust A considerable amount of noise is emitted from the inlet to the engine. This is generally in a 125Hz frequency range and is therefore difficult to attenuate normally. Inlet attenuators are available and have been used with some success, however the problem is often overcome automatically by the presence of a turbocharger. The turbocharger reduces low frequency noise. It does add high frequency tones to the noise but these may easily be attenuated.

Exhaust noise may be attenuated by standard silencers. Care should be taken that long runs of flexible pipe are not used except where essential as these tend to emit a large amount of noise. As was noted earlier, exhaust noise tends to be a factor remarked upon by drivers and it subjectively seems to be more annoying than measurements bear out. It is therefore worthwhile oversilencing systems, particularly as this is a part of the system which deteriorates rapidly. It can therefore be expected that in normal use silencers are not up to new specifications.

Design of Cab and Position of Engine Design requirements for as short a unit as possible call for the cab to be mounted directly above the engine. Many foreign cabs and some newer British cabs overcome noise problems internally by lifting the cab well above the engine. This also provides easy access for servicing and maintenance on the engine and provides a larger and more comfortable cab. With this sort of arrangement the floor can be made as one unit and may be made double skinned where possible, hence reducing the noise transmitted through the floor. Any access panels through the floor for oil checks, etc., must be made as small as possible. Older type cabs were situated lower with the engine therefore coming within the cab itself. These have obviously been associated with noise problems due to sealing problems round the various removable panels and simply by having a large area of bodywork exposed to high noise levels within the cab itself. However, careful design of such cabs with regard to noise insulation from the design stage should be able to provide such a cab with a reasonable noise environment. The cab should be designed to tilt as far forward as possible to minimise the number of servicing operations which have to be carried out through the bonnet itself. A heavier construction, or double skinning, of the bodywork panels around the engine can provide good noise insulation and careful attention to detail in the manufacture and design of seals on any opening panels can give good reductions.

Traditionally a weak point in such cabs has been the underside of the dashboard above the fan. This allows noise breakthrough into the dashboard and ventilation ducts from where the noise is distributed through the cab. More attention to detail in design of this area could result in significant reductions. This may also be overcome by situating the engine as far back as possible. This obviously improves access for servicing but in this situation care must be taken with the construction of the back of the cab, particularly where box type bodies may be used, to prevent noise being reflected up between the cab and box fans and being transmitted through the rear windows. In this situation, double glazing of the rear windows could be considered as a method of reducing noise.

Earlier comments about the positioning of intakes for heater ducts, etc., should be noted as even small holes in areas where the external noise levels are high may cause severe weakness in the cab structure.

Acoustic absorptive material in the form of headlinings and linings up the back of the cab can give a very useful subjective effect. These will reduce the high frequency content of the noise which is the familiar diesel 'knock' sound and therefore give a more pleasant tone to the noise within the cab, although on a dBA measurement they give little reduction. Such treatments should be at least 25mm (1in) thick and preferably thicker to give a useful reduction at the mid frequency range.

Proprietary barrier mats may be used to great effect as these require little space and can also be made to overlap on to other panels, giving a useful seal over any joints. Such treatments are also very useful at a remedial stage where obviously double skinned bodywork panels are difficult and expensive to produce for small runs. Reductions of up to 12dBA in internal noise levels have been achieved by the use of the barrier materials and certain vibration damping and acoustic absorptive materials in the cab.

As mentioned previously, road induced vibration in the cab structure and engine induced vibration can contribute to internal noise levels. This can be treated by mounting the cab on vibration isolators from the chassis thereby reducing vibration from both sources. This is obviously a measure to be undertaken at design stage. Barrier materials again can be useful as these will give a certain amount of vibration damping effect on the panels at the same time as performing their prime task of giving improved sound insulation. However, great care should be taken in the selection of these materials as it has been found on occasions that such materials can worsen the situation by resonating, often in the 125Hz region.

Examples On vehicles where the engine is mounted within the cab, i.e. a low cab type vehicle, the seal around bonnet covers, etc., are especially important. This was demonstrated in work carried out by SRL on a bus: a front engined Midi Bus powered by a four cylinder engine mounted with the top of the engine above the floor level. The covers over the engine were relatively small however. They simply sat on the floor, with very little to seal them to the floor. Simple replacement of seals to provide an airtight seal to the floor and from one cover to the other gave an improvement of 5dBA measured at the driver's position. Further attention to detail in seals around the cab area, and some improvement of the bonnet structure by adding barrier materials gave a further 2dBA reduction in the cab area. Very small gaps along a number of seals caused a serious weakness in the overall noise insulation of the cab.

In the extreme situation, a standard vehicle five years old was treated. This vehicle had a large number of glass fibre panels which make up the bonnet. These were awkward to replace and hence over the five years had deteriorated to such an extent that any seals which may have been fitted had been lost and the panels had not been refitted correctly. In this case improvement of the panels, provision of effective seals, and modifications to refit the panels correctly gave a reduction of the order of 10dBA in peak noise levels.

The American Department of Transportation, in hopes of a quick solution to noise from existing engines and vehicles, sponsored a programme into noise reduction from the heaviest and most powerful vehicles in use in the USA. Generally, the method used was encapsulation of the engine which involved modification of the cooling and exhaust systems. One of the vehicles used was a truck powered by a Cummins NCT350 engine which develops 350bhp. As the truck had been designed to take engines up to 500bhp, this left a considerable amount of space around the engine. This was useful as the space could be used to duct cooling air across the engine and out of the back without imposing too great a back pressure on the fan (See Fig 9).

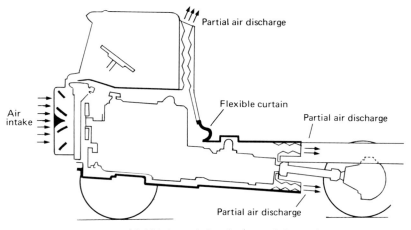

a) Initial theoretical engine/transmission enclosure

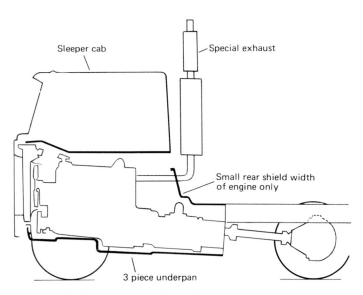

b) Enclosure as actually fitted in American investigations

Figure 9. Experimental engine enclosures

This encapsulation, combined with a kit made by Cummins which consists of glass fibre and steel shields on the sides of the engine and around the sump, an isolated induction manifold and a damped valve cover, gave a reduction on the American SAE test from 85dBA in standard form to 72dBA. Moreover, during full power tests, a noise level of only 74dBA was measured in the cab. This is an exceptional reduction. However, it requires a significant amount of space around the engine which is rarely found in British lorries. The kit also weighs between 450 and 500lb and was costly to manufacture on a production basis.

The reductions that may be achieved by raising the cab above the engine have been demonstrated in a number of cases. For example, a vehicle giving a peak internal noise levels of 78dBA. This satisfies the criterion of 80dBA given earlier and shows that this criterion can be reached with a margin to spare.

Summary Internal noise levels in vehicles may be reduced by present methods. These will give levels which, if not totally acceptable on a comfort basis, can almost certainly provide an environment in which driver concentration is not impaired and excessive fatigue is avoided. This is mainly an exercise in design for noise insulation but, as with any noise control, remedial measures are always more difficult and give less return.

External noise rightly has been, and is still, the subject of research and will be an altogether slower process than reducing internal noise. This is almost inevitably a design problem and very little can be done as a remedial measure to improve external noise without impairing accessibility to the engine for service. Hence designers of engines and vehicles should be making a major point of designing for lower external noise levels.

Plate 1. Acoustic measurements being undertaken in an anechoic test cell to ascertain noise levels from a vehicle engine.

24
Valve Noise

SOME of the most powerful noise sources in industrial plant are valves which are used to control the flow of high pressure gas in pipelines and chemical plant. The problem stems from the jets of fast moving gas on the downstream side of the valve, which mix with slower moving gas, causing the loss of kinetic energy, which causes the pressure drop across the valve. At low velocities the turbulence produced is a very inefficient means of generating noise but, as the velocities increase, the process becomes much more efficient. When the flow reaches the speed of sound, the conversion of energy into noise reaches an efficiency of 0.01% or more. Whenever the pressure drop across the valve exceeds the critical value, the speed of sound will be reached. This critical pressure ratio is surprisingly low, being about 2:1 in the case of air. This means that valves handling a pressure ratio much greater than this are quite efficient noise generators. The problem is made worse by the fact that the energy loss across a large valve handling a high pressure drop may be equivalent to many kilowatts. The result is very large sound power levels which may reach 150dB SWL or more re 10^{-12}w.

There are two main problem conditions. One occurs where valves are used to control the flow in a system by creating a pressure drop, e.g. a trimming valve. In other situations, valves normally operate either fully open or fully shut, in which case problems only occur when the valve vents to atmosphere, as in the case of an emergency dump valve, or when it is necessary to dump unwanted gas or air possibly at an intermediate stage during plant start up.

If a 500MW steam turbine trips out on full load, the steam has to be dumped until the boiler can be shut down. Even if the conversion of mechanical energy into sound energy is low, the effect of venting 500MW of steam is staggering.

If the pressure drop across the valve is increased, the velocity through the valve increases until sonic velocity is reached at the critical pressure. If the pressure drop is increased above this value, the flow remains sonic and does not become supersonic in a normal valve. The density of the gas passing through the valve does, however, increase and there is a mis-match between the flow conditions at the exit of the valve throat in the emerging fluid and downstream fluid. This results in shock waves in the flow downstream.

There are two principal ways of dealing with valve noise. These are either by reducing the noise generation at source or by controlling the noise downstream.

Controlling the Noise at the Valve The use of 'streamlined' valves which do not produce turbulence is a myth because the valves rely on the turbulence to produce the pressure drop, which is the reason for their existence. There is, however, scope for noise reduction by the use of other mechanisms to produce the required pressure drop.

A number of quiet valves have been produced which reduce the noise generated by dividing the pressure drop up into a number of small successive stages or by using flow elements which have very small passages causing very high frictional losses (Fig 1). The principle of the first type of device is that, since the efficiency of the noise generation increases with the pressure drop, the noise produced by a number of small pressure drops in succession is smaller than that produced by an equal single pressure drop. In the second form, either porous elements are used or alternatively perforated plates with a large number of small holes. (It is essential that the proportions of the holes are chosen carefully, otherwise a valve of this type may make more noise than a conventional one. Diameters close to twice the plate thickness should be avoided.) Although both principles work more or less as predicted, there is a cost and size penalty resulting from the increased complexity of the valve. There also tend to be restrictions on the range over which the valve will control successfully.

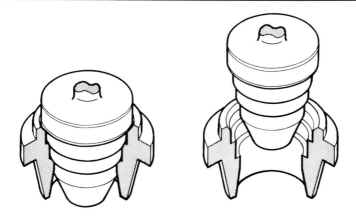

Valve using multiple stage throttling after Serck CS Trim

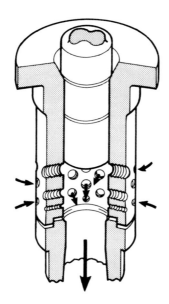

Valve using many small ports after Blakeborough 'Flash Flow'

Figure 1. Quiet valve designs

Although it is possible to predict the overall sound power generation produced by a simple valve based on the properties of the gas being handled and the pressure drop, mass flow, etc., predictions of the spectrum tend to be unreliable as these depend very much on the form of the individual valve. There are a number of computer programmes available which enable the noise generation by a valve of specific geometry to be predicted from the results of measurements of the noise on a model valve of the same geometry. Most manufacturers of control valves produce their own charts and data for predicting the noise generation of the valves that they manufacture.

Control of the Noise Downstream of the Valve One of the problems of valve noise is that the noise is generated not at the valve itself but throughout a region extending a considerable distance downstream of the valve, where the high velocity jet of gas mixes with the low velocity surrounding gas.

The principles used to control the noise downstream of the valve are to improve the mixing process so that it takes place in a much smaller space which can be more easily contained, and then to provide a conventional attenuator to control the resultant noise (Fig 2). The mixing process is normally achieved by passing the gas through a perforated diffuser or 'pepper pot' which breaks the single large solid jet up into a number of very much smaller jets. This has two effects. The first is that the mixing of high and low velocity gas takes place in a smaller space because the distance taken for a jet to merge with its surroundings depends on its diameter. A large jet takes a much greater distance than a small one. Also, frictional effects tend to destroy small eddies faster than big ones. The second effect is that reducing the jet size shifts the sound energy from the low frequency region, which requires massive attenuators, to high frequencies, which can be more easily absorbed.

Where a vent or dump valve is required to operate full bore, the perforated diffuser must be sized so that it does not cause a significant reduction in flow rate. Downstream of the mixing zone, conventional attenuator elements are used to control the noise radiated by the mixing zone. In the case of vent attenuators leading to the open air, the attenuator sections will be large so that the merging gas velocity is relatively low (typically less than 50m/sec), If the exit gas velocity is not

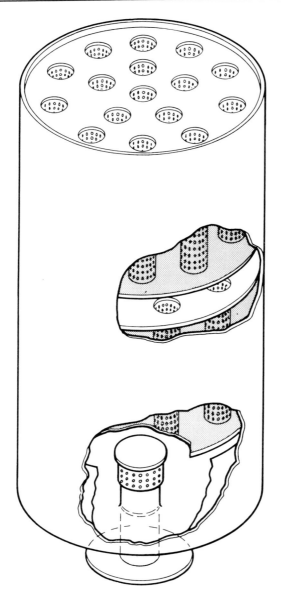

Figure 2. Blow-off attenuator

kept low, noise will be generated where the emerging jets mix with the surrounding air, making yet another sound source – this time outside the attenuator. Where a silencer is installed in a line, the outlet velocity is controlled by the size of the downstream pipework and there are no advantages to be gained by using lower velocities through the attenuator than will be handled by the downstream pipework.

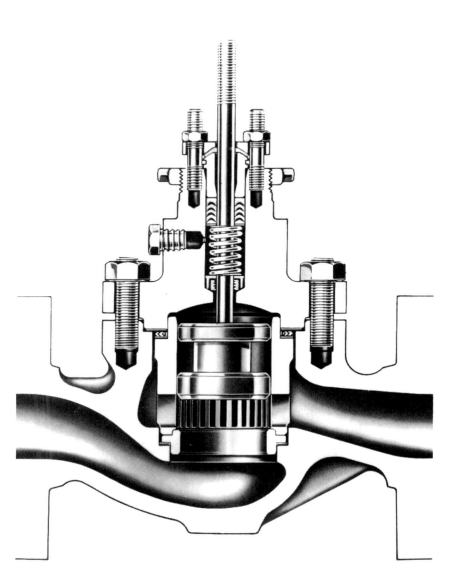

Plate 1. ***Section of control valve fitted with "Whisper trim" to reduce***
noise resulting from the pressure drop across the valve

Plate 2. *A large steam vent attenuator under construction for a power station. Only the upper dissipative section is visible*

APPENDIX 1.
ABSORPTION COEFFICIENTS OF COMMON MATERIALS

N.B. The following data should be considered only as a guide since many factors will influence the actual absorption (e.g. method of mounting, decorative treatment, thickness, properties of surrounding structure)

Material	125	250	500	1k	2k	4k Hz
Sprayed Acoustic Plaster	0.30	0.35	0.5	0.7	0.7	0.7
Board on Joist Floor	0.15	0.2	0.1	0.1	0.1	0.1
Breeze Block	0.2	0.3	0.6	0.6	0.5	0.5
Brickwork-plain/painted	0.05	0.04	0.02	0.04	0.05	0.05
Concrete, Tooled Stone, Granolithic	0.02	0.02	0.02	0.04	0.05	0.05
Cork, 25 mm Solid Backing	0.05	0.1	0.2	0.55	0.6	0.55
Fibreboard						
– solid backing	0.05	0.1	0.15	0.25	0.3	0.3
– 25 mm air space	0.3	0.3	0.3	0.3	0.3	0.3
Glass, 3–4 mm	0.2	0.15	0.1	0.07	0.05	0.05
>4 mm	0.1	0.07	0.04	0.03	0.02	0.02
Plaster, lime or gypsum						
– solid backing	0.03	0.03	0.02	0.03	0.04	0.05
– on lath studs, air space	0.3	0.15	0.1	0.05	0.04	0.05
Plywood/Hardboard, air space	0.32	0.43	0.12	0.07	0.07	0.11
Wood Blocks/Lino/Rubber Flooring	0.02	0.04	0.05	0.05	0.1	0.05
Wood Panelling, 12 mm on 25 mm battens	0.31	0.33	0.14	0.1	0.1	0.12
Carpet, Haircord on felt	0.1	0.15	0.25	0.3	0.3	0.3
Pile and thick felt	0.07	0.25	0.5	0.5	0.6	0.65
Acoustic 'blocks'	0.38	0.8	0.43	0.4	0.42	0.50
Acoustic timber wall panelling	0.18	0.34	0.42	0.59	0.83	0.68
Air Absorption (Relative Humidity = 50%) – (×) (per m³)	0.0	0.0	0.0	0.003	0.007	0.02
Audience per person	0.33	0.40	0.44	0.45	0.45	0.45
Upholstered seat	0.45	0.60	0.73	0.80	0.75	0.64
Proprietary Ceiling Tile (Typical values) A. Fixed to Solid Backing Mineral Wool Fibre	0.10	0.25	0.70	0.85	0.70	0.60
Perforated Metal, 31 mm thick absorbent infill	0.10	0.30	0.65	0.75	0.65	0.45
B. On Battens 25 mm to 50 mm thick Mineral Wool Fibre	0.15	0.35	0.65	0.80	0.75	0.70
Perforated Metal, 31 mm thick (absorbent infill)	0.2	0.55	0.80	0.80	0.80	0.75
C. Suspended Mineral Wool Fibre	0.50	0.60	0.65	0.75	0.80	0.75
Perforated Metal, 31 mm thick (absorbent infill)	0.25	0.55	0.85	0.85	0.75	0.75

APPENDIX 2

REPRESENTATIVE VALUES OF AIRBORNE SOUND REDUCTION INDEX FOR SOME COMMON STRUCTURES

Panels of sheet materials

	Thickness mm	Superficial weight kg/m²	Frequency Hz							
			63	125	250	500	1k	2k	4k	8k
1.5mm lead sheet	1.5	17	22	28	32	33	32	32	33	36
3mm lead sheet	3	34	25	30	31	27	38	44	33	38
20g aluminium sheet, stiffened	0.9	2.5	8	11	10	10	18	23	25	30
22g galvanised sheet steel	0.55	6	3	8	14	20	23	26	27	35
20g galvanised sheet steel	0.9	7	3	8	14	20	26	32	38	40
18g galvanised sheet steel	1.2	10	8	13	20	24	29	33	39	44
16g galvanised sheet steel	1.6	13	9	14	21	27	32	37	43	42
18g fluted steel panels stiffened at edges, joints sealed	1.2	39	25	30	20	22	30	28	31	31
Corrugated asbestos sheet stiffened and sealed	6	10	20	25	30	33	33	38	39	42
Chipboard sheets on wood framework	19	11	14	17	18	25	30	26	32	38
Fibreboard sheets on wood framework	12	4	10	12	16	20	24	30	31	36
Plasterboard sheets on wood framework	9	7	9	15	20	24	29	32	35	38
Plywood sheets on wood framework	6	3.5	6	9	13	16	21	27	29	33
Hardwood (mahogany) panels	50	25	15	19	23	25	30	37	42	46
Woodwool slabs unplastered	25	19	0	0	2	6	6	8	8	10
Woodwool slabs plastered (12mm on each face)	50	75	18	23	27	30	32	36	39	43

APPENDIX 2

REPRESENTATIVE VALUES OF AIRBORNE SOUND REDUCTION INDEX FOR SOME COMMON STRUCTURES

	Superficial		Frequency Hz							
	Thickness mm	weight kg/m²	63	125	250	500	1k	2k	4k	8k
Panels of sandwich construction										
1.5mm lead between two sheets of 5mm plywood	11.5	25	19	26	30	34	38	42	44	47
9mm asbestos board between two sheets of 18g steel	12	37	16	22	27	31	27	37	44	48
"Stramit" compressed straw between two sheets of 3mm hardboard	56	25	15	22	23	27	27	35	35	38
Single masonry walls.										
Single leaf brick, plastered both sides	125	240	30	36	37	40	46	54	57	59
	255	480	34	41	45	48	56	65	69	72
	360	720	36	44	43	49	57	66	70	72
Solid breeze or clinker blocks, plastered (12mm both sides)	125	145	20	27	33	40	50	57	56	59
Solid breeze or clinker blocks, unplastered	75	85	12	17	18	20	24	30	38	43
Hollow cinder concrete blocks, painted (cement base paint)	100	75	22	30	34	40	50	50	52	53
Hollow cinder concrete blocks, unpainted	100	75	22	27	32	37	40	41	45	48
"Thermalite" blocks	100	125	20	27	31	39	45	53	38	62
Glass bricks	200	510	25	30	35	40	49	49	43	45

Double masonry walls

280mm brick, 56mm cavity, strip ties, outer faces plastered 12mm	300	380	28	34	34	40	56	73	76	78
280mm brick, 56mm cavity, expanded metal ties, outer faces plastered, 12mm	300	380	27	27	43	55	66	77	85	85

Stud partitions

50mm×100mm studs, 12mm insulating board both sides	125	19	12	16	22	28	38	50	52	55
50mm×100mm studs, 9mm plaster board and 12mm plaster coat both sides	142	60	20	25	28	34	47	39	50	56

Single glazed windows

Single glass in heavy frame

6	15	17	11	24	28	32	27	35	39
8	20	17	18	25	31	32	28	36	39
9	22.5	18	22	26	31	30	32	39	43
16	40	20	25	28	33	30	38	45	48
25	62.5	25	27	31	30	33	43	48	53

Double glazed windows

2.44mm panes, 7mm cavity	12	15	15	22	16	20	29	31	27	30
9mm glass panes in separate frames, 50mm cavity	62	34	18	25	29	34	41	45	53	50
6mm glass panes in separate frames, 100mm cavity	112	34	20	28	30	38	45	45	53	50
6mm glass panes in separate frames, 188mm cavity	200	34	25	30	35	41	48	50	56	56
6mm glass panes in separate frames, 188mm cavity with absorbent blanket in reveals	200	34	26	33	39	42	48	50	57	60

APPENDIX 2

REPRESENTATIVE VALUES OF AIRBORNE SOUND REDUCTION INDEX FOR SOME COMMON STRUCTURES

	Thickness mm	Superficial weight kg/m²	Frequency Hz							
			63	125	250	500	1k	2k	4k	8k
Doors										
Flush panel, hollow core, normal cracks as usually hung	43	9	9	12	13	14	16	18	24	26
Solid hardwood, normal cracks as usually hung	43	28	13	17	21	26	29	31	34	32
Typical proprietary "acoustic" door, double heavy sheet steel skin, absorbent in airspace, special furniture and seals in heavy steel frame	100	—	37	36	39	44	49	54	57	60
Floors										
T & G boards, joints sealed	21	13	17	21	18	22	24	30	33	63
T & G boards, 12mm plasterboard ceiling under, with 3mm plaster skim coat	235	31	15	18	25	37	39	45	45	48
As above with boards "floating" on glass wool mat	240	35	20	25	33	38	45	56	61	64
Concrete, reinforced	100	230	32	37	36	45	52	59	62	63
	200	460	36	42	41	50	57	60	65	70
	300	690	37	40	45	52	59	63	67	72
126mm reinforced concrete with "floating" screed	190	420	35	38	43	48	54	61	63	67
6mm and 9mm panes in separate frames, 200mm cavity, absorbent blanket in reveals	215	42	27	36	45	58	59	55	66	70

Appendix 2 chart after Sharland

APPENDIX 3.
NOISE AT WORK REGULATIONS

Action required where $L_{EP,d}$ is likely to be:- (see note 1 below)	below 85 dB(A)	85 dB(A) First AL	90 dB(A) Second AL
EMPLOYER'S DUTIES			(2)
General Duty To Reduce Risk			
Risk of hearing damage to be reduced to the lowest level reasonably practicable. (Reg 6)	●	●	●
Assessment Of Noise Exposure			
Noise assessments to be made by a Competent Person. (Reg 4)		●	●
Record of assessments to be kept until a new one is made. (Reg 5)		●	●
Noise Reduction			
Reduce exposure to noise as far as is reasonably practicable by means other than ear protectors. (Reg 7)			●
Provision Of Information To Workers			
Provide adequate information, instruction and training about risks to hearing, what employees should do to minimise risk, how they can obtain ear protectors if they are exposed between 85 and 90 dB(A), and their obligations under the Regulations. (Reg 11)		●	●
Mark ear protection zones with notices, so far as reasonably practicable. (Reg 9)			●
Ear Protectors			
Ensure so far as is practicable that protectors are:-			
— provided to employees who ask for them (Reg 8(1))		●	
— provided to all exposed (Reg 8(2))			●
— maintained and repaired (Reg 10(1)(b))		●	●
— used by all exposed (Reg 10(1)(a))			●
Ensure so far as reasonably practicable that all who go into a marked ear protection zone use ear protectors. (Reg 9(1)(b))			● (3)
Maintenance And Use Of Equipment			
Ensure so far as is practicable that:-			
— all equipment provided under the Regulations is used, except for the ear protectors provided between 85 and 90 dB(A). (Reg 10(1)(a))		●	●
— ensure all equipment is maintained. (Reg 10(1)(b))		●	●
EMPLOYEES DUTIES			
Use Of Equipment			
So far as practicable:-			
— use ear protectors (Reg 10(2))			●
— use any other protective equipment (Reg 10(2))		●	●
— report any defects discovered to his/her employer (Reg 10(2))		●	●
MACHINE MAKER'S AND SUPPLIERS DUTIES			
Provision Of Information			
Provide information on the noise likely to be generated (Reg 12)		●	●

NOTES:
(1) The dB(A) action levels are values of daily personal exposure to noise (L_{EP},d).
(2) All the actions indicated at 90 dB(A) are also required where the peak sound pressure is at or above 200 Pa (140 dB re 20 μPa).
(3) This requirement applies to all who enter the zones, even if they do not stay long enough to receive an exposure of 90 dB(A) L_{EP},d.

Source: Health and Safety Executive

APPENDIX 4.
$L_{EP,d}$ NOMOGRAM

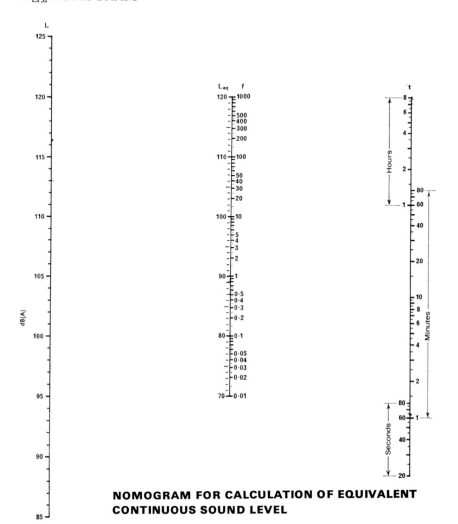

NOMOGRAM FOR CALCULATION OF EQUIVALENT CONTINUOUS SOUND LEVEL

From:

$$f = \frac{t}{8} \text{ antilog}\left[0.1(L-90)\right]$$

where t is in hours.

Also:

$$L_{eq} = \frac{\log f}{0.1} + 90$$

(1) For each exposure connect sound level dB(A) with exposure duration t and read fractional exposure f on centre scale.

(2) Add together values of f received during one day to obtain total value of f.

(3) Read equivalent continuous sound level L_{eq} opposite total value of f.

Terminology

Acoustic, airflow and vibration terminology

A

Absorption Coefficient
A measure of the quantity of sound lost at a surface.

Absorptive Attenuator
Attenuator that incorporates glass fibre and mineral wool materials, effective over a wide range of frequencies.

Ambient Noise
The existing background noise in an area. Can be sounds from many sources, near and far.

Anechoic Room
A specially constructed room in which as much sound as possible is absorbed at its boundaries. Typically achieved by using sound absorbing wedges.

Attenuation
Noise reduction

Attenuator
Noise reducing device – often colloquially known as a 'silencer'.

B

Background Noise
The existing noise associated with a given environment. Can be sounds from many sources, near and far.

Bottoming
See Solid State.

Breakout
The escape of sound from any source enclosing structure, such as ductwork and metal casings.

C

Crosstalk
The transfer of airborne noise from one area to another via secondary air paths, such as ventilation ductwork or ceiling voids.

Cut-off Frequency
This is a figure of merit used to indicate the potential lowest frequency to which a given acoustic wedge size can be employed to absorb 99% of the sound applied. A term often used when evaluating the performance of an Anechoic Room.

D

Decibel
The decibel is a unit of sound level using a logarithmic scale.

dBA
Approximately equivalent to the human ear frequency response. Increasingly used in Europe for certain design criteria.

dBA dBB dBC dBD
Specific measuring scales achieved by electrical weighting networks fitted in a sound level meter. Gives a single figure rating to a broad band sound.

dBB
Out of favour at present, not used. Originally designed for moderately high noise level measurement.

dBC
Approximate linear, flat frequency response – has practical uses when fitted to a sound level meter.

dBD
Used for aircraft noise measurement (See also PNdB).

Directivity Factor
When sound radiates from any source sound levels can be higher in certain directions than others. This is called 'Directivity'. Directivity Factor is the ratio of the increased level to the average value.

Directivity Index
Is directivity factor expressed in decibels (dB).

Discrete Frequency
A single frequency signal.
Dissipative Attenuator
Attenuator that incorporates glass fibre and mineral wool materials, effective over a wide range of frequencies.
Disturbing Frequency (Hz)
A frequency at which a machine produces vibration. Often the speed of rotation of the machine.
Dynamic Insertion Loss (DIL)
A measure of the acoustic performance of an attenuator when handling the rated flow. Not necessarily the same as Static Insertion Loss because it may include regeneration.

E

End Reflection
End reflection occurs when sound energy radiates from a hole. The sudden expansion to atmosphere causes some low frequency noise to be reflected back towards the source. Expressed in decibels (dB), the effect is dependent on hole size and frequency. Maximum at lowest frequency from smallest hole.

F

Flanking Transmission
The transfer of sound between any two areas by any indirect path, usually structural.
Flutter Echo
A rapid succession of reflected echoes from one initial sound, e.g. a handclap. Often occurs in empty offices.
Free Field
A sound field which is free from all reflective surfaces. A simulated free field can be produced inside an anechoic room.
Frequency (Hz) – Sound
The number of sound waves to pass a point in one second.
Frequency-vibration
The number of complete vibrations in one second.

H

Hertz (Hz)
The unit of frequency equivalent to one cycle per second.

I

Impact Isolation Class (IIC)
An American rating given to carpets, floor tiles, floating floors, etc. denoting their ability to reduce tapping and footstep noises.

Impact noise Rating (INR)
An American rating given to the impact transmission loss of vibration isolators, carpets, floor tiles, floating floors etc.

Insertion Loss
The reduction of noise level by the introduction of a noise control device. Established by the substitution method of test.

Insulation (Sound)
The property of a material or partition to oppose sound transfer through its thickness.

Inverse Square Law
The reduction of noise with distance. In terms of decibels, it means a decrease of 6dB for each doubling of distance from a point source when no reflective surfaces are apparent.

Isolation (Sound)
The reduction of airborne sound transfer from one area to another.

Isolation (Vibration)
The reduction of vibrational force into a structure.

Isolation Efficiency
The amount of vibration force absorbed by an isolator and thus prevented from entering the supporting structure, expressed as a percentage of the total force applied to the isolator.

L

Lamina Flow
Colloquially used to describe the preferred state of airflow. Strictly means undisturbed flow at very low flow-rates where the air moves in parallel paths.

M

Masking (Sound)
Extra sound introduced into an area to reduce the variability of fluctuating noise levels or the intelligibility of speech.

Mass Law
Heavy materials stop more noise passing through them than light materials. For any airtight material there will be an increase in its "noise stopping" ability of approximately 6dB for every doubling of mass per unit area.

N

Natural Frequency
A frequency of a system or material at which it freely vibrates when a force is applied and removed, (e.g. kicked).

Near Field
The area close to a large noise source where the inverse square law does *not* apply.

Noise
Unwanted Sound.

Noise and Number Index (NNI)
Gives a single figure assessment of aircraft noise, taking into account the measured sound level and number of flights.

Noise Criterion Curves (NC)
An American set of curves based on the sensitivity of the human ear. They give a single figure for broad band noise. Used for indoor design criteria.

Noise Rating Curves (NR)
A set of curves based on the sensitivity of the human ear. They are used to give a single figure rating for a broad band of frequencies. Used in Europe for interior and exterior design criteria levels. They have a greater decibel range than NC curves.

Noise Reduction
Used to define the performance of a noise barrier. Established by measuring the difference in sound pressure levels adjacent to each surface. (See also Sound Reduction Index).

O

Octave Bands
A convenient division of the frequency scale. Identified by their centre frequency, typically 63 125 250 500 1000 2000 4000 8000 Hz.

P

Perceived Noise Level (PNdB)
A measure of noise level used exclusively for aircraft noise.

Phon
The phon is a unit of loudness level. Used when establishing the sensitivity of the human ear.

Pink Noise
Noise of a statistically random nature, having an equal energy per octave band width throughout the audible range.

Pure Tone
A single frequency signal.

R

Random Noise
A confused noise comprised from large numbers of sound waves, all with unrelated frequencies and magnitudes.

Reactive Attenuator
An attenuator in which the noise reduction is brought about typically by changes in cross section, chambers and baffle sections, e.g., car exhaust silencer.

Regeneration
The noise generated by airflow turbulence. The noise level usually increases with flow speed.

Resonance
This is the build up of excessive vibration in a resilient system. It occurs when the machine speed (disturbing frequency) coincides with the mounted machine natural frequency, or support system.

Resonant Frequency (Hz)
The frequency at which resonance occurs in the resilient system.

Reverberation
Reflected sound in a room, that decays, after the sound source has stopped.

Reverberation Room
A calibrated room specially constructed with very sound reflective walls, e.g., plastered concrete. The result is a room with a "long smooth echo", in which a sound takes a long time to die away. The sound pressure levels in this room are very even.

Reverberation Time
The time taken in seconds for the average sound energy level in a room to decrease to one millionth of its originally steady level after the source has stopped, i.e., time taken for a 60dB decrease to take place.

Room Constant
The sound absorbing capacity of a room, usually expressed in |m².

S

Sabine's Formula
Predicts the reverberation time of a room or enclosure from known room volume and absorption characteristics. Becomes inaccurate when absorption is high.

Silencer
Colloquialism for attenuator, spoken by optimists.

Sinusoidal
Sine wave shape, the shape of an ideal wave.

Solid State (Bottoming)
Vibration Isolation – The unwanted situation when a spring can be compressed no further and the coils are in contact.
Electronics – The description of circuitry using semi-conductors instead of valves, e.g. transistors.

Sound Conditioning
Supplementary sound introduced into an area to reduce the variability of fluctuating noise levels or the intelligibility of speech.

Sound Insulation
The property of a material or partition to oppose sound transfer through its thickness.

Sound Level Meter (Noise Meter)
An instrument for measuring sound pressure levels. Can be fitted with electrical weighting networks for direct read-off in dBA, dBB, dBC, dBD and octave or third octave bands.

Sound Power
A measure of sound energy in watts. A fixed property of a machine, irrespective of environment.

Sound Power Level (SWL)
The amount of sound output from a machine, etc. Cannot be measured directly. Expressed in decibels of SWL.

Sound Pressure Level (SPL)
A measurable sound level that depends upon environment. A measure of the sound pressure at a point in N/m². Expressed in decibels of SPL at a specified distance and position.

SPL Direct Field
The direct components of a sound level field are calculated from a given SWL by using inverse square law and directivity etc.

SPL Reverberant Field
The reverberant component of a sound level calculation from a given SWL by using room constant values from reverberation time and volume.

Sound Reduction Index (SRI)
A set of values measured by a specific test method to establish the actual amount of sound that will be stopped by the material, partition or panel, when located between two reverberation rooms. Average SRI can be calculated by averaging the set of values in the sixteen third octave bands from 100Hz to 3150Hz.

Sound Spectrum
The separation of sound into its frequency components across the audible range of the human ear.

Sound Transmission Class (STC)
An American rating given to the "noise stopping" ability of building structures. Has similar uses to transmission loss and sound reduction index.

Standing Waves
These occur due to room geometry. Sound levels at some locations in the room at certain frequencies will be intensified by additive interference of successive waves, and in other locations reduced by cancellation.

Static Deflection
The distance vibration isolators compress when loaded.

T

Transmissibility
This is the amount of vibratory force that is transferred to the structure through an isolator, expressed as a percentage of the total force applied.

Transmission Loss
American preferred description for sound reduction index. A set of values measured by a specific test method to establish the actual amount of noise that will be stopped by the material, partition or panel when placed between two reverberation rooms.

Threshold of Audibility
The minimum sound levels at each frequency that a person can just hear.

Threshold of Pain
The sound level at which a person experiences physical pain. (Typically 120dB).

Threshold Shift
A partial loss of hearing caused by excessive noise, either temporary or permanent, in a person's threshold of audibility.

Third Octave Bands
A small division of the frequency scale, three to each *octave*. Enables more accurate noise analysis.

Turbulent Flow
A confused state of airflow that may cause noise to be generated inside, for example, a ductwork system.

V

Vibration Isolation
Any of several means of reducing the transfer of vibrational force from the mounted equipment to the supporting structure, or vice-versa.

W

White Noise
Noise of a statistically random nature having an equal energy level per Hertz throughout the audible range.

Wavelength
The distance between two like points on a wave shape, e.g. distance from crest to crest.

Weighted Sound Level
See dBA,dBB,dBC and dBD for specific scale descriptions.

INDEX